ABSTRACTS OF
BUCKS COUNTY,
PENNSYLVANIA
WILLS

1685-1785

F. Edward Wright

Willow Bend Books
Westminster, Maryland
2000

Willow Bend Books

65 East Main Street
Westminster, Maryland 21157-5026
1-800-876-6103

WB0887

Source books, early maps, CDs—Worldwide

For our listing of thousands of titles offered
by hundreds of publishers see our website
<www.WillowBendBooks.com>

Visit our retail store

International Standard Book Number: 1-58549-372-4

Printed in the United States of America

INTRODUCTION

These wills were abstracted under the auspices of the Historical Society of Pennsylvania in the early 1900s. Copies were made available to various libraries in Pennsylvania and microfilm copies made by the Genealogical Society of Utah (LDS). Only a few abstracts of the early administrations were included. We have made a couple of additions. We hope to publish abstracts of other probate records of Bucks County in the near future.

We extend our appreciation to the staffs of the Historical Society of Pennsylvania (1300 Locust Street, Philadelphia, PA 19107) and encourage use and support of its facilities and to the Genealogical Society of Pennsylvania whose collections are housed in the Historical Society Library. We also encourage membership in the Genealogical Society of Pennsylvania (address same as HSP).

F. Edward Wright
Westminster, Maryland
1995

Bucks County Townships

DURHAM
BRIDGETON
SPRINGFIELD
NOCKAMIXON
HAYCOCK
TINICUM
RICHLAND
MILFORD
EAST
ROCKHILL
BEDMINSTER
PLUMSTEAD
WEST
ROCKHILL
SOLEBURY
HILLTOWN
BUCKINGHAM
NEW
BRITAIN
DOYLESTOWN
UPPER
MAKEFIELD
WARRINGTON
WRIGHTS
TOWN
WARWICK
NEWTOWN
LOWER
MAKEFIELD
WARMINSTER
NORTHAMPTON
MIDDLETOWN
UPPER
SOUTHAMPTON
LOWER
SOUTHAMPTON
FALLS
BENSALEM
BRISTOL

Book A. Vol. 1

Page 8. Henry Comely, of County of Bucks. June 26, 1684. Proved 4th mo., 10th day, 1685. Wife Joan - Son Henry, 200 acres bought of Governor and 100 acres "on which I live." Daughter Mary, 100 acres, uncultivated land. Friends Wm. [Edmd.?] Bennett, David Davis, and Wm. Paxson, exrs. to act with advice of monthly meeting of friends.
Wit: James George. Letters granted to David Davis, others refused.

Page 9. William Bennett of Longford, Parish of Hammondsworth, County of Middlesex, Yeoman. August 9, 1683. Proved 9th mo., 12th day, 1685. Wife Rebecka, extx. Son William Bennett 1 shilling. Dau. Mary Chandler wife of --- Chandler. Daus. Elizabeth, Rebecka, Anne and Sarah each 200 acres; "hereafter to be alloted to one in Pensilvania."
Wit: John Stevens, Thomas Turner, and Thomas Burromby.

Page 12. Henry Gibbs of County of Bucks, Carpenter, no date, Proved 10th mo., 16th day, 1685. Wife Elizabeth Gibbs, (extx.) 130 acres in Bucks County. Gives daughter Elizabeth to Anne Harrison for term of 2 years, gives son, John to Edmond Lovet for 2 years. "John Bainbridge owes me 7 shillings, 6 pence." Edmond Lovet and Phineas Pemberton to appraise goods.
Wit: John Kinsey and Jacob Turner.

Page 13. William Hiscock, (nuncupative). 10th mo., 21st day, 1685. Proved 11th mo., 8th day, 1685. Wearing apparell to Joshua Boare(Bore). Plantation to John Webster, flitch of Bacon to Robert Lucas, overplus to those in greatest need in County of Bucks. Letters granted to Wm. Beaks and Robert Lucas. Signed Joshua Boare and Margaret, wife of said Joshua.

Page 14. John Worthington of Parish of Cheadle in Old England on Ship Friendship of Liverpool. January 16, 1684. Proved 11th mo., 8th day, 1685. Mother Dorothy Worthington, Brothers, Roger and Henry and Sister Anne Worthington. Jacob Hall and Wm. Kenerly, exrs. (Letters granted to Jacob Hall.)
Wit: Peter Dix, Bartholomew Coppock and Willm. Stockdale.

Page 17. Ralph Smith. 2nd mo., 9th day, 1685. Proved 3rd mo., 2nd day, 1686. After House is built, money remaining to sister Jane Lloyd and Susannah Pike of Shaules Town in New England. Sister Susannah, 193 acres back of Pennsbury called "Little Money Hill" with new House there on now to be built by Charles Brigham. Priscilla wife of John Rowland. 110 acres joining Robert Hall, Richard Lundy and Edmond Lovet, to be sold. James Harrison and James Atkinson, exrs. (letters granted to Harrison).
Wit: John Martin, Richard Wilson, Jon. Clark.
Appraisers Henry Baker, Lyonel Brittain.

Page 18. Thomas Wigelsworth, now living on "Neshaminah Creek" in Pennsylvania. 9th mo., 13th day, 1682. Proved 3rd mo., 24th day, 1686. Wife Allis, residue of estate, and sole extx.

Brother's and Sister's children, each 5 shillings.
Wit: Nicholas Waln, Alexander Giles.
Appraisal made 1st mo., 11th day, 1683 by Nicholas Waln, James
Dillworth, Thomas Stackhouse and John Eastburne.

Page 34. Thomas Dickinson [also Dickerson]. 5th mo., 23rd day,
1687. Proved 10th mo., 29th day, 1687. Wife Alice, land on
which I live and to be sole extx. 200 acres of land in "Writes
Town" to kinsman Thomas Coleman.
Wit: Wm. Biles, John Cuff, Robt. Lucas, Tho. Dickenson.
Indorsement on will dated 5th mo., 25th day, 1687, declares
bequest to wife to be to her and her heirs.

Page 35. Michael Huff. 4th mo., 3rd day, 1685. Proved 11th
mo., 24th day, 1687. Wife Joan. Daughter Mary Huff. Signed
Michel Huf.
Wit: John Otter, Edmund Lovet.
Appraisal made 6th mo., 26th day, 1687 by James Boyden and Edmond
Bennett.

Page 36. Thomas Dungan, of Cold Spring, County of Bucks. 12th
mo., 3rd day, 1686. Proved 11th mo., 24th day, 1687. Wife
Elizabeth, sole extx. 3 sons, Thomas, Jeremiah, and John. Daus.
Elizabeth West, Mary, Rebecka, and Sarah Dungan. Sons William and
Clement.
Wit: Arthur Cooke, John Cook, Wm. Dungan.
Appraisal made 12th mo., 4th day, 1687 by Edmond Lovet and
Abraham Cox.

Page 40. Robert Jeffs [Jeffes], now of Falls of Delaware, Bucks
Co. 1st mo., 13th day 1688. Proved 2nd mo., 3rd day, 1688.
Wife Mary, extx. Daus. Elizabeth and Mary. Governor beseeched
to take notice of unfair Treatment by Tho. Fairman about
Plantation at Frankford.
Wit: Robert Lucas, Charles Biles.
Signed Robert Jeffes.

Page 42. Thomas Staples, servant of Robert Lucas, of County of
Bucks, nuncupative, made 1st mo., 16th day, 1688. Proved 2nd
mo., 6th day, 1688. "All that he had" to John, son of Robert
Lucas. Refers to any property due him in Great Britain or
Ireland. Letters granted to Elizabeth Lucas, widow.
Wit: Joseph Chorley, Elinor Beakes. Signed Elizabeth Ridgway.

Page 44. John Clowes of County of Bucks, Yeoman. Dated 11th
mo., 29th day, 1686. Proved 7th mo., 4th day, 1687. Wife
Margery, 500 acres adjoining Delaware River called by one "The
Clough" at her death to son William, Daus. Margery, wife of
Richard Hough, and Sarah, wife of John Bainbridge of West New
Jersey, dau. Rebecka Clowes. Son Joseph, wife Margery extx.
Wit: Phinehas Pemberton, Richard Ridgway.

Page 48. Joshua Boare of County of Bucks, husbandman
(nuncupative), made 1st mo., 28th day, 1688. Signed 2nd mo., 7th
day, 1688. attested 3 mo 22rd day, 1688. Son Joshua. Dau.

Mary. Richard to take dau. Mary. William Biles and Richard Ridgway, exrs.
Signed by Thomas Coverdale, Jane Coverdale, Daniel Hawkins, Elinor Beakes.

Page 52. Thomas Woolfe of County of Bucks. (nuncupative), Made 11th of 3mo. 1688. Signed and attested 4th mo., 6th day, 1688. Being told by Edmond Lovet that if he had not disposed of what he had his sisters would share with Abraham Cocks and Sarah, his wife. Said "they would not come over" and "wold have Abraham and Sarah have all he had." Letters granted to Abraham Cocks.
Signed Edmond Lovet and Elizabeth Curton.

Page 50. Thomas Adkinson of County of Bucks. 8th mo., 10th day, 1687. Proved 3rd mo., 21st day, 1688. Wife Jane, extx., to sell 100 acres bought of Jos. English, Bro. John Adkinson, 100 acres. Children, Isaac, William, and Samuel.
Wit: Joseph Kirkbride, Richard Londes.
Signed Thomas Adkinson.
[Thomas Adkinson died 31st of 8th month, 1687. See admin.]

Page 59. William Sanford, Planter, of County of Bucks. March 25, 1689, Proved 8th mo., 17th day, 1692. Upper Mill Creek. Wife ---. Eldest son William. Son William Homer, Dau-in-law Ester Homer. 2 children, Mary and Ester.
Wit: Thomas Hartly, Scrivener, George Porter.
Codicil. No date. Son William to be put with Daniel Sutton, Taylor, for 11 yrs. Son-in-law William Homer. Wit: to Codicil James Boyden, Junr.
Neighbor James Boyden and Daniel Sutton, exrs.

Page 61. John Wood of Crookhorn, County of Bucks, Yeoman. March 20, 1692. Proved 9th mo., 12th day, 1692. Son Joseph Wood, Lands in West Jersey, purchased of Richard Ramsdell and John Champion on Crosswicks Creek. Three Daus. Hester, wife of Isaac Smalley, Sarah, wife of Charles Biles, and Mary, wife of Thomas Coleman. Land bought of John Latham. Son in law, Isaac Smaley and son, Joseph Wood, exrs.
Wit: Roger Parke, William Taylor, and William Emley.
Letters granted to Joseph Wood.

Page 66. Joane Betredg of Southampton, County of Bucks, Widow. 12th mo., 2rd day, 1692/3. Proved 2nd mo., 18th day, 1693. Sons Mark and William Betredg, dau. Joan Betredg. John Swift, exr. and trustee.
Wit: George Randle, Mark Betredg, John Smith.

Bucks County Wills. Book No. 1.

Page 1. William Dungan of County of Bucks, Yeoman. Aug. 21, 1711. Proved Dec. 16, 1713. Wife Deborah, extx. Sons, Thomas, William and Jeremiah. Daus. Deborah and Elizabeth Dungan.
Wit: John Smith, Ester Clay, Rebecka Smith.
Signed Willm. Dungan.

4

Page 2. Agnes Priestly of County of Bucks, Widow. Sept. 4, 1713. Proved Sept. 28, 1713. Son John. Daughter Elizabeth. Youngest dau. Agnes extx.

Page 3. John Griffith, of Township of Woodbridge, East Jersey. June 27, 1713. Proved Oct. 27, 1713. Wife Elizabeth and son-in-law James Heaton, exrs. Daus. Susannah Carter, Ann Heaton, Mary and Martha Griffith, Cousin Abraham Griffith. Wit: Ephraim Heaton, Diana Griffith, John Morris.

Page 4. James Moon of County of Bucks. Dated Jan. 20, 1710/11. Proved Jan. 9, 1713. Wife. --- Eldest son James 1 shilling. Sons Jonas and Jasper each 1 shilling. Daus. Mary and Sarah. granddaus. Sarah Curtis and Elizabeth Moon. Son Roger, exr. Wit: Richard Hill and Nathaniel Tyler.

Page 5. Benjamin Collins of the Town of Bristol, County of Bucks. 1st mo., 23rd day, 1713. Proved April 17th day, 1714. Nathaniel Cleamans, Carpenter Tools, axes, etc. Ezekiel Cleamans coat, etc. Lydia Cleamans. Abraham Cleamans £3.10. Wife Elizabeth Collins, residue of estate, real and personal, and sole extx. Friend George Clough to assist her. Wit: Henry Tomlinson, Thomas Marriott, William Atkinson.

Page 6. Henry Wells of Bucks Co. April 1, 1714. Proved June 11, 1714. Wife Elizabeth, sole extx., use of plantation during widowhood. Son William, Old House and 1/2 Plantation at age of 24 years. Sons Joseph, John, Peter, James, Henry, Samuel, and Edward. Dau. Mary. Wife with child. Trustees Thomas Watson of Buckingham and Joseph Fell of same place Seniors. Wit: Richard Saunders, David Williams, Henry Burges. Signed by mark.

Page 8. William Cutler of Southampton, Bucks County. 5th mo., 23rd day, 1714. Proved July 30, 1714. Mother Isabel Cutler £4 per annum during life. Bro. Thomas Cutler, Sis. Margaret Briggs, Ellin and Jane Cutler. Elizabeth, Mary and Benjamin Cutler, children of John Cutler, Sister Ellin Cutler, sole extx. Wit: John Routledge, John Wildman, John Cutler.

Page 9. Samuel Burges of Hall Twp. Bucks Co. Oct. 14, 1713. Proved Aug. 21, 1714. Wife Eleanor. Eldest Son Joseph Burgess, 1 shilling. Son John 1 shilling. Daus. Priscilla and Sarah Burges £40 each. Son Daniel Burges, land and residue of estate. Son Samuel inadvertently omitted. Sons Daniel and John exrs. Wit: Peter Webster, Nehemiah Blackshaw, John Thornton.

Page 11. John Hart of Warmister Twp. Bucks County. Sept. 14, 1713. Proved Nov. 5, 1714. Wife. --- 200 acres heretofore given to son John Hart. Son Thomas 200 acres as per agreement. Son Josiah Lots in Phila. Dau. Mary. son John, sole exr. Wit: John Morris, Thomas Reed, Joseph Todd.

Page 12. John Baldwin of New Bristol, Co. of Bucks, Yeoman. Aug. 24, 1714. Proved Nov. 29, 1714. Wife Sarah, sole extx. 400

acres on Neshaminey Creek to be appraised. Sons John, Richard, and Joseph. Dau. Sarah £50 and lot of 1/2 acre, land adj. Richard Mountain.
Wit: Benjamin Collins, John Large, John Rowland.

Page 15. Johannes Vansant of Bensalem, Bucks County, Yeoman. Oct. 30, 1714. Proved Jany. 6, 1714. Wife, all Personal estate. Son John 40 shillings land in Maryland to be sold for support of wife and children. Stophel Vansant and Bartholomew Jacobs, Trustees. If land is not sold to be divided between two Sons paying Sisters equal shares. Wife Leah, extx.
Wit: Thomas Stevenson, Hannah Vansant, Nicholas Van Hooren.

Page 16. William Beal of Bucks Co. Yeoman. Jan. 1, 1714. Proved Jan. 6, 1714. Wife Elizabeth, sole extx. Son Alexander 325 acres of land in Buckingham adjoining Mathew Hughes North and by East. Son John 225 acres residue of Tract bought of Thomas Stevenson, when 21. Wife Elizabeth residue of real and personal estate during life then to Daus. Ann, Elizabeth, Rebecka, and Martha.
Wit: Abel Higston, William Baker, James Smyth, William Beal.

Page 18. Thomas Hearl of Makefield Twp. County of Bucks, Carpenter. Apr. 13, 1715. Proved Apr. 28, 1715. Wife. --- Samuel Baker and Neighbor John Burroughs, exrs. Son Joseph £5. Son John, land at Pigeon Swamp near Bristol. 4 Daus. Sarah Duncan, Catharine Wilmerton, Ann and Mary Hearl Tract of land at Wrights Town except 50 on side next John Pidcock's Creek devised to cousin John Hawkins.
Wit: John Burroughs, Hannah Downey.

Page 19. Rachel Hayhurst of Middletown. 9th mo., 6th day, 1714. Proved July 18, 1715. Money due for goods sold by way of London as admix of husband Wm. Hayhurst. Bros-in-law John Cutler and John Hayhurst exrs. to bind out the children where they are or elsewhere. Residue of estate for maintenance of youngest daughter. exrs. to act with advice of People called Quakers at Middletown.
Wit: Cornelius MacCarty, Susanna Carter, Margery Cutler.

Page 21. Edward Radcliffe of County of Bucks. 8th mo., 25th day, 1714. Proved Nov. 15, 1715. Wife Phebe. Sons James and John (minors). Wife to have use of childrens money until they come of age toward bringing them up. Wife Phebe and Brother Rihard Radcliffe, exrs.
Wit: George Clough, John Bown, William Atkinson.
Signed Edward Radcliffe.

Page 22. William Crosdale of Town of Bristol. 1st mo., 30th day, 1715. Proved Jan. 10, 1715. Grandson William Hill. Daughter Agnes Hill, extx. Son-in-law Richard Hill. Sis. Mary Smith's 8 children, Sis. Alice Pott's 10 children, Sis. Bridget Cougill's 4 children, Bro. John Croasdale's (dec'd.) 2 daus. Money in hands of William Bleakey to People called Quakers at Bristol Meeting. George Clough and John Hall to have care of

same. Brother-in-law John Cutler and David Potts. Balance
between me and Bro. Wm. Smith to Elizabeth Smith. Bal. between me
and Marrah Wildman to her daughter Ruth Croasdale.
Wit: Joseph Bond, James Moon, and William Atkinson.

Omitted. Will of Mary Baker, widow. Proved 1715. Recorded Book
1. Page 19.

Page 24. John Rowland, Yeoman. Dec. 3, 1715. Proved Mch. 3,
1715. Dwelling House, Boulting House, and lot in Bristol to use
of Church forever. Mary wife of Henry Tomlinson £50. Residue to
Thomas Rodgers and he to be sole exr. Anthony Burton and Robert
Cobbert, Trustees. Lita to have her freedom and £10 at marriage.
Wit: John Large, John Hall, Timothy Town.

Page 26. Samuel Burges of Makefield. Feb. 13, 1715. Proved
Mch. 25, 1716. Wife Ann, sole extx. 3 daus., Margaret, Rebecka,
and Ann Burges.
Wit: Samuel Beakes, Saml. Bunting, Wm. Biles.

Page 27. William Buckman of Newtown. 7th mo., 4th day, 1716.
Proved Oct. 26, 1716. Wife Elizabeth and eldest son William exrs.
Son Thomas, land at Newtown when 21 years of age. Son David. 2
youngest daus. Elizabeth and Rebecca Buckman. Dau. Ruth Blaker,
son-in-law Edward Beck and his children, Sarah, Francis, and
Edward. Dau. Mary Strawhen and her five children Ruth, Sarah,
William, Henry, and John.
Wit: Stephen Twining, John Frost, Joseph Fell.
Signed William Buckman.

Page 31. John Frost of Newtown. 8th mo., 20th day, 1716.
Proved Nov. 16, 1716. Two daus.-in-law, Margaret Hillborn and
Isabella Carter. Margaret's son, Samuel Hillborne when 21. Thos.
Hillborne and John Stackhouse Trustees for him. Brothers Joseph,
Edmund, Samuel, Isaac, and Thomas Frost, Sis. Elizabeth Francis.
to John Carter my servant man John Jones. John Wildman, exr.
Wit: Robert Streator, Isaac Williams, Robert Carter.

Page 32. George White of Town of Bristol. Dec. 19, 1716.
Proved Jan. 8, 1716. Wife Unity, House and Lots in Bristol and
Tract of land in Middletown. Also all other estate and sole extx.
Wit: George Clough, Ben Harris, Wm. Atkinson.

Page 33. Robert Heaton of Middletown, Yeoman. April 16, 1716.
Proved July 16, 1717. Wife Alice sole extx. Sons Robert, James,
and Ephraim. Sons-in-law Thomas Stackhouse and Henry Comely. Son
Robert and Henry Comly Trustees.
Wit: John Ledyard, Robert Heaton, Junr., Henry Comely.
Signed Robert Heaton.

Page 35. James Carter of Southampton. Dec. 5, 1714. Proved
Mch. 15, 1714. Wife Susanna. Eldest son William when 21, 200
acre lot of father-in-law, John Griffith. Son John when 21, 50
acre lot of Samuel Griffith. Dau. Ann Carter's 5 youngest
children James, Richard, Joseph, Benjamin, and Ann Carter.

Jeremiah Langhorn and John Cutler, both of Middletown, exrs.
Wit: Robert Cobbert and Jeremiah Bartholomew.

Page 37. John Lucas of Fall Twp., Yeoman. Sept. 7, 1712.
Proved Oct. 20, 1719. Mother. --- £5 during life. Cousin Mary
Poole, dau. of Nathaniel and Mary Poole of Phila. Sis. Rebecca.
Bros. Edward and Robert Lucas, exrs.
Wit: Joseph Kirkbride, Junr., Peter Webster, and Jeffrey Burges.

Page 38. Thomas Stevenson, Co. of Bucks. Nov. 10, 1717. Proved
Oct. 19, 1719. Wife Sarah 1/3 of real and personal estate
absolutely. Lands in New Jersey and Pensylvania to be sold. Sons
Samuel and Edward (minors). Daus. Ann and Sarah, so much as will
make their legacies from their grandfather Jennings £50. Daus.,
Elizabeth and Alliss. Bros. William's and John's children. Wife
and Joseph Kirkbride exrs.
Wit: Anna Marriott, John Oxford, Benj. Field.
Codicil dated April 29, 1719. Proved Oct. 19, 1719. Wife Sarah
and Jos. Kirkbridge, Trustees to sell land and hold proceeds for
use of wife and children.
Wit: to Codicil. John Jones, Charles Brockden, Joseph Fox.

Page 42. John Penquite of Town of Bristol. 2nd mo., 14th day,
1714. Proved Jan. 11, 1719. Wife Agnes. Eldest son John, 200
acres in Wrightstown. Son Nicholas 200 acres on west side of
Neshaminey Creek bought of William Pickering. 4 daus. Hester,
Joan, Jane, and Agnes Penquite at 21 or marriage. Wife Agnes and
son John exrs.
Wit: Thos. Stackhouse, Thomas Baynes, John Cutler.

Page 44. Mary Paxson of Town of Bristol, Widow. 10th mo., 25th
day, 1718. Proved Feb. 23, 1719. Daus. Mary Appleton and Grace
Carter. Grandaus, Rebecca and Susanna Appleton, Mary and Martha
Carter, Mary Chase and Elizabeth Aldridge. Grandsons Robert and
William Carter. Dau. Grace, extx.
Wit: George Clough, Thos. Clifford, William Atkinson.

Page 45. Thomas Wiate of Newtown, Weaver. 1st mo., 7th day,
1719. Proved Apr. 15, 1720. Bro. William Wiat, of Stanton Parish
in Glostershire, Great Britain and Jane Wiat of Westbury Parish
Glostershire, Henry Nelson of Middletown and Abraham Chapman of
Wrightstown, exrs.
Wit: Thomas Hillborne, Elizabeth Hillborne, Katharine Hillborne.

Page 46. Robert Hillborn of Newtown. 1st mo., 24th day,
1719/20. Proved Apr. 25, 1720. Wife Mary, Father-in-law Thomas
Hardin and Brother-in-law Thomas Hardin, Junr. exrs. Son Thomas
all land at Newtown, when 21.
Wit: Abraham Chapman, Amos Watson, Katharine Hillborn.

Page 48. Stephen Twining of Newtown. 12th mo., 20th day,
1719/20. Proved May 19, 1720. Sons John and Stephen, Plantation
at Newtown bought of John Ward adj. land formerly Michael
Hough's. Son John, land left me by Government of New England.
Sons Eleazer and Nathaniel, land adj. Wm. Buckman, where Jos.

Lupton lived, 230 acres. To daus. Rachel Twining and Mercy
Lupton, grandchildren each 5 shillings Sons Stephen and Nathaniel
exrs.
Wit: James and Agnes Yeates and Abrm. Chapman.

Page 50.   John Cutler of Middletown.   11th mo., 7th day, 1718.
Proved June 6, 1720. Wife Margery, sole extx.   Son Benj. 56 acres
in Middletown at age of 21. Daus. Elizabeth and Mary Cutler.
Neighbors John Stackhouse and Brother-in-law John Hayhurst.
Wit: Henry Barton, Thomas Thwaite, Cuthbert Hayhurst.

Page 52.   John Webster of Falls Twp., Yeoman.   Dec. 13, 1720.
Proved Dec. 24, 1720. Brother Peter Webster 5 shillings Kinsman
Richard Saunders, money on Bonds of John Sotcher, Wm. Stockdale,
John Hough, Jonathan Cooper and Thomas Thwaite.   Richard
Saunders' son-in-law, Thomas Lamb. Kinsman James Yeates, Agnes
his wife and their children. Friend Nehemiah Blackshaw £3.15. due
from Anthony Burton.   Mary wife of Nehemiah Blackshaw and their
two daus. Nehemiah Blackshaw, exr.
Wit: Benj. Eastburne, Wm. Ashburn, Jos. Siddal.

Page 53.   Margery Hough of County of Bucks, Widow.   11th mo.,
27th day, 1715.   Proved Feb. 6, 1720. Sons, Richard, John and
Joseph.   Daus. Sarah Atkinson and Mary Atkinson.   Grandchildren,
Hannah, Jane, William, John, Mary, and Thomas Atkinson and
Richard Hough.   Son-in-law Wm. Atkinson exr.
Wit: George Clough, John Large, James Watson.

Page 55.   Zebulon Heston of Wrightstown.   Feb. 20, 1720/1.
Proved Apr. 4, 1722. Wife Dorothy and John Routledge, exrs.
Eldest son Zebulon (minor), rest of children, Rachel Lacey, John,
Jemimy, Stephen, Jacob, Isaac, and Thomas Heston.   Grandchildren,
Rachel and Mary Lacey.   Land purchased of John Estaugh.
Wit: John Wildman, Joseph Wildman.

Page 56.   Reece Preese of Middletown.   Feb. 20, 1720.   Proved
Mch. 11, 1720. Wife Mary, extx., all estate.
Wit: John Wildman, Joseph Wildman, John Worshall.
Signed Reece Preese.

Page 57.   William Baldwin of Co. of Bucks.   6th mo., 21st day,
1720.   Proved Sept. 28, 1720. Wife Mary and Son John (under 21)
all estate.   500 acres in place called "Hilltown." Brother John
Baldwin, Richard Hill of Phila. and Jos. Kirkbride, Junr.
Wit: Daniel Jackson, Joseph Headley, Edward Tuckett.

Page 58.   William Ellet of Co. of Bucks.   12th mo., 9th day,
1714.   Proved Sept. 15, 1721. Wife. ---- Son-in-law, James
Towney, (exr) Plantation. Daus. Ann Shallcross, Elizabeth
Doudney, Mary Hawkins, Sarah Bidgood.
Wit: Benj. Harris, Mary Atkinson.

Page 59.   Isaac Atkinson of Co. of Bucks.   Dec. 23, 1720.   Proved
Dec. 5, 1721. Wife Sarah, extx.   3 children, John, Jane, and
Thomas (under age). Samuel Baker to assist wife.

Wit: John Clowes, Richd. Brock, Wm. Atkinson.

Page 60. Henry Johnson Vandike, of Middletown. Apr. 4, 1717. Proved Nov. 11, 1721. Wife Yanica, sole extx, during life at her death son-in-law Christian Barnson. Son-in-law Paulus Vanoley. 5 shillings to grandau., Susanna Vanoley. Wit: Ury Puff, Elizabeth Vanhorne, Jeremiah Langhorne.

Page 61. John Johnson of Co. of Bucks, Yeoman. Nov. 2, 1721. Proved Jan. 13, 1721. Wife Margaret (sole ex'rx) youngest son William, daughter Hannah Seven. Children, John, William, Peter, Williamet, Mary, Elizabeth, and Hannah. Wit: Neils Laicon, Francis Rawle, Susanna Laicon.

Page 62. William Williamson, Of Bensalem Twp. Dec. 15, 1721. Proved Jan. 22, 1721. Wife Elizabeth sole extx., and guardian of children during minority. Sons Jacob, Abraham, John, William, and Peter. 600 acres with mansion house on River Delaware. Wit: John Evans, Thomas Cutler, Jeffy. Pollard.

Page 64. Joseph Hembry of Makefield Twp. Worsted Comber. June 15, 1721. Proved April 9, 1722. Joseph Kirkbride, Edward Lucas and John Thacher, executors. Samuel Coombes £10. James Downey £10. Jos. Higginbotham £5. Wit: Thomas Jones, Elizabeth Cutifer.

Page 65. Francis Searle of Bensalem Twp., Yeoman. Jan. 26, 1721/2. Proved May 28, 1722. Wife Joan, rent of 100 acres that son Thomas settled. Son Arthur and dau. Mary, wife of Henry Walmsley, exrs. Grandchildren, Grace and Mary Searle daus. of Thomas. 300 acres in Bensalem to Arthur. 200 acres in Southampton, 28 acres in Bensalem, 200 acres in Horsham and Plantation in Abington Phila. County to daughter Mary Walmsley. Wit: Thomas Tomlinson, Joan Tomlinson, Thom. Rodgers. Byberry mtg. to choose 2 members to see will fulfilled.

Page 67. William White of Bucks Co. 6th mo., 13th day, 1722. Proved Oct. 15, 1722. Wife. ---. Thomas Lambert and Joseph Kirkbride, Junr., exrs., Plantation to be sold for benefit of wife and children, son John to have privilege of buying it when 21. Wit: Thos. Watson, John Sotcher, Abel Janney.

Page 68. Thomas Hillborn of Newtown, Yeoman. 11th mo. (Jan), 10th day, 1717. Proved May 13, 1723. Wife Elizabeth, sole Executrix. Son Robert. Land adj. Bowman's and Samuel Hillborn's not to be sold before son Thomas cometh of age. Three youngest children, John, Joseph, and Rachel. 4 daus. Mary Watson, Elizabeth Darlington, Katharine and Rachel Hillborn, Grandson Samuel, son of Samuel and Margaret. Land at Egg Harbor to John and Joseph. Wit: John Twining, John Penquite, John Kirk.

Page 68. Joseph Tomlinson of Southampton, Yeoman. Oct. 30, 1722. Proved June 7, 1723. Wife Mary, 200 acres I now live on

until children come of age. Sons Thomas, Joseph and Benjamin,
exrs. Bro. Henry Tomlinson and Joseph Walker, overseers.
Wit: Richard Sands, Philip Dracott, Joseph Walker.

Page 73. Henry Paxson of Marsh Gibbon, Bucks Co., Yeoman. 2nd
mo. (Apr.) 23, 1723. Proved July 30, 1723. Cousins James, 250
acres, Thomas 250 acres and Reuben Paxson 238, sons of nephew Wm.
Paxson 500 acres I now live on and 238 purchased of George
Pownall adj. his other land. Mary Walmsley's two daus. Mary and
Elizabeth £20 each. Nephew Henry Paxson's daughter Elizabeth £20
at 21 or marriage. Son-in-law John Plumly's son John and nephew
Wm. Paxson's son Henry tract of land near North Wales "about 12
miles from Edward Farmer's Mill." Nephew James Kirkham, land at
Conistogoe. To Amy his sister, tract of land at Newtown. Mary
wife of Samuel Jacobs, Sarah wife of Thomas Knight, Junr.
Abigail widow of nephew William Paxson. Ester daughter of nephew
Wm. Paxson. Residue to son-in-law John Plumly, nephews William
and Henry Paxson, and makes them executors.
Wit: Mathew Durham, John Bowne, William Atkinson.
Signed by mark.

Page 75. Margery Cutler of Middletown Twp., Widow. 12th mo.,
22nd day, 1722. Proved Aug. 20, 1723. Son Benjamin to dwell with
his uncle Cuthbert Hayhurst until of age. 2 daus. Elizabeth and
Mary to be under their uncle's care and advice. Brothers John and
Cuthbert Hayhurst, executors.
Wit: Joseph Walker, Ann Stackhouse, and Thomas Thwaite.

Page 77. Samuel Darke of Falls Twp. Apr. 22, 1722. Proved Dec.
4, 1723. Wife. ---- sole extx. Plantation and all estate except
£50 to cousin John Darke.
Wit: Thomas Worrall, Wm. Lacey, Robert Thomas.

Page 78. Claus Johnson of Bensalem Twp. Nov. 25, 1723. Proved
Jan. 10, 1723. Wife Walburth. Sons John, Lawrence, and Richard,
all lands (640 acres) Three daus. Gartha, Barbary, and Elizabeth.
Sons John and Lawrence, exrs. Land formerly Michael
Frederickson's.
Wit: Jeffy Pollard, John Johnson, Jacob Vankirk.

Page 81. James Ray of Wrightstown, Date Feb. 25, 1723. Proved
Mch. 14, 1723. Robert Ray, son of beloved friend David Ray of
Freehold, Monmouth Co. East New Jersey, if he lives to age of 21.
Plantation in Wrightstown. Joseph Hampton and Garret Vansant of
Wrightstown, exrs.
Wit: Richard Tuney, Edward Milnor, Abraham Chapman.
Signed by his mark.

Page 82. Henry Poynter of Southampton. Nov. 4, 1723. Proved
June 8, 1724. Wife Sarah and mother Mary Poynter, exrs. Son Henry
(under 14) "moveables to be divided between rest of children."
Wit: James Stone, John Towne, Daniel Brock.

Page 84. Elizabeth Smith widow of John Smith of Bristol Twp.,
Blacksmith. 6th mo., 2rd day, 1724. Proved Sept. 18, 1724. Sons

John and Robert. Robert exr.
Wit: George Clough, Wm. Atkinson.
Signed by mark.

Page 85. Peter Webster, Co. of Bucks, Aug. 1, 1724. Proved Sept. 28, 1724. Daughter Agnes Yeates' children, Joseph Yeates, and her other children. Grandson-in-law, William Ashburn. Grandson Thomas Lamb. Granddaughter Sarah Ashburn. Son Wm. Webster.
Wit: Joseph Linton, Benjamin Linton, Mary Blackshaw.

Page 86. John Routledge of Neshaminey Creek, Yeoman. Wife Margaret sole extx. Seven children. "Tract of land I hold of Joshua Tomkins," by indenture, dated 1st mo., 10th day, 1721 to wife. Wm. Paxton and Thom. Chalkley, overseers.
Wit: Adam Harker, Grace Harker, Wm. Paxson, Mary Paxson, Thom. Chalkley.

Page 88. George Haworth of Buckingham. 11 mo. (Jan.), 27th day, 1724. Proved May 6, 1725. Wife Sarah, Plantation while she remains a widow and at her marriage "to be divided among all my children." Wife and brother-in-law John Fisher, exrs.
Wit: John Searbrough, Lawrence Bearson, Ambrose Barcroft, Joseph Sidell.

Page 90. Thomas Greasley of Richland Twp., Yeoman. 1st mo., 4th day, 1725/6. Proved Aug. 25, 1726. Wife Dorothy and Father John Creasley, exrs. Sons, Thomas, John, William and child unborn.
Wit: Wm. Nixon, Edward Roberts, Abraham Griffith.

Page 91. John Moore of Bristol, Glazier. Aug. 28, 1726. Proved Oct. 1, 1726. Sister Sarah Moore. Edward Southwood, Nicholas Allen, Joseph Jackson, Joseph White, John Double, John Welch, Samuel Haker and John Emmet, pallbearers, each pr. of gloves. £5 toward flooring church at Bristol. Richard Glover, James Higgs and Joseph Thornton, exrs., all estate here in this Province or in the Jerseys.
Wit: George Clough, Henry Betts.

Page 92. Margaret Jones of Hill Town, Bucks Co. April 3, 1727. Proved May 11, 1727. Eldest son John. Youngest son Thomas. Sons Edward, Robert and Richard. Eldest dau. Elizabeth. Youngest Margaret. Daus. Ann. Dau. Elizabeth's 3 children. Brother Thos. Clayton. Sister Jane's son. Plantation of 200 acres to son Richard, exr.
Wit: Bernard Young, Thomas Morris.
Signed by mark.

Page 94. William Kitchin of Solesberry, Bucks Co. Gent. July 18, 1723. Proved May 15, 1727. Wife Rebecca. Son Thomas all Real estate. Son William £5. Ruth, Olive, and Mary Kitchin each £3 at 21 yrs. of age. Joseph Ashton, of Phila. Co. and John Wells of Bucks Co., exrs.
Wit: John Holcombe, Samuel Coate.

Page 95. Stephen Whitten, of Northampton. April 9, 1728.
Proved April 23, 1728. Wife Sarah and nephew James Whitten, exrs.
and sole legatees. Codicil Thomas Harmon £10.
Wit: Robert Heaton, John Shaw, Daniel Brock.

Page 112. Daniel Bankson, Bensalem Twp. Mch. 30, 1727. Proved
Apr. 11, 1727. Wife Elizabeth, extx. and sole legatee.
Wit: William Hote, John Williamson, Jeffrey Pollard.

Page 97. Robert Harvey of the Falls Twp., Yeoman. Mch. 13,
1726. Proved Apr. 24, 1727. Wife Susanna sole extx. Sons Robert
and John, Plantation and meadows called "Cadwallader Swamp" and
"Birtch Swamp" the latter purchased of Samuel Darke. Agreement
with Thomas Walthell for sales of Mault House and Lot to be
fulfilled by Trustees and exrs. Joseph Peace, John Sotcher, and
Jos. Kirkbride, Junr., Trustees.
Wit: Josiah Patterson, Wm. Eaton, Clear Smith.

Page 99. Ralph Dunn, Northampton Twp. Mch 30, 1727. Proved May
1, 1727. Wife. ---- sole extx. Son William land in Munor or
Moorland. Sons Ralph and George land "here at home" Daus.
Margaret, Mary, Sarah, Rephane, Rebecca, and Hannah. "Young
Thomas Hardin" and Robert Hittin, Trustees.
Wit: William Dunn, Jonathan Davis.

Page 101. Rachel Pidcock of Richland Co. of Phila. (?) Dated
Mch. 23, 1726/7. Proved May 8, 1727. Brother John Buckman,
trustee and exr. Land to be sold for use of children. Son Stephen
to have two parts, the other two one part.
Wit: Silas McCarty, Francis Lewis, Samuel Watson.

Page 102. Henry Margerum of Maxfield, Bucks Co. Pa. May 3,
1727. Proved Aug. 24, 1727. Wife Jane and eldest son Richard,
exrs. Farm "on which I dwell." Son Abraham Farm on which Wm.
Snowden dwells and right in Proprietary in New Jersey. Eldest
dau. Elizabeth and her 4 children, Elizabeth, Mathias, Mary, and
Henry Harvey. Youngest dau. Jane under 20 yrs. of age. Wife's
daughter Margaret Yeates and her husband Joseph Yeates and her
children, John, Robert, and Margaret Pearson, and Jane and Joseph
Yeates. Friend William Rigg.
Wit: James Downey, Alexander Pickey, Francis Parrell.

Page 105. William Searbrough of Solbury, Turner. 2nd mo.
(Apr.), 27th day, 1727. Proved Sept. 24, 1727. Son William, 200
acres left me by will of Father John Searbrough (see below).
Brother John, exr. to occupy and enjoy same until debt is paid to
loan office. Son William to live with him. Son Uclides 60 acres
I now live on, son Uclides to be put apprentice to John Head, to
learn art of making German Wheels. 3 daus. Lydia, Martha, and
Sarah.
Wit: Henry Paxson, Thomas Canby, Benjamin Canby.

Page 107. John Searborough of Solberry, Yeoman. 1st mo., 13th
day, 1726/7. Proved Oct. 2, 1727. Wife Mary and sons John and
William, executors. Wife 200 acres having the Lake Meadow

therein. Son Robert. Daus. Sarah Haworth, Elizabeth Fisher, Hannah Searbrough, and Mary Pickering. Grandchildren, James Haworth, John, Elizabeth, Mary, and Susanna Brock and Samuel Pickering. Son William 60 acres and 200 acres on death of wife.
Wit: Thos. Canby, Henry Paxson, Joseph Fell.

Page 110. Mary Tomlinson of Southampton, Widow. 9th mo., 19th day, 1727. Proved Feb. 12, 1727. Children to be bound to trades. 3 sisters Sarah, Rebecca, and Jane. Joseph Walker and John Wildman, exrs.
Wit: Thom. Eastburne, Wm. Ring.

Page 111. Josiah Mark lately from Old England and living with uncle Thomas Watson of Straberry in County of Bucks, Province of Penna. Dated 6th mo., 4th day, 1727. Proved Oct. 21, 1727. Goods as per inventory signed by me to be sold, proceeds to "cozens" Mark Watson and John Watson.
Wit: John Socther, Amos Watson, Benjamin Linton.

Page 116. Joseph Pidgeon of Falls Twp. Sept. 7, 1728. Proved Dec. 4, 1728. Wife Ann, extx. Sons Joseph and William each £1000. Wife, residue of estate, real and personal.
Wit: Thos. Groome, Wm. Biles, Thos. Biles.

Page 114. Gabriel Bains of Falls Twp., Yeoman. 9th mo., 19th day, 1727. Proved Feby. 12, 1727. Wife Ellin, Mark Watson, and Robert Sotcher, exrs. To be buried in graveyard at plantation of neighbor Thos. Watson. £1 to said Thos. Watson, toward repairing fence around said graveyard. Son Bryan Bains, Plantation at 21, if he die without issue, to Brother Thomas Bains. Sister Agnes Wood, Cousin Ann Hillburne and Cousin Deborah Lee's 2 children, John and Deborah Lee.
Wit: Nehemiah Blackshaw, John Sotcher, Jos. Kirkbride, Junr.

Page 117. James Robinson, no residence given. 12 mo. (Feby), 6th day, 1728. Proved Mch. 14, 1728. Sarah Haworth, extx. and legatee. Stephanus Haworth, Thomas Haworth. Thomas Holcombe. Mary Fisher, dau. of John 40 shillings toward fencing graveyard at Buckingham.
Wit: John Fisher, Lawrence Pearson, Jacob Holcombe.

Page 118. John Brown (nuncupative). Feb. 2, 1727. Proved Oct. 1, 1728. "Feby 2, 1727, Then our Brother John Brown departed this life." Plantation to 4 brothers, George, Thomas, Alexander, and Joseph Brown. Legacies to George's 3 children, John, Jonathan, and Susanna. Thomas' 4 children, Ann, Mathew, Hannah, and Moses Brown. James Shaw's wife and her children, Joseph, Samuel, and John. Sister Hester Brown.
Signed by Thomas Brown, Mary Brown, George Brown.

Page 119. Willoughby Warder of Makefield. Mch. 5, 1728. Proved Mch. 31, 1728. Wife Mary, ex'rx. Brother Saml. Baker to assist her. Son Jeremiah £5 when of age, if he dye to Kinsman Henry Baker.
Wit: Robert Pidcock, Thos. Craven, Rachel Baker.

Page 120. Henry Large of Plumstead, Yeoman. 1st mo., 10th day, 1728/9. Proved May 22, 1729. Wife Elizabeth, personal estate she and Bro. Jonathan, exrs. Bro. Large, Plantation paying wife value thereof.
Wit: Thomas Brown, Joseph Fell.

Page 121. Thomas Watson, Junr., of Buckingham. Oct. 21st 1728. Proved May 22, 1729. Wife Elizabeth, sole extx. Son John. Daus. Elinor, Mary, and Sarah. Brothers John Watson of Buckingham and William Smith of Wrightstown, Trustees.
Wit: John Thomas, Amor Preston, Joseph Fell.

Page 123. John Dunkan of Bensalem, Yeoman. Jany. 24, 1728. Proved June 20th day, 1729. Wife Margaret and son William, exrs. and sole legatees. 60 acres whereon I live to William.
Wit: John Kelohr, Sarah Dunkan, F. Parrell.

Page 124. Robert Smith of County of Bucks. Sept. 24, 1729. Proved Nov. 10, 1729. Wife Mary and John Burges, exrs. Son Joseph, House and Lot in Town of Bristol. Daus. Hannah and Elizabeth.
Wit: Tho. Marriott, David Palmer, Wm. Atkinson.

Page 121. James Lewis of Hilltown Twp. Nov. 11, 1729. Proved Mch 24, 1729. Wife Elizabeth and Father Lewis Thomas, sole exrs. mother. Only son James, Tract of land I live on at age of 21 yrs. Brother Thomas Lewis. Sisters. David Evans and Jenkin Evans of Montgomery, Trustees.
Wit: William Thomas, Barthw. Young, Benjm. Phillips, Benjm. Griffith.

Page 127. Jeremiah Lewis of Hilltown Twp., Yeoman. Nov. 28, 1729. Proved Dec. 10, 1729. Wife Mary, sole extx. Martha only child 200 acres of land at 18. Brothers Thomas and John. Son of Brother James, dec'd. Sisters Jenet and Elinor. Limon Butler and Bernard Young, Trustees.
Wit: Simon Butler, Thomas Jones, Griffith Owen.
Signed by mark.

Page 129. George Hulme of Middletown, Yeoman. June 9, 1729. Proved Jan. 8, 1729. Wife Ruth and Brother-in-law Jonathan Palmer, exrs. Children.
Wit: Joseph Kirkbride and Thomas Pugh.

Page 130. Morris Lewis of Hilltown Twp., Yeoman. Oct. 21, 1729. Proved Nov. 9, 1729. Wife Dorothy, Bartholomew Young and Griffith Owen, exrs. Son Henry. Daus. Mary and Martha (all minors). Bro. Henry.
Wit: William Thomas, Evan Evans, Bernard Young, Benj. Phillips.

Page 132. John Darke of Makefield, Yeoman. April 27, 1730. Proved July 23, 1730. Wife Jane, sole ex'rx, all estate real and personal, paying children 5 shillings each.
Wit: Edward Lucas, William Gregory, Stephen Edwin.

Page 133. John Sotcher of Falls Twp., Yeoman. Dec. 6, 1729. Proved Feby. 26, 1729. Son Robert, exr., all real estate. Sons-in-law Joseph Kirkbride, Junr., Mahlon Kirkbride and Mark Watson. Daus. Mary Kirkbride, and Anne Watson. Grandchildren, Stacy Kirkbride, Mary Kirkbride, dau. Mahlon and Joseph Watson. Falls Mo. Mtg. £5.
Wit: Joseph Kirkbride, Willm. Paxson, Abel Janney.

Page 136. John Teeton of Middletown, Miller. Feby 24, 1730. Proved Mch. 8, 1730. Wife Hannah, sole extx. Children of Uncle William Roberts of Phila. Co. vist. John, Timothy, Edward, William and Elizabeth.
Wit: Tho. Stackhouse, Richard Jones, William Toliffe.

Page 134. Leonard Shallcross of Co. of Bucks. Feby. 28, 1729/30. Proved Nov. 16, 1730. Wife Sarah, sole extx. Sons William, Joseph, and Leonard and John. Dau. Rachel.
Wit: James Higgs, Wm. Atkinson.

Page 137. Benjamin Harvye of Makefield Twp., Yeoman. Mch. 17, 1728. Proved Mch. 8, 1730. Wife Susanna and Bro. Mathias Harvye, exrs. Sons Benjamin and John, Daus. Sarah and Mary (all minors).
Wit: Wm. Russel, John Brown, Charles Bryan.

Page 139. Francis Richardson of New York, Merchant. 5th mo., July 7, 1688. Pr. July 16, 1688. To be buried at Friends Burying ground at Flushing. Wife Rebecca (sole extx) 400 acres of land in Twp. of Chltenham and 1/3 of other estate. 3 children, Francis, Rebecca and John at age of 21, 2/3 of estate. Wm. Richardson, Arthur Cooke, and John Delavall, overseers.
Wit: John Lawrence, William Dearing, George Heathcote and Richard Van Dam.
Pr. and certified from Boston Feb. 14, 1688. John Wat. Depty Sec'y.

Page 141. Joseph Growden of Trevose, Bucks Co. Gent. July 25, 1730. Proved Dec. 28, 1730. Wife Ann, sole extx., son Joseph, Plantation, "Richelieu" and water mill adj. Francis Searle, Herman Vansandt leaving off encumbrance to Collet. Dau. Hannah Growdon, Plantation adj. Duncan and Arthur Searle, formerly in possession of Francis Lucas. Dau. Ganifeir Cooper, grandson Francis Richardson, son of Francis Richardson late of Phila., goldsmith, Joseph Richardson his brother. Son Lawrence 5 shillings. son-in-law David Lloyd 5 shillings.
Wit: Tho. Stackhouse, John Stackhouse, Wm. Watson, Griffith Owen.

Page 143. George Clough of County of Bucks. 10th mo., 26th day, 1729. Proved Mch. 30, 1731. Wife Pleasant. Son George. Dau. Mary Shaw. Dau.-in-law Isabel Heyworth. £5 to Friends Mtg. of Bristol. Dwelling House and Boulting House to be sold. Son-in-law Joseph Shaw and Wm. Atkinson, exrs.
Wit: Tho. Clifford, William Silverstone, Benjamin Harris.

Page 144. Thomas Watson, Senr., of Buckingham. 1st mo., 5th day, 1731. Proved May 14, 1731. Wife Jane, extx. Grandsons John

and Thomas Watson.
Wit: Andrew Wright, Andrew Dunbar, Reece Davis.
Appraisers Math. Hughes and John Cadwallader.

Page 145. John Beakes, of Falls Twp. (nuncupative), Declared
June 21, 1731, Signed July 2, 1731. Proved July 30, 1731.
Children of sister Mary Hamilton, Elizabeth, James, William,
Mary, Jenitt and Stephen Hamilton. John Howard, son of sister
Grace Howard. Residue to sisters Mary Hamilton and Grace Howard.
Wit: Richard Pritchard, Ann Browne, Mary Clarke.

Page 146. Cornelius McCarty of Middletown, husbandman. Mch. 13,
1726. Proved Dec. 7, 1731. Wife Judey and Bro.-in-law Nicholas
Cruse, exrs. "child or children."
Wit: Derrick Cruse, Ann Edmonson, Jeremiah Croasdale.

Page 149. John Johnson of Newtown. July 9, 1731. Proved Oct.
12, 1731. Wife Margaret. Sons Lawrence and Abraham (minors).
Brother Abraham Johnson. Euclides Longshore and John Wildman,
exrs.
Wit: Rachel Janney, William Curny, Thomas Heard.

Page 151. William Brelsford of Middletown, Carpenter. Nov. 22,
1731. Proved Nov. 8, 1732. Wife Elizabeth. Sons John and
Abraham and Isaac. Dau. Lydia. Joseph Headly and John Sisom,
exrs. Plantation whereon I live to John. House Mill St. Bristol
adj. Benj. Harris. Lot in Bristol adj. John Priestly. share in
Milford Mills to be sold if necessary.
Wit: Richard Jones, Hanah Headly, Samuel Brelsford.

Page 153. Jane Sharp of Buckingham, Widow. 6th mo., 8th day,
1729. Proved Nov. 13, 1731. Sons Samuel Ogburn, Joseph Hampton,
Benjamin Fitzrandel, dau. Sarah Kinsey. Dau. Mary's 3 daus. Son
Joseph Hampton's dau. Mary and Elizabeth Kinsey. Son-in-law
Edmund Kinsey and Joseph Fell, exrs.
Wit: John Hill, Elizth. Fell.

Page 155. Derrick Cruson of Southampton, Yeoman. Jan. 4, 1729.
Proved Dec. 25, 1731. Wife Elizabeth. Sons Garret, Francis,
Nicholas, John Derrick, Henry. Dau. Catharine. Plantation in
Southampton to wife for life. Sons Garret and John, exrs.
Wit: Jacobus Vansand, Jacob Stricklin, John Hart.

Page 159. Jane Watson of Buckingham, Widow of Thomas. Oct. 6,
1731. Proved Nov. 13, 1731. Son-in-law John Watson and his 3
children Joseph and Thomas, granddau. Sarah Watson. Grandson
John Watson, son-in-law Thomas Watson, dec'd. Elizabth Reed,
wid. of Bro. John Reed, dec'd. and her children. Richard
Mitchell of Wrightstown, exr.
Wit: Math. Hughes, Mary Dunbar, Jane Bradfield.

Page 160. Amos Palmer of Makefield, Weaver. 8th mo., 23rd day,
1731. Proved Feb. 26, 1731. Brother Daniel. Bro. Jonathan's
children. Bro. David's son David. Bro. John's 2 eldest sons.
Sister Ruth Hulme and her son John Hulme. Bro.-in-law James

Thackeray's 2 sons. Bro-in-law Thom. Clowes dau. Sarah. Brother Daniel, exr.
Wit: Mary Bulls, Thomas Miles.

Page 162. David Palmer of County of Bucks. 9th mo., 1st day, 1731. Proved April 17, 1732. Wife Mary and Brother-in-law Samuel Allen, exrs. 3 children, David, William, and Samuel. House and Lot in Bristol.
Wit: Edward Southwood, Wm. Atkinson, Rebeckah Burges.

Page 163. Abraham Margerum of Maxfield. Mar. 24, 1731. Proved April 26, 1732. Wife Margaret and Mother Jane Margerum, exrs. (wife now sick) Elder Bro. Richard.
Wit: Saml. Coombe, Hanah Coombe, F. Parrell.

Page 165. John Plumly of County of Bucks, Yeoman. Mch. 24, 1731/2. Proved Apr. 27, 1732. Wife Mary and Son Charles, exrs. Sons Charles and William Tract of land 600 acres joining Neshaminey Creek, son Wm. the part adj. land formerly Daniel Jackson. Dau. Sarah Carter. Son John. Cousins Wm. Paxson and William Atkinson, Trustees.
Wit: Robert Shewell, William Murdaugh, Sarah Bullock.

Page 168. Nathaniel Donham of Co. of Bucks, Yeoman. Mch. 28, 1732. Proved May 12, 1732. Wife Hannah, sole ex'rx. and guardian of son Ephraim. Dau. Elizabeth House and Lot in Newtown now rented by John Frohock. Son Ephraim 48 acres in Newtown purchased of Joseph Lupton.
Wit: James Yeates, Sarah Twining, John Frohock.

Page 169. Joseph Reeder of County of Bucks, Yeoman. Dec. 6, 1731. Proved May 31, 1732. Wife Margaret and Timothy Smith of Makefield, exrs. Children Sarah, Charles, John, William, Isaac and others that may be born.
Wit: Elijah Doane, John Headlee, John Dillon.

Page 171. John Clark of Falls Twp., Yeoman. Nov. 28, 1731. Proved June 24, 1732. Wife Rachel and father-in-law Solomon Warder and Jos. Kirkbride, exrs. Sisters Sarah Richards, Ann Brown, Elizabeth Brown, Mary and Christian Clark. 400 acres in Makefield adj. London Co. Tract of land in Hunterdon Co. N.J. which Father John Clark agreed to sell to John Hart of Co. of Hunterdon. Plantation I live on to be sold except Grave Yard. 3 Sons Charles, Joseph, and Wheeler.
Wit: Enoch Anderson, Eliakim Anderson, John Bates.

Page 175. Clement Dungan, of Northampton, Senr. Aug. 26, 1732. Proved Sept. 25, 1732. Brother Jeremiah, sole exr. All lands. Thomas Dungan of Warminster. Nephew Wm. Dungan to pay Judey McCarty £6 due me. James Carrell to pay Bro. Thomas Dungan £3 and £3 to our new meeting house and be quit of debt he owes. Edward Doial to pay Jeremiah Dungan's youngest dau., Mary.
Wit: David Drake, George Dungan, Daniel Brock, Jenkin Jones of Phila. and Joseph Earton of North Wales. Bond due from John Hart.

Page 175. Jacob Coffing of Northampton, Senior. Aug. 26, 1732. Proved Oct. 9, 1732. Sons William and Abraham, exrs. All lands. Eldest Son Jacob 5 shillings.
Wit: Robert Heaton, John B. Brock, Danl. Brock.

Page 177. Sarah Wally of Newtown, Widow of Shadrack Wally, late of Newtown. Aug. 28, 1732. Proved Dec. 15, 1732. Son John Wally, his wife Elizabeth, son John and his dau. Damaris. 4 grandchildren, children of John and Elizabeth. £4 due from Tho. Story. Abraham Chapman, exr.
Wit: Jos. Yeates, Margaret Yeates, John Frohock.

Page 181. William Stockdale of Northampton Twp. 3 mo. (May) 12, 1727. Proved Jany. 30, 1732/3. Wife Dorothy, sole extx. with advice of Mo. Mtg. of People called Quakers. Sell lands.
Wit: Robert Heaton, Abraham Gray, Daniel Brock.

Page 178. John Bye, of Solebury, Shoemaker. 6th mo., 23rd day, 1723. Proved Nov. 13, 1732. Wife Sarah, extx. Sons Enock and Hezekiah. daus. Elizabeth Mitchell, Sarah, Deborah, Mary and Martha Bye (son Hezekiah 194 acres, son Enock 50 acres).
Wit: Nathaniel Bye, Andrew Ellicot, Thomas Bye.

Page 182. Martha Darke, Widow, of Falls Twp. Mch. 7, 1725/6. Proved Dec. 26, 1732. Friend Samuel Beakes, exr. Brother John Worral of Chester County. Cousins Ellin, Elizabeth, and Martha, daus. of Thomas Worrall, Martha dau. of Robert Thomas of North Wales. Mary Darke.
Wit: Henry Margerum, Samuel Coomb, Jane Margerum, Junr. Letters of Admr.c.t.a. granted to William Mead. Jane Margerum was Jane Scarborogh at the time of Proof of Will.

Page 185. Richard Tillbram, of Burrough of Bristol. 6th mo., 18th day, 1732. Proved Jan. 5, 1732/3. Joseph Peace and Wm. Atkinson, exrs. Sister Mary Church. Cousin William Church and his son. £5 to Bristol Mtg. Friends Henry Tomlinson, Thomas Tomlinson, Mary Tomlinson, Joseph Tomlinson, Sarah Tomlinson, Elizabeth Tomlinson, Thomas Clifford, David Murray, John Priestly, Junr., John Hall, Thomas Marriot, and Joseph Kirkbride's son Thomas. Jonathan Church son of Sister Mary.
Wit: John Priestly, Mathias Keen, John Bishop.

Page 187. Thomas Harding, of Southampton, Yeoman. Feby. 4, 1728/9. Proved Dec. 26, 1732. Wife Mary. Sons-in-law Wm. Crodell, Jos. Arbuckel and Kinsman Thos. Gill, exrs. Daus. Mary Arbuckle and Grace Croasdell. Dau.-in-law Mary Harding. 9 grandsons, John, Abraham, Isaac, and Henry Harding and Thomas Harding, Thomas Hillburn, John Arbucke and John Croasdale. goddaus, Mary, Sarah, Rebecca Croasdale, Mary Harding, Grace and Hannah Arbuckle. Thomas Butler and his sister Mary.
Wit: Mary Simcock, Jacob Simcock, Junr., John Simcock. Land where Mark Butteridge formerly divdt. Land in Phila. bot of Penn in 1688. Land in Newtown.

Page 193. John Swift of Bensalem Twp. Feby. 17, 1732/3. Proved

Mch. 15, 1732/3. Grandson Samuel Swift, exr. Plantation and Mill known as Alberson's. Only daughter Mary Fisher. Granddaus., Frances Wood, wife of Josiah Wood, Elizabeth English wife of John, and Hannah Swift. £50 to Baptist mtg. of Phila. Wit: Cornelius and Jacobus Vanostin and Philip Amus.

Page 195. James Yates, of Newtown Twp., Yeoma. Dec. 31, 1730. Proved Apr. 2, 1733. Wife Agnes and son Joseph, exrs. Sons Joseph, James, Peter, and Robert. Daus. Agnes, Isabel, Sarah, and Margaret. Wit: Margaret Thornton, Jos. Frohock, Joseph Thornton.

Page 197. Stephen Sands, of County of Bucks. 11th mo., 25th day, 1730/1. Proved Feby. 15, 1732/3. Wife Elizabeth. Sons Richard and John, exrs. Sons, Edmund, William. Dau. Elinor Hough. Plantation where I live to Richard. Wit: Tho. Stackhouse, Wm. Atkinson, Margaret Eastburn.

Page 199. John Morris, of Southampton Twp. Feby. 16, 1732/3. Proved Mch. 5, 1732/3. Wife Mary. Cousin John Morris (son of Bro. Richard) now living in Great Britain 300 acres in Phila. Co. joining Theophilus Williams, if he come into this Province. Cousins Richard and James Morris 700 acres in Phila. Co. bal. of 1000 acres tract. Cousin William Morris (son of Bro. Thomas) 600 acres in Southampton on which I live with stock and implements in hands of Stephen Watts provided he come into this Province and to male heirs forever. If he fail to come within one year to cousin Richard Morris above mentioned if he come into Province if not, then to cousin James Morris above mentioned. Hannah Davies £10. Henry Harris and his 3 sisters £20 each. Stephen Watts and his 3 children. George Eaton. Joseph Eaton Sr. and Jenkin Jones, Minister of the Gospel, exrs. Benj. Griffith of New Britain. Wit: John Hart, Thomas Dungan, Joseph Shaw.

Page 205. Thomas Bailey of Makefield. Jan. 4, 1732. Proved May 1, 1733. Wife Mary. Sons Thomas and Edward, exrs. Daus. Mary Ellet and Ann Gumley. Granddaus. Mary Ellet and Deborah Gumley. Plantation formerly James Makcomes 280 acres to son Thomas. Plantation formerly Amos Janney's 269 acres to son Edward. Wit: Alexander A. Rickey, James Downey, Richard Hough.

Page 207. John Humphrey of New Britain, Yeoman. Dec. 17, 1733. Proved Mch. 13, 1733/4. Wife Ann, sole extx. Son and 2 daus. in Great Britain. Dau. Ann. Wit: John Rowland, William Jones, Reese Lewis.

Page 209. Thomas Walthell of County of Bucks. Apr. 13, 1733. Proved Apr. 21, 1733. Son John,. Daus. Mary, Rachel and Joannah, Joseph Peace, exr. Wit: John Gale, Jonathan Bourne, Wm. Atkinson.

Page 211. Abraham Wood, of Makefield, Mason. June 2, 1733. Proved Sept. 29, 1733. Wife Ursula and uncle Abraham Lidden of City of Phila., exrs. Son Abraham. Dau. Elizabeth and child unborn. Bro.-in-law Benj. Taylor, Trustee.

Wit: John Clowes, James Tomlinson, Chas. Bryan.

Page 213. William Paxson of Middletown. Jan. 17, 1731/2.
Proved Feby. 11, 1733. Wife Mary, extx. Son Thomas 200 acres
formerly William Bryan's. Son John 200 acres s. side road leading
from Neshaminey to Falls adj. Jer. Langhorne, Stophel Vansant,
John Plumly with swamp called Pear's Swamp. Son James 200 acres
adj. Adam Harker, and land formerly Danl. Jackson. Eldest son
William 406 acres on which I live. Son Henry lots in Bristol
bought of John Forrest. Brothers-in-law Nathan and Mark Watson
Trustees to complete division of land bequeathed to eldest son
William by (?) John Plumly by Uncle Henry Paxson. Dau. Deborah
Paxson.
Wit: Jael Beckerdike, Joseph Richardson, Wm. Atkinson.

Page 217. Thomas Buckman, of Newtown. 5th mo., July 1734.
Proved Sept. 12, 1734. Wife Agnes and Abraham Chapman, exrs. Son
Thomas and daus. Rebecca and Agnes and child unborn.
Wit: Mary Gibson, Esther Buckman, David Buckman.

Page 219. Cuthbert Hayhurst. 6th mo., 20th day, 1733. Wife
Mary. Eldest son William, place I live on. Sons John and James.
Daus. Elizabeth (eldest) and Ruth. No exr. mentioned. Cuthbert
Hayhurst and Benjamin Cutler, Trustees.
Wit: James Thackeray, Benj. Cutler. Letters c.t.a. granted to
Mary Hayhurst.

Page 220. Thomas Kimber, of Sassafrass Neck, Md. Dec. 10, 1734.
Proved Feby. 12, 1734/5. Brother-in-law Walter Shewell, exr.
Nephews Joseph and Thomas Barton, Elizabeth Kimber dau. of Bro.
John. Elizabeth and Catharine Kimber daus. of James Kimber.
Nephew John Stephens.
Wit: Abraham Richards, Sr., Robert Smith, Daniel Griffith.

Page 222. Mary Palmer, Widow David Palmer of Bristol. July 1,
1735. Proved Aug. 9, 1735. Bro. Samuel Allen and Brother-in-law
John Palmer, exrs. 3 sons David, William, and Samuel Palmer
(minors).
Wit: Thos. Marriott, Wm. Atkinson,, Mary Robinson.

Page. --. John Naylor, of Southampton, Yeoman. Feby. 24,
1732/3. Proved Aug. 16, 1735. Son John and his son John. Sons-
in-law Benjamin Scott and Arthur Searle, exrs. Grandchildren,
Thomas and Benjamin Tomlinson (sons of Joseph and Mary,
deceased). Children of daughter Sarah Evans, by name, Ralph and
George Dunn, Thomas Evans and Mary Searle. 4 acres of plantation
for Public Burying Ground forever, for use of inhabitants of the
neighborhood on north side of Phila. Road.
Wit: Richard Studham, Thomas Eastburn.

Page 225. Richard Jones, of Borough of Bristol. Oct. 9, 1735.
Proved Nov. 18, 1735. Having sent to Michael Jones my brother for
some goods from England to be consigned to myself and Thomas
Clifford, he to receive same and send remittance back. Friends
Wm. Beckley of Burlington. John Campbell of Phila. Thos.

Clifford, Junr. Medicins, Instruments, etc. Thomas Clifford, exr.
Wit: Wm. Atkinson, Richard Glover.

Page 226. James Higgs, of "Burrough of Bristol." 11th mo., 10th
day, 1735/6. Proved Jan. 22, 1735/6. Wife Elizabeth. Son James.
Children, Mary, Elizabeth, Jane, James and Ann Higgs. Wife to
have use of children's legacies until they are 14. Samuel Cary of
Newtown and Samuel Bunting of Bristol, exrs.
Wit: Benjamin Harris, Richard Glover, Wm. Atkinson.

Page 228. Margaret Routledge, Widow. April 27, 1735. Proved
Feby. 9, 1735. Sons Thomas and John. Daus. Rachel Yeates, Sarah
Cooper, Mary Strickland, Isabella and Elizabeth Routledge. Son-
in-law John Strickland, exr.
Wit: Wm. Buckman, Thomas Butler.

Page 229. John Johnson, of Bucks Co., Weaver. May 10, 1736.
Proved June 18, 1736. Wife Mary, extx. Sons Peter, John and
Dennis. Thomas West overseer.
Wit: Ethan Sayre, Abigail Sayre, Plain Wilkinson.

Page 231. William Jemison, of Milford Twp., Cordwainer. Sept.
11, 1736. Proved Mch. 8, 1736/7. Wife Jane and son John, exrs.
250 acres of land. Bro. John Jemison.
Wit: John Lewis, Thos. Roberts, Joshua Richards.

Page 233. Sarah Cooper, Widow of Abraham, of Warminster Twp.
4th mo., 1st day, 1736. Proved Mch. 18, 1736/7. Son Joseph
Cooper. Daus. Lucretia and Tabitha. Jeremiah Langhorne and
William Huddleston, exrs.
Wit: John Jones, Penman, Robert Pugh.

Page 235. Joseph Strickland, of Northampton Twp., Taylor. May
1, 1737. Proved June 13, 1737. Wife Sarah and Brother-in-law
John Hillborne, exrs. 5 children, Miles, Mary, Ruth, Sarah, and
Rachel.
Wit: Samuel Blaker, William Cooper, Abraham Chapman.

Page 236. Samuel Allen, of Bensalem, Cordwainer. Nov. 13, 1735.
Proved June 22, 1737. Son Samuel 60 acres I live on conveyed to
me and my wife Jane by Thomas Fairman. Sons William, Richard
(defect in sense), John and Nicholas. Daus. Ann Palmer, Jane
Knight, Priscilla, Marsha and Sarah Allen. Brothers-in-law
Richard Waln, sons Saml., Nicholas and Wm., exrs.
Wit: John Baldwin, Samuel Baldwin, Richard Johnson.

Page 238. Thomas Ash, of County of Bucks. Feby. 21, 1736/7.
Proved July 13, 1737. Wife Ellinor and Joseph Kirkbride, Junr.,
exrs. Bro. Edmund Ash, son-in-law William Swift, dau.-in-law
Lydia Hurst.
Wit: Joseph Wood, Henry Kirkpatrick, Anne Wood.

Page 239. Arthur Searle, of Middletown. 6-20-1737. Proved Oct.
3, 1737. Sons Thomas, Arthur, and John. Son-in-law Samuel
Stevenson. Daus. Jane, Mary, Rebecca, and Sarah Searle, and

Elizabeth Stevenson. estate bequeathed by Father-in-law John
Naylor, dec'd. Land in Newtown purchased of Agnes Yeates to son
Thomas, exr. 400 acres in Middletown to 3 sons.
Wit: Grace Weasley, Jos. Wildman, Thos. Jenkins.

Page 241. John Evans, of Northampton Twp. Oct. 4, 1737. Proved
Nov. 12, 1737. Wife Judith. Son John and child unborn. Son-in-
law Cornelius McCarty. Jeremiah Croasdale, exr. Lease of land
from Isaac Pennington.
Wit: Lawrence McSorely, James Ellit, Joseph Wildman.

Page 246. Samuel Rowland, of New Britain Twp., Yeoman. Jan. 14,
1737. Proved Jan. 30 1737/8. Wife Priscilla. Son John. Daus.
Elinor and Margaret, Elinor 4 acres adj. house where she and her
husband live.
Wit: James Davis, John James, Barthw. Young.

Page 244. Daniel Jackson, of Burrough of Bristol. Dec. 20,
1736. Proved Nov. 25, 1737. 3 children, Joseph Jackson, Hannah
Keen, and Susanna Bourne, exrs. Son Joseph's 2 sons Daniel and
Samuel. Bro. Richard's daughter Rebecca Ryland. Andrew Hamilton,
Trustee to see that son John's son John is not wronged in
division of land in Buckingham given to my children by father-in-
law Joseph Baynes and that he is not wronged out of what he is
right heir to in Broad-Kill Sussex Co.

Page 247. William Silverstone, of Borough of Bristol. Jan. 22,
1733. Proved Feby. 24, 1737. William Atkinson, exr. and Trustee
for son William Silverstone.
Wit: John Cross, Nicholas Allen, Edward Southwood.

Page 249. Richard Sunly, of Wrightstown, Yeoman. Dec. 25, 1736.
Proved Mch. 4, 1737. Sister Ann Appleby's children by Thomas
Appleby. Sister Dorothy Well's children by --- Wells, 3 tracts of
land in Wrightstown and one in Buckingham. £10 to use of
Buckingham meeting. Thomas Canly and John Hill, Trustees thereof.
Thos. Brown of Plumstead and Robert Smith of Buckingham, exrs.
Wit: Philip Williams, Eleazer Doane, and Thomas Canby.

Page 254. Thomas Watson, late of Straberyhone but now of Bristol
Boro., Dated 12-13-1737. Proved Aug. 15, 1738. Wife Rebecca,
house and lot in Bristol with privilege of wharf I built. Son
Nathan, house he lives in purchased of William Paxson. Son Mark,
(Exr.), plantation at Straberyhone. Son John. Dau. Mary Paxson.
Dau.-in-law Frances Croker. Eldest grandson Thomas Watson, Amos'
eldest son and his two brothers and two sisters.
Wit: William Atkinson, Henry Tuckney, Matthias Keen.

Page 251. Joseph Kirkbride, of Bucks Co., Yeoman. June 5, 1736.
Proved April 18, 1738. Wife Mary and sons Joseph and John, exrs.
Son Joseph 536 acres on River Scoolkil in Phila. Co. 1666 acres
in Hunterdon County, N.J. and my part of tract of land on Morris
River in Salem Co., N.J. held in partnership with heirs of Thomas
Lambert and William Biles. 3 sons Joseph, Mahlon, and John, 6052
acres at Suckasunning, Hunterdon Co. Son Mahlon, 650 acres in

Hunterdon Co. afsd. at Grat Bog Meadow, surveyed by me in company with Thomas Lambert and John Reading. Son John, plantation on which I live (wife Mary 1/2 int. therein during life) also plantation in possession of James Gray, bought of James Sutton, Ruth Hulme, and Thomas Pugh, 528 acres also tract of 900 acres in New Britain bought of John Sotcher. Also, 340 acres in Makefield in Tenor of John and James Siddal. Son-in-law Thomas Marriott, 1250 acres in Hunterdon Co., N.J. on Delaware River near Limestone Falls. Also 500 acres at Minnisinks, in said county. Dau. Martha Marriott £300. Dau. Sarah Kirkbride, plantation bought of John Biles and tract of 325 acres adjoining also £500. Dau. Jane 440 acres in Bucks Co. adjoining Edward Doyal and £500. Granddau. Hannah Murphy 250 acres in Plumstead Twp. Dau. Phebe's children £20 each. Hannah Murphy excepted. Cousins Thomas Kirkbride (£40) and Joseph Kirkbride (£10). Wife Mary all the residue of Real estate including tract in Jersey on South Branch of Raritan River bought of John Budd and William Bidle. To Son Joseph and Dau. Sarah, Liberty lands and Lotts in Phila. share and share alike. Son Joseph to sell interest in partnership land on Morris River and put £100 at interest towards raising a Fund toward maintaining a Free School at or near Falls Meeting House.
Wit: John Hutchinson and John Beaumont.

Page 256. Mary Poynter, of Southampton. Sept. 2, 1738. Proved Sept. 15, 1738. Grandson Henry Poynter and granddau. Mary Poynter, exrs. Farm to grandson Henry Poynter. Dau. Sarah Stone. Dau. Elizabeth Hyder. "Hannah Hyder, late Hannah Poynter" Mary and Sarah Poynter.
Wit: Henry Kreusen, Thomas Evans, Richard Davis, Junr.

Page 257. William Stockdale, of Warminster, Yeoman. May 17, 1738. Proved Oct. 30, 1738. Wife Phebe and Bro. William Atkinson, exrs. Bro. Ralph Stockdale's son. Sister Isabel and Sister Amey's children, cousins William and John Atkinson and cousin Mary Child.
Wit: Richard Sands, Mary Sands, Margaret Lewis.

Page 259. Phebe Stockdale, of Warminster Twp., Widow. Dec. 27, 1738. Proved Jan. 24, 1738/9. Sister Margaret Atkinson, Brother-in-law William Atkinson Sons, James Radcliffe and John Radcliffe, exrs. Cousin Rebecca Smith.
Wit: Samuel Gilbert, William Gilbert.

Page 261. John Vastine, of Hilltown Twp. Dec. 31, 1730. Proved Feby. 21, 1738/9. "Aged and Weak of Body" wife Abigail, house and lot in Phila. and 100 C. land. Sons Abraham, Jeremiah, Benjamin, and John. Dau. Mary Wilson. Benjamin and John, exrs.
Wit: Owen Evan, Edward Milnor, Benj. Griffith.

Page 262. John Dyer, of Plumstead Twp., Yeoman. 11 mo. (Jan.) 20th day, 1738/9. Proved Mch. 3, 1738/9. Wife Elizabeth. Sons Samuel, John, and Josiah. Dau. Hester Brown. Grandsons Abraham, Scot, Joseph, Josiah, Thomas, and John Dyer, and Josiah Brown. G. dau. Elizabeth Brown. Samuel and John, exrs.

Page 272.   John Griffith, of Bucks Co., Miller.   4th mo., 1st day, 1738.   Proved Sept. 9, 1739. Wife Ann, extx. All estate real and personal to be sold, 1/3 to herself, 2/3 to 3 children, Hannah, Sarah, and Samuel. when of age.
Wit: Robert Colket, Abraham Griffith.

Page 265.   Samson Cary, of Borough of Bristol.   Feby. 9, 1732. Proved Sept. 11, 1739. Wife Mary, £100 and profits of Real estate during life. Brother John's children, viz., Hannah, Thomas, William, John, Mary, and Samson. Brother William's children, viz. Samuel, Margaret, Abigail, and Jane.   Brother William's son William, Brother William's son Samson, living in Bristol. Brother Samuel's sons Sharp and Samuel, the latter, exr. and residuary legatee. Every of wife's children £10.   £10 toward enclosing Friends Burying Ground at Bristol.
Wit: John Priestly, Joseph Burleigh, Wm. Atkinson.

Page 267.   William Biles, Esq. of Falls Twp.   Dec. 3, 1737. Proved Sept. 27, 1739. Wife Sarah.   Sons William, Charles, Langhorne, 2000 acres in Sagalen, Hunterdon Co., N.J.   Son Langhorne 600 acres in Whitpain sd. county. Daus. Sarah and Elizabeth each 1000 acres in Chepack sd. county. Dau. Ann wife of Isaac Pennington and Hannah, wife of Thomas Janney 1000 acres at Morris River, New Jersey. Grandchildren, William, Jeremiah, and John, Sarah and Hannah Beates, grandchildren, Edward, Mary and Sarah Pennington, Thomas and Margaret Biles, last two, 500 acres in Quohlockin, Salem Co., N.J. Son Lunhorne, 400 acres at same place.   Sons William, Langhorne and Charles, exrs.
Wit: Wm. Fry, Garret Vandike, John Duncan. Codicil. Island to wife for life then to son Wm. except 20 acres to Thomas, son of Thomas.

Page 270.   Daniel Howell of Solebury, Yeoman.   Apr. 14, 1739. Proved Sept. 28, 1739. Son Benjamin Howell.   Son-in-law Job Howell.   William Rettinhouser of Amwell and Joseph Howell of Bethlehem, County of Hunterdon, N.J., exrs. All lands except 1/8 of a Proprietary Right purchased by Father Howell.
Wit: Daniel Howell, Edward Milnor, Christn. Search.

Page 273.   John Wildman, of Middletown, Yeoman.   9th mo., 28th day, 1738.   Proved Sept. 9, 1739. Wife Mara.   Son-in-law John Woolston.   Bro. Joseph Wildman.   Sister Alice Nelson.   Bro. Joseph's 6 children, viz., Rebecca, Mary, Rachel, Joseph, John and Isaac.   Nephew James Woster.   Bro. Mathew Wildman. Land where Thomas Jinks lives formerly Thomas Musgraves, annuity due wife from her son Thomas Croasdale.   Son-in-law John Woolston, exr.
Wit: Thomas Marriott, David Wilson, Jos. Richardson.

Page 275.   Andrew Breckenridge, of Warwick Twp.   Oct. 9, 1739. Proved Nov. 19, 1739. Alexander Jamison, exr. and sole legatee.
Wit: John Loock, John Carver, Robert Jamison.

Page. --.   Isaac Cadwallader, of Warminster.   9th mo., 10th day, 1739.   Proved Nov. 25, 1739. Wife Mary. Children, Abraham, Isaac, Mary, Elizabeth, Margaret and Sarah. Father John Cadiwallader.

Bro. Jacob. Thomas Kinderdine, John Roberts of Montgomery and John Roberts of Abington, guardians, Trustees, and Overseers. Brother-in-law Robert Comly and Bro. John Cadwallader, exrs. Wit: John Cross, Joseph Naylor.

Page. --. Bernard Verkerk, of Bensalem, Yeoman. May 29, 1736. Proved Dec. 3, 1739. Son Jacob, 100 acres bought of Joseph Growden. Son John's children, dau. Mary wife of Neels Boon, dau. Constant wife of James Fitchet, dau. Dinah wife of James Keril. Granddaus. Rebecca and Rachel Underwood. Sons Jacob and John, exrs. Wit: Benj. Harris, Wm. Atkinson, Margaret Atkinson.

Bucks County Wills, Book No. 2.

Page 2. Henrick Breece of Bensalem Twp., Yeoman. Feby. 2, 1736/7. Proved Apr. 26, 1739. Wife Hana. Youngest daus. Sarah and Hana of age in year 1747. Sons Henry and John. Dau. Nealeha, Create, Sarah, and Hana. Wife and Philip Tilyer of Byberry Phila. Co., exrs. Wit: Abraham Messer, Mary Staats, Peter Staats.

Page 3. Joseph Wildman, of Middletown. 1st mo., 20th day, 1739/40. Proved May 7, 1740. Wife Sarah and son Jacob and Thomas Jenkins, exrs. Son Jacob 2 tracts of land bought of Robert Heaton and Thomas Yeates in Middletown. Son Joseph. plantation "on which I dwell" when 21 years of age. Son John. Daus. Rebecca, Mary, and Rachel. Wit: Euclides Longshore, John Hunter, Benj. Field.

Page 5. Edward Lucas, of Falls Twp. 11th mo., 23rd day, 1737. Proved June 2, 1740. Wife Bridget and son John, exrs. Son John, plantation. Son Robert, land lying between Wm. Paxson's and Widow Darke, formerly Bro. John's. Son Samuel. Son-in-law Thomas Bayley. Bro. Giles. Daus. Ann, Elizabeth, Mercy, Mary, and Margaret. Wit: J. Watson, Jos. White, Wm. Atkinson. Codicil dated 12th mo., 6th day, 1739/40.

Page 7. William Russell of Makefield, Taylor. Sept. 25, 1729. Proved July 28, 1740. "Intending to voyage by sea." Benj. Harvye and Benj. Taylor, exrs. Kinsman Jacob Hooper (Residence unknown). Kinswoman Mary Divowyhous (?) of Phila. Benj. Harvye's children. Benj. Taylor's children. Wit: Edward Sands, Peter Yates, Charles Bryan.

Page 8. Egra Croasdale of Middletown. 2 mo. (Apr.) 17, 1727. Proved Aug. 2, 1740. Wife. ---, sons William (eldest) and Jeremiah exrs. Grandsons John Croasdale, son of Wm. Egra Croasdale, son of Jeremiah 200 acres in Solebury. Land in Newtown and Middletown. Wit: Jonathan Carlile, Elizabeth Carlile, Elizabeth Randal.

Page 9. Jane Margerum, of Maxfield, Widow. Oct. 3, 1728.

Proved Aug. 18, 1740. Son William Riggs. Grandsons John Pearson, Robert Pearson, Abraham Harvye (and his brothers and sisters) and Henry Margerum son of Richard. Grandchildren, Margaret Pearson, Jane, Providence, Joseph, William, and Hannah Yates. Children, Elizabeth Harvye, Richard Margerum, and Jane Scarborough.
Wit: Wm. Russell, Hannah Coombe, Junr., Hannah Coombs, and Francis Parrell.

Page 10. Mary Strawhen of Bethlehem Co. of Hunterdon N.J. Jan. 7, 1738. Proved Sept. 10, 1740. Daus. Ruth and Sarah. Son Jacob Strawhen (Exr.). William, Henry, and John Cooper.
Wit: Daniel Ashcraft, Robert Hazlet, Richard Mitchell.

Page 11. Godfrey Kirk, of Wrightstown, Mason. 8th mo., 8, 1740. Proved Nov. 14, 1740. Wife Rachel. Bro. Isaac Kirk and Thos. Lancaster, exrs. Son Samuel, plantation at 21. Daus. Jane and Sarah Kirke.
Wit: David Sphere, Janet Craig.

Page 12. Andrew Ellicott, Junr., of Solebury, Weaver. Dec. 20, 1740. Proved Oct. 5, 1741. Wife Ann, extx. To child at her death.
Wit: Thos. Bye, John Price, Wm. Saterthwait.

Page 13. Jonathan Carlile, of Bucks Co., Date 8th mo., 28th day, 1741. Proved Nov. 3, 1741. Sons John and Jonathan, plantation in Plumstead bought of Richard Hill. Dau. Elizabeth. Alexander Brown and Benj. Cutler, exrs.
Wit: Samuel Stackhouse, Agnes Strickland, Elizaeth Ellit.

Page 12. Jonathan Woolston of Middletown. Sept. 20, 1741. Proved Oct. 7, 1741. Son Samuel and John, exrs. Samuel, lot where I live from road to back wall of house where John Stackhouse lives with Smith Shop and Tools. Bal. of said tract to be sold and proceeds divided among my daus. Son Jeremiah, land bought of Christian Van Horn joining Jos. Richardson. Son Benjamin, land adj. Thos. Stackhouse Mill Pond bought of Edward Glover.
Wit: James Thackeray and John Stackhouse, Junr.

Page 14. Rebecca Watson, of Burrough of Bristol, Widow. 11th mo., 5th day, 1741/2. Proved July 31, 1742. Codicil dated April 1742. Sons Nathan and Mark, exrs. Son John. His dau. Hannah. Nathan's daus. Mary, Margaret, and Sarah, and his sons Isaac and Thomas. Daus. Mary Paxson, Mary Watson, Ann Watson. Granddaus. Mary Richardson and Deborah Paxson and Mark's dau. Rebecca. Son Amos's children, Thomas Watson, and Hannah, Jacob, Samuel and Deborah.
Wit: John Cross, Malachi Walton, Wm. Atkinson.

Page 16. Thomas Edwards, of New Britain Twp., Yeoman. July 29, 1742. Proved Sept. 18, 1742. Wife Jane, Bro. John and William Edwards, son of Bro. John, exrs. Son Peter (weakly) other children and child unborn. exrs. to confirm to Thomas Lewis 40 acres on N.E. side of Great Road as per contract.
Wit: Robert Thomas, Grace Thomas, Benj. Griffith.

Page 17.   Sarah Mitchell, of City of Phila., Widow. Aug. 9, 1742. Proved Sept. 21, 1742. Daus. Elizabeth Barbur, Martha Janney, and Sarah Clark. Sons John and Henry. Son John and John Bessonett of Middletown, exrs.
Wit: Jacob Shoemaker, Elizabeth Shoemaker, Rebecca Roberts.

Page 17.   Matthias Harvye, of Makefield Twp., Yeoman. Aug. 19, 1742. Proved Oct. 9, 1742. Wife Elizabeth and son-in-law Joseph Simcock, exrs. Sons Henry, Mathias, (land bought of John Whitacre, Junr. leased to Thos. Scott) John and Abraham (land on which I dwell adj. Bro. Thomas). Daus. Elizabeth, wife of Randal Hutchinson, Mary wife of Joseph Simcock, and Sarah and Jane Harvye.
Wit: Jos. Baker and Chas. Bryan.

Page 19.   Samuel Stackhouse, son of John Stackhouse of Middletown. 7th mo., 13th day, 1742. Proved Oct. 13, 1742. Sisters Grace and Sarah. Bro. James. Niece Rachel Stackhouse, dau. of Bro. Thomas.
Wit: Jeremiah Croasdale, Grace Croasdale, James Thackeray.

Page 23.   George Lewis, of New Britain Twp., Yeoman. Dec. 1, 1742. Proved Dec. 23, 1742. Sons Peter, Abel, and Isaiah. Dau. Sarah to live with Benj. Griffith. John Bartholomew, Thomas Edmunds, and David Evans, exrs.
Wit: Bernard Young, Daniel Pennington, Mary Edwards.

Page 24.   Edward Perry, of Southampton, Yeoman. Dec. 17, 1742. Proved Dec. 31, 1742. Wife Ann, sole extx. Dau. Hannah Perry (a minor).
Wit: Job Walton, Isaac Walton, George Randall, Henry Noden.

Page 19.   Jeremiah Langhorne, Esq. of Middletown. May 16, 1742. Proved Oct. 23, 1742. Nephews Langhorne Biles and Lawrence Growden, exrs. Thos. Biles, son of nephew Thos. Biles, dec'd., Langhorne Park, where I live, 800 acres in default of issue to niece Sarah, wife of Lawrence Growden. Negroes Cudgo and London to remain thereon and have profits thereof to Mch. 25, 1751. All negroes to be free at 24 yrs. of age. Negroes Jo. and Cudgo, 150 acres where Nathaniel West liveth, after Mch. 25, 1751. Servant Wm. Finley. Children of niece Ann Pennington, viz. Edward, Mary, and Sarah. Children of niece Grace Bates viz. Wm., Jeremiah, John, Sarah and Hannah. Nephew Charles Biles, land where he dwells (sic) bought of Benj. Scott and Arthur Searle. Margaret Biles, dau. of nephew Thomas, dec'd., 100 acres adj. Robert Shaw, nieces Sarah Growden and Hannah Janney, 1000 acres near Perkasey. James and Andrew Hamilton, sons of friend Andrew Hamilton, dec'd., 1000 acres Kinsman Thomas Langhorn now or late in service of Lord Lonsdale and Kinsman Wm. Jackson, Woolen Draper, of London, 500 acres at Forks of Delaware. Sister Sarah, widow of William Biles. Friends Joseph Turner of Phila., merchant, and Buckridge Simms who liveth with sd. Turner. Good friend Wm. Allen. Furniture in Parlor and Room over it not to be removed but kept with House as Heirlooms. Residue of estate to Langhorne Biles and Lawrence Growden.

Wit: Matthew Rue, Benj. Scott, Jno. Duncan.

Page 25. Mary Warder, of Falls Twp. Sept. 17, 1739. Proved
Apr. 18, 1743. Joseph Kirkbride, exr. Charles Clarke, Wheeler
Clarke, Rachel Cross and Joseph Cross (each £2.10) Mary
Carruthers and Rachel Carruthers, Junr. (each 20 shillings).
Wit: John Wescombe, Henry Wilson.

Page 25. William Smith, of Wrightstown, Yeoman. 10th mo.,
(Dec.) 13, 1740. Proved Apr. 20, 1743. Wife Mercy. Sons
William (eldest), Thomas, Joseph, Ralph, John, Samuel, and David.
Daus. Margaret Pearson, Sarah Blaker, Mary Atkinson, Hannah Lee,
Lydia Heaton, Esther and Elizabeth. John Penquite and Joseph
Chapman, exrs. Land adj. John Chapman, Abrm. Chapman and John
Turning.
Wit: Rachel Penquite, Abrm. Chapman, Wm. Chapman.

Page 26. Robert Heaton, Senr., of Hampton Twp. Mch. 17, 1743.
Proved July 23, 1743. Wife Susanna. "Son and Heir" Robert
Heaton, exr. Daus. Sarah Walker (eldest), Grace Croasdale,
Elizabeth Noble, Alice Plumly and Anna Heaton (youngest). Bond
agt. Wm. Noble.
Wit: Thos. Cooch, Wm. Cartar, Henry Noden. Codicil dated Mch.
25, 1743.

Page 28. Thomas Banes, of Middletown, Yeoman. Jan. 8, 1742/3.
Proved July 25, 1743. Son-in-law Daniel Doane and Ann his wife,
exrs. and sole legatees.
Wit: Jos. Richardson, Stephen Leighton, Jno. Duncan.

Page 29. David Murray of Bristol, Gent. Jan. 7, 1742. Proved
Sept. 7, 1743. Wife Mary (£250). Father and Mother in Great
Britain. Bro. Alexander Murray, Minister of the Gospel in
Scotland. Sons Alexander and John. Bro. James and sisters Isabel
and Ann. Son Alexander, Joseph Peace, and father-in-law John
Snowdon and John Abraham Denormandy, exrs.
Wit: Jo. Jackson, John and Elizabeth Frohock.

Page 30. John Chapman of Wrightstown, Yeoman. Apr. 6, 1743.
Proved Sept. 16, 1743. Wife Ruth, Bros. John and Abraham and
cousin John Wilkinson, Junr., exrs. Bro. Abraham's grandsons,
John and Abraham Chapman. Son John, plantation I live on and land
where William Giffon lives, also tract lying by River Delaware
where Joseph Don liveth. Thomas Wilson, 100 acres where John
Lucas lives in Jerseys upon Pohatcunk, share in Grist Mills at
Pine Run, and share of saw mill to Bro. Joseph. Cuzon, Thomas
Croasdale, 100 acres in Jerseys. Cuzons Joseph and Elizabeth
Chapman.
Wit: Luke Sevens, Jer. Bowman, Mary Wilson.

Page 31. William Leedom, of Southampton, Yeoman. Sept. 11,
1743. Proved Sept. 21, 1743. Wife Sarah and James Arbuckle,
exrs. Father Richard Leedom. Children, Richard, Wiliam, and
child unborn. Land in tenure of Samuel McGraudy.
Wit: Nicholas Tucker, Thos. Justice, John McGraudy.

Page 32. Solomon Boom, of Bristol Twp. Dec. 6, 1743. Proved Dec. 20, 1743. Sons Solomon, Ralph, Joseph, dau. Elizabeth. John Baldwin, John Cross, and son Solomon, exrs.
Wit: John Johnson, Wm. Atkinson.

Page 34. Daniel Doane, of Newtown Twp., Carpenter. Oct. 24, 1731. Proved Dec. 20, 1743. Wife Mary and Joseph Wildman, exrs. Children Daniel, Eliezer, Elijah, and Joseph Doane, Lydia Stradling and Rebecca Randal. Son-in-law George Randall. My children by wife Mary, viz., Samuel, Mary, Thomas, Sarah, and Ebenezer Doan.
Wit: Henry Nelson, Joseph Yeates, John Worstall. Codicil dated 11th mo., 9th day, 1742, Euclides Longshore, exr., Jos. Wildman above named being dec'd.

Page 35. John Morgan, of Richland Twp., Yeoman. 11th mo. (Jan.), 4, 1741. Proved Mch. 9, 1743. Present wife Deborah, late Deborah Woodruff, exr. Sons Isaac, John, James. Dau. Sarah, Susannah, and Deborah. "All children of wife, Deborah" 400 acres in Richland and 25 acres in Abington. Wm. Nixon and Morris Morris, guardians.
Wit: John Ball, Sr., John Ball, Jr., Chas. Maycock.

Page 37. John Samuels. Dec. 8, 1741. Proved Mch. 26, 1744. Wife Isabel. Sons John and Robert. Dau. Ann Samuels. Moses Crawford, Wm. Aberneth, Alexander McKinstry, each 1/2 crown. Alex McKinstry, Wm. Abernethy and James Pock, exrs.
Wit: William Bol, Mary Stevenson.

Page 40. Alexander Quintin, of Makefield Twp., Yeoman. Aug. 6, 1744. Proved Aug. 23, 1744. Wife Mary. Wm. Maxwell and Benjamin Allibone, exrs. Mother. Bro. Robert Mearns. Sisters in law, Sarah, Ann, Elizabeth, ---.
Wit: James Jolly, John Slack, Isaac Ashton.

Page 37. Thomas Stackhouse, of Middletown. 12th mo., 1st 1741/2. Proved July 14, 1744. Wife Dorothy, son Isaac and son in law Euclides Longshore, exrs. Son Joseph and his sons Caleb and Joshua and Dau. Grace. Sons Thomas, Isaac, Robert, Jacob, and Samuel. Son Benjamin's children, Benjamin and Grace. Plantation adj. Wm. Paxson, Wm. Bidgood, Tho. Marriott. Daus. Sarah Carah and Ann Plumly.
Wit: Jeremiah Croasdale, James Thackery, Wm. Atkinson.

Page 41. Enoch Bye of Solebury, Yeoman. 3rd mo., 5th day, 1744. Proved Oct. 1, 1744. Mother. Bro. Hezekiah, exr. Sister Sarah Bye. Sisters.
Wit: Reece Davis, Enoch Pearson, Jr., Wm. Pearson.

Page 42. John Hough, of Solebury, Yeoman. 6th mo., (Aug.) 12, 1744. Proved Nov. 17, 1744. Wife Elenor and son William, exrs. Children, William, Mary, Daniel, Joseph, John, Richard, and Jane.
Wit: Abraham Cowgill, Dorothy Cowgill, John Hill.

Page 43. William Griffon, of Upper Makefield, Farmer. 9th mo.,

20th day, 1743. Proved Dec. 14, 1744. Wife Sarah and brother-in-law Edward Beck, exrs. Eldest son Peter, son Aaron, and dau. Sarah.
Wit: Amos Strickland, Agnes Strickland, and John Ogg.

Page 44. Nehemiah Blackshaw of Falls Twp. 6th mo., 11th day, 1743. Proved Jan. 7, 1744. Wife Mary, son-in-law Joseph Linton and dau. Phebe, exrs. Dau. Mary Linton, 300 acres in Solebury, adj. John Fisher. Dau. Rebecca Wharton 50 acres formerly Peter Websters and 200 on Stony Hill. Dau. Phebe Blackshaw, tract I live on and 40 acres called Manangers. She to maintain my Bro. Joseph. Son in law Daniel Wharton.
Wit: John Burges, Samuel Burges, Wm. Atkinson.

Page 46. John Brooks, of Southampton, Yeoman. Dec. 31, 1744. Proved Jan. 18, 1744/5. Wife Mary. Son John Brooks (otherwise John Tucker), exr. Other children, Thomas, Hannah, Humphrey, and Jacob. Robert Parsons, Senior, Trustee.
Wit: Robert Parsons, Junr., Thos. Hillborne, Jr., and Nicholas Tucker.

Page 48. Joseph Hill, of Warminster Twp., Yeoman. July 31, 1733. Proved Mch. 22, 1744. "Neece" Mary Wood wife of Thomas Wood of East Jersey, Clothier, exr. All estate for life, at her decease to her children, Joseph, William, and Richmandy Wood.
Wit: John Scott, Ann Lida, Jan. MacFarland, John Hart.

Page 49. Johannes Vandegrift, of Bensalem, Yeoman. Mch. 16, 1732. Proved Mch. 28, 1745. Wife Nealke and son Phalcort, exrs. Children, Phalcort, Jacob, Abraham, Rebecca, Christian, and Lenah Vandegrift.
Wit: Jacob Vandegrift, Wm. Baker, Wm. Smart.

Page 50. Henry Nelson, of Middletown. Apr. 11, 1744. Proved May 14, 1745. Wife Alice, son Thomas, and friend Euclides Longshore, exrs. Dau. Alice Carter, plantation near Wrightstown. her son Henry Carter. Dau. Ann Wilson, 50 acres in Bristol Twp. adj. Thos. Dowdney and River Delawre and 2 lots in Bristol Boro. Dau. Letitia Joly, plantation at Newtown between Amos Strickland and Wm. Buckman, for life then to her son Nelson Joly. Son Thomas, plantation where I live and land and mill at Newtown. Alice Carter's children, viz., Henry, John, and James Carter. Ann Wilson's children, viz., Nelson and Alice Joly. Grandchildren descended from dau. Jemimah Heaton, Robert and Thomas Heaton. Nephew Edward Worstell.
Wit: John Watson, John Woolston, Edward Worstell.

Page 52. Edward Hartley, of Solebury, Yeoman. 4 mo. (June) 13, 1744. Proved June 14, 1745. Sons, Thomas and John, exrs. Son Thomas. Dau. Jennett Hughes. Son Roger's 7 children.
Wit: David Kinsey, Tamar Kinsey, Jacob Holcombe.

Page 54. Nicholas Hellens, of Newtown, Yeoman. July 19, 1745. Proved Aug. 6, 1745. Wife Elizabeth and son Robert, exr. Sons Simon, John, and Richard. Daus. Elizabeth Griffith, Mary Dungan,

Sarah Shaw, Martha Doyle, and Patience Vanhorne.
Wit: Jos. Thornton, Wm. Ashburn, Robert Heaton.

Page 55. Robert Mearns, of Northampton Twp., Blacksmith. Apr.
10, 1730. Proved Sept. 13, 1745. Wife Jane. Children, Hugh,
Agnes, Jennett, Mary, and child unborn. Bro.-in-law Wm. Ramsey,
Bro. Samuel Mearns, exrs.
Wit: Thos. Davids, Henry Smith, John Hart.

Page 56. Robert Smith, of Buckingham. 5 mo 15th day, 1745.
Proved Sept. 26, 1745. Wife Phoebe. Sons Thomas (eldest),
Timothy, Robert, John, Joseph, Benjamin, Samuel, and Jonathan.
Thomas and Timothy, exrs. Land, late Launcelot Gibson's, adj.
Eleazer Doan.
Wit: Wm. Blackfan, Jeffrey Burgess, Thomas Ross.

Page 58. Jams Tunnecliff, of Makefield Twp., Yeoman. 3 mo. May
23, 1745. Proved Oct. 21, 1745. Wife Hannah, sole extx. Her son
and dau. John Doble and Elizabeth Collins, land in Makefield.
Deed from Thomas Bishop Vickaris and his atty. Richd. Hockley
dated Sept. 13, 1743.
Wit: Peter Larew, Jacob Hawabout, and Charles Bryan.

Page 59. Joseph Todd, wife Elizabeth, extx. Aug. 12, 1745.
Proved Oct. 28, 1745. Sons Joseph and Charles, plantation I live
on when 21 yrs. of age. Daus. Elizabeth, Rebecca, and Mary. Wife
undivided right in land in Montgomery.
Wit: Charles Stewart, Evan Jones.

Page 60. John Hutchinson, of Falls Twp., Taylor. Jan. 24,
1740/1. Proved Nov. 27, 1745. Wife. ---. Brothers-in-law John
Burges and Mahlon Kirkbride, exrs. Sons John, Joseph, Thomas,
Michel, Randal, and Samuel. Daus. Hanna Murphy, Priscilla, Phebe,
Mary and Marcy Hutchinson. Land in Quohocking in the Jerseys.
Land sold by me to Michel Reup to be confirmed to him when paid
for.
Wit: Daniel Burges, Samuel Burges, Elen Burges.

Page 62. Benjamin Town, of Bristol Twp. Sept. 2, 1745. Proved
Dec. 10, 1745. Wife Rebecca. Sons John, Benjamin, Thomas. John,
exr. Daus. Rebecca, Ryal, and Deborah Town. £40 to Friends Mtg.
at Bristol and use of quarry to fence grave yard.
Wit: Wm. Rodman, Michel Dugin, Wm. Atkinson.

Page 63. John Martin Weller, of Southampton Twp. Sept. 30,
1745. Proved Dec. 15, 1745. Wife Annake, sole extx. Son John
Boltus Weller. Dau. Rosena Maria Trimanus, wife of John Jacob
Trimanus.
Wit: Joseph Hart, Edith Hart, John Hart.

Page 64. Jacobus Vansandt, of Southampton Twp., Yeoman. Dec.
12, 1744. Pr. Jan. 9, 1745/6. Wife Rebecca. Sons, Nicholas (144
acres bought of Cornelius Egnrout), Jacob (150 acres on which I
dwell), Garret and Isaiah, Grandson Charles Ingard. Daus.
Rebecca and Elizabeth, (dec'd.). Kinsman John Vansandt and

Nathaniel Brittain, exrs.
Wit: Daniel Bankson, Thos. Duff, Robert Vernon.

Page 66. Peter Wood, of Bristol. July 10, 1745. Proved Mch.
12, 1745/6. "Cozens" Richard Saunders and William Saunders. Ann
Moore. "First wife's sister" Elizabeth Pinlett. Mtg. House Grave
Yard at Bristol £4 toward fencing. Jos. Atkinson and John
Johnson, exrs.
Wit: William Sands, John Johnson.

Page 67. William Tennent, Warminster Twp., Minister of the
Gospel. July 16, 1745. Proved May 9, 1746. Wife Kathren, extx.
of personal estate. Son Gilbert, exr. of Real estate. to sell
plantation. Grandsons William, son of Wm., Junr. William, son of
Charles. Bal. to be divided among rest of children at discretion
of exr.
Wit: Charles Beatty, Evan Jones.

Page 68. Joseph Large, of Buckingham, Yeoman. 10th mo., 21st
day, 1745. Proved June 9, 1746. Wife Deborah. Son Joseph and
son-in-law Robert Russell, exrs. Son Joseph, plantation I live
on. Son Ebenezer, plantation he live on in Plumstead. Daus. Ruth
Brown, Hannah Russell, and Elizabeth Watkins.
Wit: Thomas Ely, Sarah Hill, John Hill.

Page 69. Moses Nox, of Warwick Town, Farmer. 7th mo., 9th day,
1746. Proved Sept. 29, 1746. Wife Margaret. Bros. William and
Samuel Nox. John Ewer of Warwick, exr.
Wit: Wm. Dickinson, Jos. McMikin, Jean McCullough.

Page 70. Sarah Wansel, of Makefield, Widow. Jan. 21, 1745/6.
Proved Oct. 21, 1746. Son Joseph Tomlinson and son-in-law Robert
Whiteacre, exrs. Sons Richard (eldest), James, and John (weak
minded) Tomlinson. Daus. Mary Livezey, Elizabeth Montgomery,
Sarah Whiteacre.
Wit: Benj. Allibone, Samuel McNaire, Wm. Smith.

Page 72. James Caldwell, of Plumstead Twp., Farmer. Jan. 1,
1745/6. Proved Oct. 20, 1746. Wife Francisca. Son David. Daus.
Jean, Agnes, and Mary. Rev. James Campbell, John Wigton, Yeoman,
and Robert Jamison, Yeoman, and Alexander Harvey, Farmer, exrs.
Wit: Stephen Kitchin and Howell Thompson.

Page 73. Robert Dawson of Northampton Twp., Weaver. Nov. 7,
1746. Proved Dec. 2, 1746. Wife Mary and Robert Parsons, exrs.
Son Isaac. John Dawson, son of Benjamin Dawson of Phila.,
Hatter.
Wit: Sarah Pritchard, John Evans, Samuel Pritchard.

Page 74. Rebekah Vansandt, of Southampton, Widow. Nov. 18,
1746. Proved Jan. 13, 1746/7. Son Jacobus, exr. Sons Garrett,
Nicholas, and Esaias Vandsandt. Grandson Charles Ingard. Dau.
Rebekah Larue.
Wit: Simon Vanarsdalen, Derrick Kreusen, John Bond.

Page 76. John Burges, of Falls Twp. 9th mo., 5th day, 1746.
Proved Feby. 3d. 1746/7. Son Samuel, exr. Dau. Ellin Harvey.
Grandchildren, Mary and Mathias Harvey.
Wit: John Kirkbride, Joseph Wharton, John Nutt.

Page 77. Benjamin Abbitt, of Makefield Twp. Dec. 23, 1746.
Proved Mch. 16, 1746/7. Father-in-law John Burroughs, of
Trenton, Hunterdon Co., N.J. and Brother-in-law Thomas Whitson of
Huntingdon, Suffolk Co., New York, exrs. Children, James
(eldest), Benjamin, Edith Burroughs, Joseph, John and Hannah (all
minors).
Wit: Joseph Baker and Charles Bryan.

Page 78. Robert Naylor, of Warrington Twp., Yeoman. Feby. 11,
1746/7. Proved Mch. 27, 1747. Wife Susanna, extx. to sell 150
acres on which I live and lot of 20 acres in Merion. Son John
Naylor (under 14 yrs). Bro. Richard Naylor, Bro-in-law John
Williams and cousins Edward Foulke and Amos Griffith, Trustees
and Overseers.
Wit: Robert Nixon, Thomas Nixon, George Shoemaker.

Page 79. Thomas Betts, of Newtown. Feby. 23, 1746/7. Proved
Apr. 6, 1747. Wife Susanna, extx. 1st wife's children, Thomas,
John and Stephen Betts and Susanna Field. 2d. wife's children,
Patience, Richard, Mercy, Zachariah, Meriom, and Wm. Int. in land
in Chesterfield, Burlington Co., N.J., now in possession of
Meriom Wright.
Wit: Thos. Hillborn, Heath Horner, Jos. Davenport.

Page 81. Thomas Morris, of Hilltown, Yeoman. Aug. 25, 1743.
Proved Apr. 6, 1747. "Aged and weak" Wife, Jennett. Son Thomas,
exr. Elizabeth dau. of son Isaac, dec'd. John Batholomew of
Montgomery and Lewis Evan of Hilltown, Trustees.
Wit: Evan Thomas, Henry Jones, Benj. Griffith.

Page 82. Simon Sacket of Borough of Bristol, Date Mch. 20,
1746/7. Proved Apr. 21, 1747. Codicil dated Apr. 4, 1747. Wife
Mary. Daus. Mary, Rebecca, and Sarah. Wm. Buckley, Bristol
Boro., and Thos. Dowdney, of Bristol Twp., exrs.
Wit: John Large, Wm. Atkinson, Margaret Sheppard.

Page 84. John Gosline, of Middletown Twp., Carpenter. Mch. 24,
1746/7. Pr. Apr. 22, 1747. Wife Rebekah. Sons William, John, and
Jacob. Daus. Rebekah and Martha. Relation Wm. Burras and Friend
John Bessonet, exrs.
Wit: Peter Peterson Vanhorne, Henry Mitchell, James Bodine,
Robert Brodnax.

Page 85. Garret Vansandt, of Wrightstown, Yeoman. Nov. 12,
1746. Proved May 1, 1747. Wife Clauchey and sons Garret and
Cornelius, exrs. Daus. Rachel Dungan, Sarah Sacit, and Rebekah
Vansant. Land formerly Peter Johnson's including part of Town
Square.
Wit: Abrm. Chapman, John Lacey, John Johnson.

34

Page 87. John Riale, of New Britain Twp., Yeoman. Aug. 8, 1747. Proved Sept. 15, 1747. Wife. --- Sons Joshua and Richard, exrs. Daus. Phebe, Hannah, Mary.
Wit: Wm. Wells, Peter Wells, Jno. Frazer.

Page 88. John Davies, of New Britain Twp., Yeoman. Jan. 28, 1743/4. Proved Sept. 16, 1747. Wife Isabel. John and Tristram, exrs. Sons Nathaniel, Wm. John, Baxter and Tristram. Daus. Elizabeth Rogers and Elizabeth ---. Grandsons John Poak and John Crawford.
Wit: Richd. Walker, Benj. Snodgrass.

Page 90. John Bond, of Southampton Twp., Yeoman. Sept. 13, 1747. Proved Oct. 15, 1747. Wife Sarah, extx. Sons Benjamin, Joshua, Abraham, John and Edward. Daus. Rebecca and Hannah. Wm. Duncan of Bensalem and Bro-in-law Robert Comly of Warminster, Trustees.
Wit: Jos. Gilbert, Edmund Duncan, Mary Duncan.

Page 91. Mara Wildman, of Middletown, Widow. 5th mo., 8th day, 1746. Proved Oct. 21, 1747. Son Thomas Croasdale and his dau. -- - Croasdale. Daus. Agnes Warner, Mercy Jenks, and Elizabeth Woolston. Gr.daus. Mary Warner, Mary Jenks, and Mary Woolston. Abrm. Chapman and Jos. Chapman, exrs.
Wit: Ralph Lee, John Chapman, and William Chapman.

Page 93. Thomas Kirkbride, of Falls Twp. 8th mo., 3d. 1747. Proved Nov. 23, 1747. Wife Grace. Son Thomas and other children. John Woolston, John Kirkbride and Mahlon Kirkbride, exrs.
Wit: Samuel Woolston, Margery Woolston, Roger Moon.

Page 93. Isaac Bennett, of Northampton Twp., Yeoman. Sept. 9, 1747. Proved Dec. 11, 1747. Wife Elizabeth. Son Isaac and other young children. George Bennet, William Bennett, and Jacob Bennett, exrs.
Wit: John Shaw, Leffert Leffertson, Barendt Van Hooren, Andrew Patterson.

Page. 95. John Head, of Solebury Twp., yeoman. June 5, 1745. Proved Dec. 17, 1747. Wife Olive and Thomas Dawson, exrs. Sons John and Abraham. Daus. Mary and Rebecah.
Wit: Paul Kester and William Kitchin.

Page 96. Thomas Marriott, of Borough of Bristol. Nov. 6, 1747. Proved Jan. 20, 1747/8. Son Thomas, son-in-law William Paxson and brother-in-law Mahlon Kirkbride, exrs. Son Isaac, at sea. Son Joseph. Daus. Mary Shipley and Anna Paxson. Apprentice, Billingham Humphrie's time to son Thomas.
Wit: Wm. Atkinson, Jos. Atkinson, Mary Tuckney.

Page 98. Joseph McCreary, of Plumstead Twp., Yeoman. Aug. 31, 1747. Proved Jany. 22, 1747/8. Wife Isabella. Daus. Ann, Jennett, and Elizabeth McCreary. Samuel Hart and Wm. Means and John Gaddis, exrs.
Wit: Wm. Hart, Joseph Porter, Luke Severns.

Page 99.   James Paxson, of Marsh Gibbon, Solebury Twp.   11th mo.,
25th day, 1747.   Proved Feby. 25, 1747.   Wife Margaret and Bro.
Thomas Paxson, exrs.   Son William, part of plantation next Henry
Paxson, butting of Delaware.   Son Thomas, residue of plantation.
Sons Jonas and James.   Daus. Abigail, Hannah, Jane, Mary, and
Margaret.
Wit: John McMasters, Samuel Eastburn, Henry Paxson, Jr.

Page 101.   James Pool, of New Britain Twp. worsted comber.   Dated
Mch. 19, 1747/8.   Proved Mch. 29, 1748.   Wife Catharine, extx.   40
acres in Warwick bought of John Thompson (not survd.).   Sons
Edward and John (minors).   Daus. Matilda, Mary, Elizabeth, and
Sarah.   John William and David Morgan of New Britain, Trustees.
Wit: David Stephens, Wm. Davids, Jonathan Mason.

Page 102.   Garret Wynkoop, of Northampton Twp., Gent.   Oct. 26,
1741.   Proved Mch. 4, 1747.   Sons Cornelius and Phillipus, exrs.
Sons Garret and Nicolaus.   Daus. Mary Van De Grift, Annetie Van
Meeter.   Grandchildren, Jeanette, Garret, and Andries Van Buskirk,
children of dau. Jacomynbie, dec'd.   Land bought of George Burson
"betwixt Theodurus Hall and son Philipus.."
Wit: Nathaniel Brittain and Peter Blaker.

Page 105.   Joseph Fell, of Buckingham Twp., Yeoman.   12th mo.,
5th day, 1746.   Proved Apr. 28, 1748.   Wife Elizabeth, extx.   Sons,
Titus (plantation), Thomas, George, Joseph, Benjamin, John, and
Isaac.   Daus. Tamer Kinsey, Sarah Church, and Rachel Kirk.
Wit: John Bradfield, Junr., John Vanduren, Jacob Holcombe.

Page 104.   Joseph Stidman, of Plumstead Twp.   2nd mo., 5th day,
1748.   Proved Apr. 22, 1748.   25 acres for use of Poor of Twp.
Cousin Jane Miller, wife of Wm. Miller and "The Rest of my
Sister's children."   Cousins Jacob and Joseph Thomas.   £2 toward
building Plumstead Mtg. House, besides £3 already subscribed.
Residue toward building on and improving the 25 acres for use of
Poor of Twp.   John Brittain and Nathan Preston, exrs.
Wit: John Rich, Benj. Collins, Andrew Love.

Page 107.   Joseph Brown of Plumstead Twp.   2nd mo., 24th day,
1748.   Proved May 16, 1748.   Wife Ann.   Bro. Alexander and Friend
Nathan Preston, exrs.   Sons Abraham, Isaac, Joseph, Dawson.   Daus.
Ann and Leah.   Land on Durham Road adj. John Rich.
Wit: Arthur Allen, John Rich, Wm. Hough.

Page 108.   Joseph Kirkbride, of Makefield Twp., Yeoman.   May 21,
1748.   Proved July 22, 1748.   Wife Sarah and brothers-in-law
Nicholas Austin and Mark Watson, exrs.   Son Joseph, plantation
whereon I live when 21.   5 daus. Phebe, Hannah, Mary, Elizabeth,
and Sarah.   Land in Jerseys to be sold.
Wit: Henry Wilson, Michel Hutchinson, and Ann Hutchinson.

Page 110.   George Brown, of Buckingham Twp.   2nd mo., 29th day,
1749.   Proved July 26, 1748.   Wife Sarah.   Sons John and Jonathan,
plantation.   Daus. Susanna and Mary Brown.   Son John and bro-in-
law Joseph Shaw, exrs.

Wit: Cornelius Hilliard, Jona. Kinsey, and Jacob Holcombe.

Page 111. Joseph Simcock, of Makefield Twp., Yeoman. 4 mo. (June) 24 ---. Proved Aug. 2, 1748. Wife Mary, Uncle John Palmer and Bro-in-law Henry Harvey, exrs. Son Mathias, land I live on purchased of Thomas Clowes. under (14 yrs. of age). Daus. Sarah, Elizabeth, and child unborn. Land in Ridley, Chester Co., to be confirmed to Samuel Evans, of Marple, Chester Co., when paid for.
Wit: Anne Palmer, Charles Bryan.

Page 113. Peter Staats of Bensalem Twp., Yeoman. May 28, 1745. Proved Aug. 8, 1748. Sons Abraham and Peter, exrs. Daus. Susannah Lewis (eldest), Magdalen wife of Thomas Morgan, Agnes wife of Michael Weesley, Lucretia wife of Jacob Stickler and Elizabeth wife of Mark Overholt. Children of eldest dau. Ann Praal, dec'd.
Wit: Edmund, Isaac, and Wm. Dunkan.

Page 115. John Lucas, of Falls Twp., Yeoman. 6th mo., Aug. 9, 1748. Proved Aug. 25, 1748. Wife Isabel. "antient mother," what was left her by father's will. Bro. Robert, plantation after Mother's death. Bro. Edward, plantation where Robert lives. Bro-in-law, James Moon. Nephew Robert Margerum. Sister Mary Margerum's children. Joseph Straw's children, Wm. and Mary Goforth. Martha White, dau. of Joseph.
Wit: Willoughby Warder, Isaac Moon, Jos. White.

Page 118. Isabel Lucas, Widow of John Lucas, Falls Twp. Aug. 12, 1748. Pr. Aug. 25, 1748. Aunt Hannah Woodfoard. Sister Mary Shaw and her daus. Sarah and Anna, niece Mary Harding. Children, Richard and Mary Margerum. Sister-in-law, Mary Margerum. Joseph Shaw, Jr. Mary and Wm. Goforth. Bros.-in-law Robert Lucas, Joseph Shaw, and James Moon, exrs.
Wit: Benj. Linton, Daniel Wharton, and Joseph White.

Page 118. Jacob Holcombe, of Buckingham Twp., Yeoman. 6 mo 1748. Wife Mary, extx. Son Thomas. Kinsman Barnard Hough. Daus. Sarah, Rebecca, Mary, Elizabeth, Susanna, Hannah, and Sophia. Grandson Jacob Holcombe, spoons marked "R.H.." John Watson, Overseer.
Wit: James Bradshaw, Joel Lowther, John Hill.

Page 120. William Davis, of Bristol. Aug. 25, 1748. Proved Oct. 3, 1748. Wife Sarah and Wm. Buckley, exrs. Est. to wife and all children.
Wit: John Priestly, Samuel Jackson, John Frohock.

Page 121. Samuel Pancoast, of Solebury Twp., Weaver. Sept. 28, 1748. Proved Oct. 14, 1748. Wife Abigail and Bro-in-law John Beaumont, exrs. Children, Joshua, Hannah, Abigail, Samuel, and child unborn. Plantation in Mansfield, Morris Co., N.J.
Wit: Joshua Ely, Paul Lewis, John Heaton.

Page 122. George Pownall, of Solebury Twp., Yeoman. May 13, 1748. Proved Oct. 18, 1748. Sons Reuben and Simeon, exrs. Plantation in Solebury. Son John. Dau. Rachel Pownall.

Wit: Wm. Kitchin, Sarah Kitchin.

Page 123. Sarah Hutchinson, of Falls Twp., Widow. 8th mo., 28th day, 1748. Proved Nov. 19, 1748. Bro-in-law, Samuel Bunting, dau. Phebe, exrs. Son Samuel. Dau. Phebe, and Mary Hutchinson and Priscilla Coats. Granddau. Sarah Coats. Bond of Joseph Burgess of Buckingham to Saml.
Wit: Thomas Green, Phebe Milnor, Samuel Burgess.

Page 124. James Evans, of Buckingham Twp. Sept. 14, 1747. Proved Dec. 21, 1748. Codicil Oct. 9, 1747. Wife Elizabeth. Sons Wm. Davis, Junr. and Evan Stephens, Junr., exrs. Daus. Mary Davis, Sobilla Stephens, Margaret Hough, Elizabeth, Hannah, Sarah and Rachel Evans. Grandson Benjamin Hough. £5 to Overseers of Buckingham Mtg. towards building stone grave yard.
Wit: William George, George Hughes.

Page 126. Benjamin Jones, of Northampton Twp. Aug. 28, 1748. Proved Dec. 27, 1748. Wife Catharine, extx. Children, Malachi, Samuel, Benjamin, Derrish, Joshua, Henry, John, Elizabeth, Mary, Catharine, and Ann.
Wit: Gerrett Kroesen, Rem Van der Bilt, John Hart.

Page 127. Thomas Phillips, of Solebury, Farmer. Dec. 17, 1748. Proved Jan. 2, 1748/9. Wife Rebecca. Sons Aaron and Thomas (minors). Cousin Job Noble and son-in-law William Kitchin, exrs.
Wit: Wm. Smith, Euclides Scarbrough, John Beaumont.

Page 128. Nathaniel Bye, of Buckingham Twp., Yeoman. May 20, 1748. Proved Jan. 5, 1748/9. Wife ---. Son Joseph and Rees Davis, exrs. Son Thomas. Daus. Martha and Mary Bye and Ann Wall.
Wit: Wm. Mitchell, David Stram, and John Quin.

Page 129. Benjamin Harris, of Borough of Bristol. Dec. 27, 1748. Proved Jan. 23, 1748/9. Wife Ann and Bro-in-law Joseph Shaw, exrs. Daus. Mary and Ann Harris.
Wit: Richd. Allen, Sarah Davis, Wm. Atkinson.

Page 130. Thomas Sisom of Borough of Bristol. Jan. 11, 1748/9. Proved Jan. 23, 1748/9. Children, Samuel, Lydia, William, Thomas, Hannah, John and Rebecca. Wm. Atkinson and Enion Williams, both of Bristol Borough, exrs.
Wit: John Coats, Junr., Alex. Seaton, Wm. Rakestraw, Wm. Coates.

Page 131. John Wells, of Solebury Twp., Yeoman. July 16, 1748. Proved Jany. 23, 1748/9. William Kitchin of Solebury, Weaver, 105 acres I live on in Solebury Twp. John Wells, son of Bro. Samuel Wells, of Phila. Co., £100. Bro. Moses Wells of Lower Dublin, Philadelphia Co., his son Moses and other children. Job Noble, of Warminster Twp., Blacksmith, (£50). Lydia Tomlinson wife of Richard Tomlinson of Phila. Co. and their children, John Tomlinson excepted. Olive Head of Solebury and children of hers by John Head, dec'd. John Norton of Bucks Co. Schoolmaster. Aaron and Thomas Phillips sons of Thomas. Moses Kitchin, son of Thomas. Wm. Kitchin to wall in my Grave Yard. "My wife Mary

requested that Mary, dau. of John Head, and Mary, dau. of Paul Kester, have Doz. Diaper Napkins.." Wm. Kitchin, exr.
Wit: Thomas McMasters, John McMasters.

Page 133. Benjamin Canby, no residence given. 10th mo., 16th day, 1748. Proved Feby. 16, 1748/9. Wife Sarah. Children, Sarah, William, Anne, Thomas, and Samuel Canby. Wm. Hill, Wm. Yeardley, and Thos. Yearley, Junr., exr. "to make tryal of Iron Works" Cousin Elizabeth Head. Friend John Mills. Defect in agreement between George Ely and myself concerning premises where George Ely lives.
Wit: Randal Hutchinson, Geo. Ely, and Sarah Hill.

Page 135. Jeremiah Cooper, no residence given. Jany. 31, 1748/9. Proved Feby. 21, 1748/9. Wife Rebecca, David Kinsey, and Thos. Atkinson, exrs. Children, Isaac, Rachel, Jeremiah, Rebecca, and Job.
Wit: Wm. Lee, Jabol Cooper, Wm. Smith.

Page 136. George Haworth, of Buckingham Twp. 12th mo., 2d. 1748/9. Proved Feby. 24, 1748/9. Wife Martha, probably with child. Brothers, Stephanus (eldest) Absalom, James and John. Sister Mary Mitchener. Bro. John and Father-in-law, Mathew Hall, exrs. Bro. John, all lands.
Wit: John Scarbrough, John Fisher, Nathan Preston.

Page 137. Charles Plumly, of Middletown, Farmer. Mch. 22, 1747/8. Proved Feby. 27, 1748/9. Wife Anne. Money in hands of Samuel Cary for 1/2 acre lot in Bristol. Sons John and Goerge. Daus. Sarah and Margery. Mark Watson and Mahlon Kirkbride, exrs. to make Deed to Garret Vansant for land exchanged.
Wit: John Praal, Edward Roberts, Robert Brodmax.

Page 138. John Hill, of Buckingham, Yeoman. 11th mo., 15th day, 1748. Proved Mch. 4, 1748/9. Wife ---. Sons William and Joseph, exrs. Children, William, Thomas, Hannah, Joseph, Benjamin, John, James, Samuel, Moses, and Aaron.
Wit: Samuel Wilson, Thos. Gilbert, Junr., Thos. Ross.

Page 140. Jeremiah Croasdale, of Middletown. 11th mo., 23rd day, 1748. Proved Mch. 8, 1748/9. Wife Grace, sons Ezra and Robert, Daus. Grace, Mercy, and Ann. 4 younger children, Eber, Abijah, Macry, and Achsah. So Ezra, James Thackeray, and Cuthbert Hayhurst, exrs.
Wit: Abrm. Chapman, Junr., John Evans, John Woolston.

Page 141. Christopher Day, of Plumstead, Yeoman. Sept. 1, 1746. Proved Mch. 25, 1748/9. Wife Martha. Son Mathew, exr. Son Christopher 50 acres he lives on adj. Alex. Brown. Sons Joseph and Nathaniel. Daus. Abigail Poe and Ursula Fenton.
Wit: Clement Doyle, Jno. Watson.

Page 142. George Mitchell, of Wrightstown Twp. May 1748. Proved Mch. 17, 1748. Wife Elizabeth. Sons George, Samuel, and Enoch. Daus. Margaret, Deborah, Elizabeth. Plantation at Newtown.

Wm. Briggs of Newtown, Abrm. Chapman of Wrightstown, exrs.
Wit: James Rose, Deborah Rose.

Page 144. David Dawes of Wrightstown Twp., Yeoman. 12th mo.,
20th day, 1748/9. Proved Mch. 27, 1749. Wife Rebekah.
Daus. Sarah Twining and Elizabeth Dawes. Plantation
bounded by land of Warner, Eleazer Doan, and Bezebeel Wiggins.
Grandchildren, Elizabeth, Mary, and Joseph Twining.
John Twining, Junr., dau. Elizabeth Dawes, and Joseph
Tomlinson, exrs.
Wit: John Linton, John Hampton, Joseph Hamton.

Page 145. John Burley, of Makefield, Yeoman. June 12, 1748.
Proved Apr. 5, 1749. Wife Alice, and Friend George Logan, exrs.
Children to be put to trades at age of 14 yrs.
Wit: John Scott, Mathias Harvye, Chas. Bryan.

Page 146. Alexander Jamison, of Warwick, Yeoman. Sept. 27,
1747. Proved Mch. 29, 1749. Wife Martha and Robert and Henry
Jamison, Seniors, exrs. Sons Henry, William, Robert, Alexander,
and John.
Wit: William Miller and Anne Miller.

Page 147. Abigail Paxson, of Solebury, widow. 5th mo.,
16th day, 1742. Proved Apr. 8, 1749. Robert Smith and
John Hill, exrs. Son James and his children, William,
Abigail and Jonas. Dau. Esther Clayton and her children,
Joseph, Susanna and Margaret Clayton. Daus in law Jane
and Alice Paxson. Son Thomas's children, Joseph, Benjamin
and Oliver. Son Reuben's children, William, Jacob and
Mary Paxson. Dau. Abigail's children, Jacob and Mary
Lamplaugh.
Wit: Wm. Hill and Elizabeth Large.
Both exrs. dec'd. Letters granted to Thos. Paxson, eldest son
and heir.

Page 148. John James of New Britain, Weaver. Jan. 13, 1747/8.
Proved May 8, 1749. Son Thomas, exr. Sons William, Isaac.
Thomas (lent me £100. 18 yrs. ago). Daus. Sarah Lewis,
Rebecca Miner, and Mary James. Wm. Davis Baptist Minister
at new Meeting house where I am a member. Joseph Eaton,
Baptist Minister. Griffith Owen and David Jones,
Trustees.
Wit: Hugh Edmunds, John Edmund, and Mordecai Bevan.

Page 152. Casper Clattre of Plumstead Twp. July 25, 1748.
Proved May 23, 1749. Wife Jane. Sons Simeon and John, exrs. Sons

Paul, William, and Jacob. Daus. Ann, Lanah, Caterin, and
Elizabeth. John Rose and Matthew Hughs, Junr. exrs.
Wit: Ichabod Wilkinson, John Smith, Junr., and John Price.

Page 150. John Gray, of Warrington Twp., Yeoman. Apr. 5, 1749.
Proved May 9, 1749. Wife Margaret. Bro. Richard Walker, Rev.
Charles Beatty and Rev. --- Treat, exrs. Niece Sarah Craig living
with her aunt, Margaret. Nephews David and Robert Graham. Niece
Anna Graham. Children of Margaret Graham, dec'd. - late wife of
Robert Miller. John McKey, Senr., and John McKey, Junr., living
at Tohikon. Ann McKey, living in Ireland. Cousin Henry Gray,
living in Ierland. Second cousin John Gray, living in Ireland.
Residue of personal estate and plantation to wife for life, then
to be sold. £2 of Proceeds per annum to be paid for support of
Ministry at New Pres. Mtg. House where Rev. Charles Beatty
preaches. 1/2 of residue for use of said Beatty during his
ministry at said church. 1/2 for use of Religious Students for
the Ministry. When Beatty ceases to preach, whole profits for use
of Students.
Wit: Wm. McConnell, Jos. Weir, John Craig.

Page 154. Andrew Long, of Warwick, Yeoman. Nov. 15, 1738.
Proved June 13, 1749. Wife Isabel and Wm. Miller and John Earles,
both of Warminster, exrs. Sons and Daus. (minors).
Wit: John Scott, Jos. Kaar, Robt. Scott, and Richard Brush.

Page 155. John Frohock of. --- Dated Feby. 25, 1748. Proved
June 10, 1749. Child, Thomas Hugh. "Have lain under great
obligations to Mr. DeNormandie's family from the time I first
came into America. ..." "... now desire Mrs. Denormandie to take
my children under her care." exrs. to write to my sisters in
England "upwards to 20 yrs. since I left Europe." If any estate
there, to go to my 4 children, John, William, Thomas and Hugh.
Hon. John Coxe, Esq. and Dr. John Denormandie, exrs.
Wit: John Abm. Denormandie, Jos. White, Inkeeper, and John Allen.

Page 157. James Banes, of Southampton, Blacksmith. May 2, 1749.
Proved July 12, 1749. Wife Elizabeth. Bro. Mathew Banes and
Stephen Watts, exr. Children, Phebe, Jesse and Elizabeth.
Wit: Jos. Banes, Elizabeth Banes, John Hart.

Page 158. Stoffel Vansand, Middletown, Farmer. June 4, 1749.
Proved Aug. 21, 1749. Son John and son-in-law Lewis Rue, exrs.
Son James and his children. Daus. Elizabeth, Rachel, Olshe.
Grandson Wm. Renberry.
Wit: James Rue, Mary Rue, Robert Brodnax.

Page 160. Nicholas Williams, of Buckingham, Yeoman, Date 12 mo.
9th day, 1748/9. Proved Aug. 22, 1749. Wife Mary and Kinsman Ely
Welding, exrs. Dau. Sarah Thomas. Grandchildren, Jonathan, John,
Mary, and Ann Thomas.
Wit: John Beal, Wm. Carver, Henry Carver.

Page 161. Bartholomew Longstreth, of Warminster, Yeoman. Mch.
17, 1746. Pr. Sept. 7, 1749. Wife Ann and son Daniel, exrs. Sons

Joseph, Isaac, John, and Benjamin. Dau. Sarah, Jane, Ann,
Elizabeth. Land sold to James Robinson of Rockhill, 250 acres on
Gallows Hill Run in Bucks Co. Land in Warminster purchased of
Andrew Frazier, Thos. Fairman and George Williard, Daniel Brock,
and Daniel Pritchard.
Wit: Wm. Spencer, Joseph Hart, and John Hart.

Page 164. Richard Addis, of Northampton Twp. Sept. 19, 1749.
Proved Oct. 7, 1749. Wife Susannah. Sons John, Simon, and
Richard. Daus. Mary and Charity Addis. Brothers Jacob Benet and
John Addis, exrs.
Wit: Robert Heslet and Evan Jones.

Page 165. John Scott, of Warwick Town, Farmer. Aug. 8, 1749.
Proved Nov. 6, 1749. John Mitchell, John Mann, and Robert Scott,
exrs. Sons Robert (eldest), John, William, James, Joseph. Dau.
Mary and 3 other children.
Wit: Tristram Davis, Benj. Hair, Jos. Moore.

Page 166. Benjamin Taylor, Junr., of the Falls Twp., Blacksmith.
Oct. 18, 1749. Proved Nov. 27, 1749. Wife Sarah, Father Benjamin
Taylor and Brother-in-law Joseph White, exrs. Daus. Sarah,
Hannah, and Esther.
Wit: Henry Margerum, Priscilla Buckman, and Jane Buckman.

Page 167. Ellin Baynes, of Falls Twp., Widow. 11th mo. (Jan.)
2, 1744/5. Proved Nov. 28, 1749. Thomas Cornthwaite and Wm.
Atkinson, exrs. 1/2 of clear estate to Falls Mo. Mtg. 1/2 to be
remitted to Shipley Mtg. of People call Quakers in Old England,
(5 miles from Worminghurst) "1/2 thereof for service of Truth"
1/2 for Brothers John and Thomas Botting, living in Gillington
Parish near Broad-full Bridge, near Red Hill in County of Sussex.
Wit: Thos. Yeardley, Thos. Marriott, Mahlon Kirkbride. Letters
granted to Cornthwaite.

Page 168. William Atkinson, of "Burrough of Bristol." Sept. 22,
1749. Proved Nov. 30, 1749. "Far advanced in years." Dau. Rachel
and Son Joseph, exrs. Son Samuel, dau. Mary Bankson, and other
children. Son-in-law John Hall and Cousin Samuel Bunting,
Overseers.
Wit: Samuel Bunting, Mark Watson, Thos. Cornthwaite.

Page 169. Elizabeth Hellens, of Newtown, Widow. Aug. 30, 1749.
Codicil Sept. 4, 1749. Proved Dec. 10, 1749. Sons John and
Joseph Walley, former husband John Walley, dec'd. Elizabeth
Tomlinson, wife of James. Deborah Letch, wife of James, Sarah
Riche, wife of John. Evan Jones and wife Rebecca. Bro. Samuel
Hough. Bond agt. Joseph Stackhouse, son of Robert. Amos
Strickland to hold land leased of son Joseph Walley, and to build
a stone house at expense of estate of John Walley, dec'd. Agnes,
wife of Amos Strickland. Amos Strickland, exr.
Wit: Evan Davis, Wynchel Opdycke, Agnes Buckman.

Page 170. Thomas Harvye, Junr., of Upper Makefield, Yeoman.
Dated Nov. 14, 1749. Proved Dec. 9, 1749. Wife Magdalen and Dau.

Ann Ann Harvye. Jos. Duer and Geo. Logan, exrs.
Wit: James Logan, Henry Harvye, Abrm. Harvye. exrs. named
renounced and Letters granted to widow.

Page 171. Esther Clay, Widow of John Clay, late of Bristol,
Blacksmith, dec'd. Nov. 27, 1749. Proved Dec. 17, 1749. Dau.
Mary Aspril and her daus. Mary, Sarah, and Lydia. Daus. Sarah and
Catharine and their children. John Hall and Saml. Bunting,
Junr., exrs.
Wit: Thos. Stanaland, Thos. Stanaland, Junr., Darby Brannyn.

Page 172. Joseph White, of Burrough of Bristol, Innholder. Nov.
4, 1749. Proved Dec. 17, 1749. Wife Lydia and Kinsman John Hall,
exrs. Son Joseph and other children. Land in Kent Co., Delaware,
to be sold. Land in Bristol to be leased and profits used to
remove indebtedness to Loan Office, then to son Joseph.
Wit: Peter White, Wm. Large, John Williams.

Page 173. William Gilbert of Warminster, Yeoman. Nov. 20, 1749.
Proved Jan. 8, 1749/50. Wife Lucretia and Bro. Nicholas, exrs.
Sons Seth (eldest), Silas, and Joseph.
Wit: Robert Tomkins, John Heaton, John Hart.

Page 174. Anthony Wright, of Middletown, Farmer. Dec. 13, 1749.
Proved Jan. 6, 1749. Sons Joseph and Benjamin, and Wm. Allen,
Esq. of Phila., exrs. Dau. Lydia and other children.
Wit: Ann Carter, Jos. Bodine, Samson Cary.

Page 175. Thomas Kelly, of Hilltown, Yeoman. Dec. 13, 1749.
Proved Jan. 6, 1749. Wife Martha and Father, John Kelly, exrs.
Father and Thomas Thomas, Guardians of minor children.
Wit: Levis Evans, David George, Benj. Griffith.

Page 176. Thomas Cornish, of the Falls Twp., Cooper. Sept. 22,
1747. Proved Jan. 24, 1749. Wife Tamer and Sons John and Thomas,
exrs. Dau. Elizabeth Burroughs. Sons Thomas, 43 acres he lives on
part of tract bought of Samuel Cary, and 30 acres bought of Thos.
Cadwallader, also sword and gun.
Wit: Paul Wilmerton, Joseph Ashton, Samson Cary.

Page 177. Jonathan Nutt, of the Falls Twp., Yeoman. Dec. 14,
1749. Proved Jan. 26, 1749. Wife Ann, son Edmund, exrs. Son
John, 5 shillings. Daus. Hannah and Ann.
Wit: John Wharton, Joseph Kirkbride, Mahlon Kirkbride.

Page 178. Benjamin Field, of Middletown Twp. 10th mo., 6th day,
1749. Proved Feby. 3, 1749. Wife Sarah, extx. Sons Benjamin,
Thomas, Edward, and Jennings. Daus. Sarah Stockdale, Susanna,
Elizabeth, and Mary.
Wit: Wm. Blaker, Jos. Stackhouse, Wm. Paxson.

Page 179. Mark Watson, of the Falls Twp., Yeoman. Nov. 7, 1749.
Proved Feby. 9, 1749. Wife Ann, Bro-in-law Mahlon Kirkbride and
Nephew William Paxson, exrs. Children, Joseph, Benjamin, Ann,
Mark, Amos, Rebecca, Deborah, and Isaac Watson, the five youngest

minors.
Wit: Jos. Ahton, Thos. Watson, Joseph White.

Page 181. Pieter Van Hooren, of Middletown, Yeoman. Feby 12,
1749/50. Proved ---. Wife Elizabeth. 2d. son Gabriel, exr.
Eldest son, Bernard, 3d. Peter, 4th Benjamin, 5th Richard, 6th
John, 7th Garrett. Eldest dau. Catharine, wife of Thomas Craven.
2d. Charity, wife of Isaiah Vansant. 3d. Jane, wife of Edmond
Roberts. 4th Elizabeth, wife of Peter Praul. 5th Mary, wife of
William Gosline.
Wit: John Vansandt, Francis Titus, Garret Vansant.

Page 183. Mary Vandegrift, Widow of Abraham Vandegrift, late of
Bensalem Twp., dec'd. Feb. 12, 1749/50. Proved Mch. 3, 1749/50.
Eldest son Leonard Vandegrift, exr. Son Abraham under 21 and
youngest son Garret. Youngest dau. Jemima Vandegrift.
Wit: Abraham Vandegrift, Patt. Kelly, Thomas Evan.

Page 184. Joseph Hutchinson, of the Falls Twp. 9th mo., 21st
day, 1749. Proved Mch. 5, 1749. Wife Sarah and Brothers Michel
and Randal, exrs. Children, Mary, Sarah, Hannah, Martha, and
Joseph.
Wit: Laurence Terry, John Kirkbride, Junr., Henry Addington.

Page 185. John Vansandt, of Middletown, Farmer. Dec. 7, 1749.
Proved Mch. 6, 1749. Wife Rebekah, extx. Crispin Collet and Alex.
Edwards, Trustees. Children, Ann, Elizabeth, Caterin, Mary,
Rebecca, and John.
Wit: Joseph Rue, Benj. Vanhorn, Richard Vanhorn. Letters granted
to Crispin Collet and Alex. Edwards.

Page 186. John Nield, of Makefield Twp., Yeoman. 12th mo., 1st
day, 1728. Proved Oct. 6, 1747. Wife Judith. Son John, exr. Sons
John and James, 236 acres I live on. Daus. Martha and Jane Neild.
Wit: Abel Janney, Junr., Thomas Watson, and Leonard Shallcross.
Handwriting of Thomas Watson pr. by his son Mark Watson, Abel
Janney of Makefield testifies as witness.

Page 188. John Barwis of Bristol Twp. Mch. 20, 1740/1. Proved
Mch. 22, 1749. Wife Margaret, extx. Son Thomas. Daus. Margaret,
Esther, Phebe, and Jane Barwis. Children by 1st wife each 1
shilling.
Wit: Wm. Atkinson and Margaret Atkinson. Signatures of wits. pr.
by Rachel Atkinson, a dau. of Wm. and Margaret, and by John Hall
who had married antoher of their daus.

Page 189. William Carter, of Southampton, Yeoman. Feby. 7,
1749/50. Proved Mch. 22, 1749/50. Wife Sarah and Bro-in-law John
Plumly and James Thackeray, exrs. Daus. Sarah and Mary. Sons
James and William.
Wit: David Wilson, James Stuart, John Hart.

Page 191. Edward Roberts, of Boro. of Bristol, Miller. Nov. 12,
1749. Proved Mch. 22, 1749/50. Wife Mary and Dau. Mary. Wife and
Father-in-law John Hall, exrs.

Wit: John Baldwin, Junr., Elizabeth Hutchinson, Margaret Baldwin.

Page 191. Thomas Stuart, of Tinnecome, Yeoman, Date Dec. 10, 1749. Proved Mch. 22, 1749/50. Wife Jean. Sons, Samuel, Robert, Thomas, and William estate I live on and tract of land on Deep Run adj. Robert Barnhill and land late William Wells. Daus. Lilley, Jean, Elizabeth, son John's dau. Martha. Jean Wigton. Wit: John Patterson, Joseph McKinney, and Andrew Patterson. Letters granted Aug. 30, 1750.

Page 193. James Logan, of Lower Makefield. Mch. 16, 1749. Proved Mch. 26, 1750. Wife Margaret and John Duer, exrs. Son Thomas "4 of my children," viz., Mary, George, Henry, and Dorcas Logan.
Wit: Noah Gates, Allen Dunlap, Geo. Logan.

Page 194. John Norton, of Solebury, Schoolmaster. Feby. 17, 1749/50. Proved Mch. 27, 1750. Nephew Samuel Crook, all estate, "what is not used in bringing up to be paid him when 21," if he dye, to Rev. Charles Beatty, for use of Presbyterian College. Bro-in-law William Kitchin, exr.

Page 195. John Lawrenson, of Makefield Twp. Feby. 2, 1749. Proved Mch. 27, 1750. Wife Olive, sole extx. and legatee. Wit: Geo. Logan, John Enoch, and Thomas Yeardley, Junr.

Page 195. Archibald Finley, of New Britain, Mason, nuncupative, Declared Mch. 11, 1749/50. Signed Mch. 12, 1749/50. Proved Mch. 27, 1749/50. Wife Margaret and 2 eldest sons, John and Henry, exrs. estate to be divided among children "as the law directs." Simon Butler of New Britain and Isaac James of Montgomery (sic) Phila. Co., Trustees. Signed by Robert Lalor, Henry Kelso, and James Finley. Letters granted to Margaret and John Finley.

Page 196. Debora Morgan, of Richland Twp., Widow. 9th mo., 11th day, 1749. Proved Mch. 30, 1750. Son Jonathan Haycock, exr. Son John 100 acres and overplus of 30 acres within the lines of the 200 acres left him and Isaac by his father, and which I purchased of Joseph Jones, after my husband's death. 3 Daus. Sarah Dennis, Debora Morgan, and Susanna Haycock. 5 grandchildren, Rachel, Ann, Sarai Haycock and Sarah Morgan, and Josiah Dennis.
Wit: Jonathan, Benjamin, and Abraham Griffith.

Page 197. Thomas Darrogh, of Bedminster Twp. Mch. 16, 1749/50. Proved Apr. 3, 1750. Wife Mary and William Means, exrs. Sons Robert (190 acres), Thomas (180 acres), William, Henry and James. Daus. Agnes, wife of John Davis, Esther, wife of George Scott, and Susannah Darrogh.
Wit: Francis McHenry, Thomas Morris.

Page 205. Nicholas Allen, of Bristol Borough. 1st mo., 13th day, 1750. Proved May 1, 1750. Wife Margaret and Bro. Samuel Allen, exrs. Daus. Mary and Sarah Allen.
Wit: Thos. Marriott and Wm. Large.

Page 199. John Thomas, of New Britain Twp., Weaver. Feby. 13, 1748/9. Proved Apr. 3, 1750. Wife Margaret, extx. Bro. John Thomas of Kent Co. on Delaware, Weaver. 2 sons of Dau. Sarah, Abijah and John, £20 to be paid to their grandfather, Wm. Davis. Plantation to wife for life then to eldest son of Dau. Sarah (only Dau.).
Wit: Stephen Rowland, Abel Griffith, Benj. Griffith, Junr.

Page 201. Samuel Hart, of Plumstead, Yeoman. Mch. 28, 1750. Proved Apr. 20, 1750. Wife Elizabeth. John Gaddis and James Hart, exrs. Sons James (eldest), William, Joseph, John, Samuel. Daus. Mary McGlaughin, Jane Mathers, Nellie and Elizabeth Hart.
Wit: Charles Williams, William Logan.

Page 201. Elizabeth Hart, of Plumstead, Widow, Date Apr. 3, 1750. Proved Apr. 20, 1750. Sons Joseph and Samuel. Daus. Nellie and Elizabeth Hart. Gd. Daus. Elizabeth McGlaughlin, Elizabeth Hart, and Elizabeth Mathers.
Wit: Charles Williams, Wm. Logan. Eldest son James renounces, Letters granted to son Joseph.

Page 203. Elinor Williams, of New Britain, Widow, Relict and Administratix of David Williams late of New Britain, dec'd. Nov. 3, 1749. Proved Apr. 27, 1750. Dau. Elizabeth £10. Bal. of Est. to be equally divided between all children. Eldest son Isaac and Bro. Thomas Lewis of New Britain, exrs. Said Thomas Lewis and Jenkin Evans, guardians of minor children.
Wit: Daniel Davis and Benjamin Griffith.

Page 204. Silas McCarty of adjacent of Springfield. Jan. 13, 1749/50. Proved May 1, 1750. Wife Sarah, son Carell and Bro-in-law Robert Tomkins, exrs. To wife, plantation for life, then to all children, Carell excepted. Carell, 100 acres adj. Congregation of Baptists 1 acre on east side of tract where a Meeting House now stands.
Wit: Thos. Lancaster, Benjamin Gilbert.

Page 206. John Leedom, of Southampton, Yeoman. Aug. 9, 1743. Proved May 7, 1750. Wife Susanna. Sons John, Samuel, and Allijah. Daus. Ann and Hannah and child unborn. Cuthbert Hayhurst of Northampton and Benj. Cutler of Middletown, exrs.
Wit: Nicholas Tucker, Thos. Hillborne and Thomas Prichard.

Page 207. Christopher Moor. Dec. 11, 1749, Proved May 14, 1750. Share of father's estate to 2 children. Michel Moor, exr.
Wit: John Moor, Garet Moor, and Melicha Kite.

Page 208. Thomas Smith of Upper Makefield. Apr. 21, 1750. Proved May 18, 1750. Wife Elizabeth. Sons Thomas and Samuel, Tract I live on, on road leading from Canby's Ferry to Wrightstown adj. John Trago. 2 youngest sons, Ephraim and Jacob. Daus. Elizabeth, Mary, and Margaret Smith. Sons Thomas and Samuel, exrs. Bro. Wm., Trustee.
Wit: Thos. Atkinson, Wm. Lee, Junr., and Ezekiel Atkinson.

Page 212. Catharine Sparway, of Bensalem Twp. Jany. 9, 1750.
Proved June 17, 1750. Surviving children and grandchildren. John
Sands and John Baldwin, Sr., exrs.
Wit: John Gilbert, Thomas Gilbert, Stephen Sands.

Page 209. Thomas Canby of Solebury Twp., Yeoman. 9th mo.,
(Nov.) 18, 1742. May 25, 1750. Wife Jane. Sons Benjamin and
Oliver, exrs. Son Thomas. Daus. Sarah Hill, Elizabeth, Mary,
Phebe, Esther, Lydia, Rachel, and Ann. Martha, Jane and Rebecca
Wilson. Son Benjamin, Real estate in Partnership with Anthony
Morris, Land, Mill, and Saw Mill.
Benj. being dec'd. and Oliver a non-resident and also having
renounced Executorship. Letters granted to Wm. Hill, Wm.
Yeardley, and Thos. Yeardey (sic), Jr., exrs. of Benj. Canby.

Page 211. Robert Newton, of Tunnekum, Bucks Co., Yeoman. Jan.
26, 1748/9. Proved June 6, 1750. Wife Elizabeth and Friends
George and Henry Newton, exrs. Daus. Jean and Ann. Children to
conform to Church of England.
Wit: John Houey, Geo. Scott.

Page 213. James Cumings. July 1, 1750. Proved Aug. 13, 1750.
Caveat filed July 27, 1750. Wife Jane. Bro. Robert, Rev. Chas.
Beatty and Rev. Richard Treat, exrs. Bro. Robert, his wife Mary,
sons John and James and dau. Jane. Bro. John and his sons Robert
and James. Sister Margaret wife of John Gallasby of the Kingdom
of Ireland. Kinsman Jacob Lindsey and James Lindsey, son of
David. Daniel MacLean. £50 to Rev. Charles Beatty and Rev.
Richd. Treat in Trust for use of Presbyterian Church at Newtown.
Wit: Jonathan Bavington, David Lindsey, and John Hart.
Caveat filed July 27, 1750 by widow, Jane Cummings. John Hart
testified to writing will at dictition of Testator, other wits.
and Evan Jones, testify. Pr. Aug. 30, 1750 before Abraham
Chapman, Richard Mitchell and John Abrm. Denormandie, Justices of
Court of Common on Please and Lawrence Growden, Dep. Register.

Page 217. Thomas Butler, of New Britain, Miller. Aug. 25, 1750.
Proved Sept. 7, 1750. Wife Sarah and her children, Thomas, Isaac,
and Thamer Jones. Son Joseph and dau. Mary Butler. Wife and uncle
Thomas Gill, exrs.
Wit: David Eaton and Cephas Child.

Page 218. John Laycock of Wrightstown, Yeoman, Dated, Aug. 20,
1750. Proved Sept. 12, 1750. Wife Mary and Dau. Mary, sole
legatees. Dau. Mary and son-in-law John Trago, exrs.
Wit: John Gibson, Jos. Johnson, Rachel Johnson.

Page 219. Joseph Armstrong, of Bedminster Twp. Aug. 4, 1750.
Proved Oct. 11, 1750. Bro. Samuel, exr. To provide for Father
during life. Sister Agnes Creighton. Nefew Jean Creighton. Bro.
James Armstrong. Lawful Heirs of Bro. William, dec'd. Bro-in-law
James McMullen. Nefew Christopher Hues.
Wit: Robt. Smith, Adam Armstrong.

Page 220. William Lowther, of Buckingham, Weaver, Date Sept. 12,

1750. Proved Nov. 1, 1750. Benj. Fell, exr. Son-in-law James Bradshaw, £60 he to give security to provide to my gd. dau. Hannah Lowther, dau. of son Robert. Bal. of Est. equally among all children, Joel excepted. He to have 2 shares.
Wit: John Thomas, Abraham Tucker, John Watson, Junr.

Page 223. Neill Grant, of Makefield Twp. May 12, 1749. Proved Feby. 14, 1750/1. Wife Elizabeth and son Robert, exrs. Son Amos to be provided for being by accident rendered uncapable of helping himself. Son Thomas. Daus. Elizabeth, Catharine, Margaret, Mary, and Anna.
Wit: Joseph Duer, Wm. Nixon, Chas. Bryan.

Page 222. Ephraim Fenton, of Buckingham, Yeoman. Sept. 7, 1738. Proved Dec. 24, 1750. Wife Mary. Eldest son Ephraim, 180 acres off east end of tract where he lives. Sons Josiah and Samuel, bal. of tract. Land in N.J. to 3 sons. Dau. Mary. Nehemiah Blackshaw of Falls Twp., exr.
Wit: Mathew Hall, Benj. Fell, Chas. Bolton. (Exr. named and also eldest son being dec'd. Letters granted to Josiah Fenton.).

Page 224. John Rose of Solebury, Yeoman. Feby. 4, 1750. Proved Mch. 25, 1751. Wife Magdalen and son Christopher, exrs. Children, Christopher, Alice, Mary, Margaret, Ursula, Elizabeth, and Ann. Real Est. and Personalty in West New Jersey to be sold. Plantation in Solebury to son Christopher after wife's death, and to male heirs forever, in default of issue to John Rose, eldest son of Bro. Andrew, in default of male issue to his brother Henry and male heirs forever.
Wit: Stephen Townsend, States Jewell, and Samuel Armitage.

Page 225. John Wilkinson, of Wrightstown, Yeoman. Feby. 1750/1. Proved Apr. 23, 1751. Wife Mary. Sons John and Joseph, exrs. Son Josiah. Dau. Plain Ball.
Wit: Peter Josts, Rachel Kibbs, Thos. Chapman.

Page 227. John Beelet, of Tinicum, Yeoman. Oct. 18, 1750. Proved June 13, 1751. Wife Elizabeth. Sons James and John, land I live on and 150 acres in Swamp. Dau. Mary. 5 youngest children, viz., Elizabeth, Ann, Jean, Susanna, and Rebecca. Sister Jean. John Wigton, James Johnson, and Samuel Stewart, exrs.
Wit: Joseph McKinney, Robert Patterson, and John Wallace.

Page 228. Benjamin Butler, of New Britain, Yeoman. Apr. 7, 1750. Proved June 13, 1751. Wife Elizabeth and only child unborn. Bro. Simon, exr. Bro. Simon's children - eldest is Abiah. Friends and relations Isaac James and Griffith Owen, Trustee. Cousins John and Edward Mathew, Guardians. Plantation and Saw Mill.
Wit: Simon Morgan, Lodowick Workman, John Hartshorn.

Page 230. Margaret Johnson, of Bristol Twp., Widow. Aug. 29, 1749. Proved Sept. 9, 1751. Dau. Mary, wife of Edward Britten. Dau. Elizabeth, wife of Patrick Kelly. Grandchildren, Wm. Harry, Elizabeth and Mary Harry. Granddau. Margaret, wife of John

Baldwin, Junr. Grandchildren, Jonathan, Jacob, and Phebe Hibbs.
Mary and Lydia Johnson, Mary, dau. of John Johnson, granddau.
Lydia Johnson, £50 in lieu of £50 devised to her mother Hannah by
will of her father John Johnson. Grandson Thomas Lacey. Thomas
Thacher, son of Nicholas. Residue to John Bessonett of Middletown
and Nicholas Allen of Bristol Boroug., Shopkeeper, exrs in Trust
for dau. Elizabeth, at her death to grandchildren, Jonathan,
Jacob, and Phebe Hibbs.
Wit: Thos. Bartholomew, Jos. Brelsford, Wm. Brelsford, and John
Duncan.

Page 232. Moses Crawford, of Warwick Twp., Joiner. Sept. 2,
1751. Proved Oct. 31, 1751. Wife Isabel and Robert Scott of
Warwick, exrs. Sons Archibald, Robert, John, James, Moses and
Samuel. Daus. Elinor, Anne and Jane.
Wit: William Abernethy, James Pook, Elinor Poak.

Page 233. James Hambleton, of Solebury Twp., Yeoman. 7th mo.,
9th day, 1751. Proved Nov. 8, 1751. Wife Mary. Son Stephen and
son-in-law Samuel Armitage, exrs. 200 acres to be sold. Residue
to son Stephen. Son William. Grandsons James and John Armitage.
Daus. Grace and Gennett.
Wit: John Scarborough, Joseph Skelton, Saml. Eastburn.

Page 234. Ephraim Leech, of Warrington, Yeoman. Jan. 6, 1751.
Proved Nov. 30, 1751. Wife Mary, £70 beside £40 part of her
former husband's estate, now in hands of her son Thomas Nixon.
Sons Simon (£30 if he appear to demand it), William, and John.
Cousins Thomas and John Robinson £5 each to pay their passage to
their native country. Sister Katrin Robinson of the City of
Dublin, Ireland. Mr. Stephen Sibtrop, Esq. of Newtown, near
Drauchadaice, Ireland. £4 for use of Church at White Marsh. £4
for use of Pres. Meeting House and Grave Yard at Neshaminy. 1
acre of land at S.E. corner of plantation joining County Line for
School House, forever. Archibald McLean and Wm. Birney of
Horsham, Phila. Co., exrs.
Wit: Thomas Barr, Thomas Ross. Codicil Oct. 5, 1751.

Page 239. Mary Kirkbride, of Falls, widow of Joseph. 6th mo.,
(Aug.) 26, 1751. Proved Jan. 3, 1752. Son John and sons-in-law
Israel Pemberton, Jr. and Samuel Smith, exrs. Dau. Jane Smith,
children of dec'd. dau. Sarah Pemberton, Mary, Rachel, Sarah,
Israel, and Joseph. Grandson John Kirkbride. Children of son-in-
law, Joseph Kirkbride, viz. Phebe, Hannah, Mary, Elizabeth, and
Sarah. Children of son in law Mahlon Kirkbride, Mary, Sarah, and
Letitia. Granddau. Anna Paxson. Kinswoman Grace Kirkbride.
Wit: Thos. Cornthwaite, Mary Kirkebride, Junr., Mahlon Kirkbride.

Page 236. Christian Van Nooran (Van Horn), of Northampton,
Yeoman. June 18, 1748. Proved Dec. 12, 1751. Wife Williamakee.
son Barnard and Nicholas Wyncoop of Northampton, exrs. Sons
Barnard, Henry, John and Christian. Daus. Ann, wife of Cornelius
Corson,. Catharine, wife of Henry Hageman,. Jane, wife of John
Hageman,. and Charity, wife of Godfrey Vanduren. Barnard, 205
acres where I dwell lateley surveyed by Benj. Field adj. 50

conveyed to him on Neshaminey Creek. Son Henry, plantation of 200 acres at Newtown and privilege of purchasing bal at 20 shillings per acre. John, 32 acres in Northampton, Christian, 187 acres in Northampton. Charity, 40 acres on road leading from Robert Heaton's Mill adj. Grave Yard and son John.
Wit: Edmond Cahill, Catharine Spicher, Jno. Hart.

Page 240. Henry Tomlinson, of Burrough of Bristol. Mch. 22, 1748/9. Proved Jan. 6, 1752. Sons Thomas and Joseph, exrs. Dau. Sarah Tomlinson.
Wit: Andrew McFarland, Wm. Large, Wm. Atkinson. Letter granted to Joseph.

Page 241. John Atkinson, of Upper Makefield, weaver. Dec. 10, 1751. Proved Jan. 15, 1752. Sons William and Thomas (exrs.), 200 acres on which I live paying rent due London Company. Dau. Mary Atkinson. Bro. Wm. Atkinson. Sons Ezekiel, Christopher, Cephas. Servitude of apprentice Joseph Heaton to son Cephas.
Wit: Henry Child, Cephas Child.

Page 242. William Beal, of New Britain, Yeoman. Dec. 24, 1751. Proved Mch. 11, 1752. Wife Grace, her father Thomas Gill and my cousin Thos. Watson, exrs. Sons Thomas and Joseph, plantation when 21. Dau. Sarah.
Wit: John Fell, John Watson, Junr.

Page 244. Elizabeth Archibald, of Buckingham, Widow. Jan. 10, 1748. Proved Mch. 11, 1752. Only surviving, absent some time, supposed to have gone out of Province. Dau. Margaret, plantation for life then to her children and children of brother John Clerk, living in Scotland and Sister. Wm. Ramsey and Robert Bready of Warwick, exrs.
Wit: Moses Crawford, John McCllow (?). Letters to Ramsey.

Page 245. Henry Benson, of Northampton Twp. Dec. 14, 1751. Proved Mch. 11, 1752. Father Thomas Benson, Sister Elizabeth Benson, Wm. Ramsey and Thomas Benson, exrs.
Wit: John Comnes and James Boyd.

Page 246. Joseph Chapman, of Wrightstown, Yeoman. 7th mo., 6th day, 1746. Proved Mch. 13, 1752. Son Isaac, tract called Neshamyne Hollow, also 30 acres bought of Jos. Kirkbride and lot where Andrew Vanbuskirk lives, both sides of road leading to Richard Mitchells Mill, with Saw Mill. Youngest daus. Mary, Jane, and Margaret Chapman. Daus. Sarah Wilkinson and Ann Chapman. Land adj. Meeting House and land in tenure of James Hill. Son Isaac and Dau. Ann, exrs.
Wit: Abraham Chapman, Benjamin Chapman, Joseph Hamton.

Page 248. Richard Stout of New Britain. Feby 7, 1752. Proved Mch. 31, 1752. Son Joseph. Daus. Sarah, wife of John Lambert, and Elizabeth Stout. Cephas Child and Daniel Pennington, exrs.
Wit: Frances Wilgus, Clement Doyle, and Wm. Pennington.

Page 248. Isaac Stout, of New Britain, Carpenter. Jan. 27,

1752. Proved Mch. 31, 1752. Wife Hester. John Embley, of West
Jersey, and Cephas Child, of Plumstead, exrs. Sons James and
Thomas. Daus. Catharine, Elizabeth, and Rachel Stout and Dyer
Deme.
Wit: Clement Doyle, Samuel Wells, and Matthew Day. Emley
renounced. Letters to Child.

Page 250. Lewis Rue, of Middletown, Farmer. Dec. 5, 1751.
Proved Apr. 4, 1752. Wife Rachel and Bro. Richard and Bro-in-law
Garret Vansant, exrs. Sons Lewis and Christoffell. Daus. Anne,
Elizabeth, Catharine, Rachel, and Jesinah.
Wit: John Bessonett, Francis Titus, Saml. Rue. Letters granted to
Rachel Rue and Garret Vansant.

Page 251. Edmond Lovett, of Co. of Bucks, Yeoman. 12th mo., 2nd
day, 1720/1. Proved Sept. 28, 1752. Son Edmond Lovett, exr.
Daus. Mary Large, (£50), Susanna Nutt (£14). Granddau. Martha
Lovett. Residue to Edmond.
Wit: John Schofield, John Scott, Wm. Atkinson.

Page 251. John Thomson, of Warwick Twp., Yeoman. Nov. 22, 1752.
Proved Dec. 6, 1752. Wife Ruth. Sons William and John, exrs.
Daus. Ruth, Hester, Elizabeth, and Rebecca. Sons James and
Daniel. Jos. Hough and Isaac Fell, Trustees.
Wit: Jos. Hough, James Meredith, Owen Roberts.

Page 253. Henry Wilson, Falls Twp., Nuncupative, Declared Nov.
5, 1752. Signed Nov. 9, 1752. Proved Apr. 2, 1753. "At usual
place of abode at House of Sarah Kirkbride, in Falls Twp.." All
estate after payment of debts to sister Hannah Burges. Signed by
Nicholas Austin and Sarah Kirkbride. Letters to Hannah Burges.

Page 254. William Creighton, of Warrington Twp., Turner. Aug.
16, 1746. Pr. June 17, 1747. Wife Agnes, plantation during life
or widowhood for use of children. exrs. Richard Walker and John
Gray of Warrington, Planters, Thomas Craig of Forks of Delaware,
Esq., Richard Graham of Twp. of Rocky Hill and Joseph Armstrong
of Bedminster Twp. Moveable to be sold to help clear the place
and make a purchase thereof.
Wit: John Gourley, Saml. Harper, Saml. Kennedy. Letters granted
to Thos. Craig only on Mch. 12, 1753.

Page 255. James Kelly, of Warminster Twp., Yeoman. Feby. 9,
1749. Proved Mch. 28, 1753. Wife Margaret and son John, exrs.
Grandsons John Kelly and James Kelly.
Wit: Charles Beatty, Ann Beatty, Hugh Johnston. Letters to John
Kelly.

Page 256. Daniel Davis of New Britain, Yeoman. Sept. 27, 1751.
Proved Apr. 13, 1753. Wife Mary, sole extx. Eldest son John, 40
acres adj. David Evans and Benj. Griffith. 2d. son Abel, 40 acres
adj. Jenkin Evans and Jonathan Drake. 3d. son David Davis, 130
acres I live on. Dau. Mary Davis.
Wit: Benj. Griffith, Junr., Benj. Griffith, Isaac Williams.
Codicil dated Mch. 2, 1753. Wit: Thos. Bartholomew.

Page 259. Thomas Stanaland. Sept. 17, 1747. Proved May 11, 1753. Wife Mary. Eldest son John, youngest Thomas. Dau. Nanney. (no Wits., no exr.). Proved by Rebecca Hands, late Wetherill. Widow renounces Letters and they are granted to Thomas.

Page 260. Sarah Winner, of Bristol Twp. June 8, 1753. Proved July 23, 1753. Son Anthony Hooper. Joseph Smith, exr. Mary Stanaland for "Docerting and other just debts.." Trencher at Richd. Allen's.
Wit:. --- Stanaland, Sarah Marthas.

Page 261. Thomas Nelson, of Middletown. June 4, 1753. Proved Aug. 4, 1753. Sister Ann Wilson "as long as she remains Ann Wilson or goes to live with her husband again." Her son Thomas Wilson and her youngest children, Ann and Jonathan Inslee, alias Wilson. Sister Letitia Bell and her dau. Ann Bell. Friend Phebe Hibbs, dau. of William Hibbs, and her son Valentine Nelson alias Hibbs and any child or children of hers begat by me. Naomi Nelson alias Wildman, dau. of Hannah Wildman. Cousins Robert and Thomas Heaton, sons of my sister Jemima. Cousins Martin Wildman and John Worstall and James Worstall. 1 acre for Public Burying Ground and land for road to same from Greate Road leading from Bristol to Newtown 20 ft. wide. Real estate to Valentine Nelson, alias Hibbs. Robert Heaton, Wm. Ashburn, and Cuthbert Hayhurst, exrs.
Wit: Thos. Longshore, Giles Olphin, Anna Dunn.

Page 264. John Eaton, of Warminster, Yeoman. Sept. 26, 1753. Proved Nov. 8, 1753. Wife Martha, extx. Sons Joseph (eldest), John, David, and Ed.

Page 264. Christian Trueby of Hilltown Twp. Nov. 6, 1753. Proved Nov. 26, 1753. Wife Catharine and Joseph Panchoke, exrs. Six children now living.
Wit: John Bartholomew, Blaze Weaver. Widow renounces.

Page 266. Christian Vanhorn, Northampton, Yeoman. Nov. 18, 1753. Proved Dec. 13, 1753. Wife Jane. Daus. Margaret and Williamkee under 18. Cousin Christian Vanhorn, son of Bro. Henry. Garret Wyncoop and Evan Jones of Northampton, exrs. and Trustees.
Wit: Benj. Dyer, John Shreeve, and Elizabeth Wesley.

Page 267. Thomas Biles, of Middletown. Jan. 14, 1754. Proved Feby. 8, 1754. Wife Sarah and uncle Langhorne Biles, exrs. Est. to be disposed of as under Intestate Laws.
Wit: Benj. Biles, Dan. Byles, Saml. Biles.

Page 268. Benjamin Allman, of Bristol Twp., Yeoman. Feby. 9, 1754. Proved Mch. 20, 1754. Wife Mary and Philip Johnson, exrs. Son Lawrence. Daus. Rachel and Brichet each 1 shilling bal to wife.
Wit: Saml. Johnson, Wm. Bollard. Letters granted to Mary Allman only.

Page 269. John Johnson, of Solebury, husbandman, 4th mo., Aprl.

11, 1754. Proved May 8, 1754. Wife Lydia and bro-in-law Thomas
Paxson, exrs. Son Jonathan. Dau. Ann (under 14).
Wit: Timothy Smith, Hezekiah Bye, John Garrison.

Page 275. William Chestnut, of Plumstead. Oct. 19, 1754.
Proved Jan. 24, 1755. Wife Mary "good will of place I live on."
Children, John, William, and Margaret. John Brittain and Thos.
Moore, exrs.
Wit: Wm. Ramsey and Joseph Stewart.

Page 269. William Clinkenbird, of Northampton Twp. May 15,
1741. Proved June 4, 1754. Wife Johanna, all Est. for life, then
to children and grandchildren, viz, William Clinkenbird, Barbara
Cooney, Else Broadast, Mary West, Elizabeth Vanhorn, Johanna
South, William Clinkenbird, son of son John, dec'd., Johanna and
Josiah daus. of Josiah Clinkenbird, dec'd. Barnard Vanhorn of
Northampton Twp., Yeoman, and Solomon Fussell, of City of Phila.,
Chainmaker, exrs.
Wit: Geo. Wilson, Henry Kreusen and John Pickering.

Page 271. Jonathan Drake, of New Britain Twp. Dec. 15, 1751.
Proved July 30, 1754. Wife Mary. Sons George and Jonathan and
Simon Butler, Junr., exrs. Sons George, William, Jonathan, and
Thomas. Daus. Mary Bevan (eldest), wife of Mordecai Bevan, £30
for life then to her children. 3 youngest daus. Deborah,
Catharine, and Aphie Drake, £40 each. Son-in-law Mordecai Bevan
£5 in consideration of his charge for building house he lives in.
Thomas Humphrey and Isaac James both of Moungomery, exrs.
Wit: John Marks, Alexander Wright, Benjamin Griffith.

Page 272. William Freame of Plumstead Twp. Sept. 24, 1754.
Proved Oct. 16, 1754. Wife Anne. Sons Thomas (5 shillings),
Archibald (5 shillings), James (5 shillings). Daus. Elizabeth (5
shillings). Residue to sons, William and John. George Logan and
Robert Barnhill, exrs.
Wit: Chas. Stewart and Joseph Stewart.

Page 273. William Philpot of Newtown Twp. July 2, 1754. Proved
Jan. 9, 1755. Wife Jane extx. Plantation and all Est. for life
then to children.
Wit: Richard Yeardley and John Carr.

Page 274. William Buckman, of Newtown, Yeoman. Sept. 15, 1751.
Proved Jan. 13, 1755. Wife Hester and son Jacob, exrs. Son Jacob
"Plantation I live on" to line dividing mine and son Wm.'s land.
Son William, bal. of plantation, if he dye to his wife Jane and
son William. Son John (5 shllings), Joseph (5 shillings), Thomas
(£50), Isaac, Bond agt. son John. Dau. Sarah Taylor.
Wit: Charles Stewart, Thomas Buckman, Junr., Wm. Ashburn.

Page 276. Joannah Johnson, of Bensalem Twp. Dec. 3, 1755 (?).
Proved Mch. 1, 1755. Sister Mary Alman. Bro. Philip Johnson.
Mother Mary Johnson. Sarah Inslee. Bro. Samuel Johnson. Sister
Bridget Goheen. Sister Ann Anderson. Bro. Nicholas Johnson. Bro.
Philip, exr.

Wit: Sarah Baldwin, Phebe Hibbs, John Baldwin.

Page 276. Elizabeth Dyer, Widow of John Dyer of Plumstead. 8th mo., 19th day, 1747. Proved Mch. 15, 1755. Son Josiah Dyer and son-in-law Alexander Brown, exrs. Grandson Abraham Scott, dau. Esther Brown.
Wit: John Rich, Nathan Preston.

Page 277. Abraham Chapman, Wrightstown, Yeoman. Jan. 9, 1752. Proved Mch. 21, 1755. Wife Susanna and Sons John and Abraham, exrs. Son John land bought of John Routledge adj. John Linton, Bro. John and Jno. Laycock and Jos. Hampton. Son William land adj. John Chapman Sr. and Town Square. Daus. Jane Lacey and Elizabeth Chapman. Son Thomas. Joseph. Benjamin, Tract of land at Tohickon "over against son William's shop." Mtge of Mathew VanScar and Jane his wife. Land conveyed to me by John Parsons for use of John Verity's children, to be conveyed to John Verity eldest son of John Verity, dec'd. Bond of John Lacey Sr. to dau. Jane Lacey.
Wit: Ann Chapman, Sarah Wilkinson.

Page 279. Yorus Neffus of Northampton, husbandman. Apr. 12, 1744. Proved May 14, 1755. "Aged and infirm" wife Williamkee. Sons Cornelius and John, exrs. Son Peter, "to have this place" bal. Est. equally divided amongst all children.
Wit: Rem. Vanderbilt, James Edams, Andrew Patterson. Codicil Apr. 17, 1744.

Page 280. Simon Mathews, New Britain Twp., Yeoman. Dec. 28, 1751. Proved July 9, 1755. "Aged and sickly" Sons John (20 shillings), Simon (£10), Benjamin (20 shillings), Edward 1/2 part of Grist Mills, Bolting Mill and Dwelling House on Mill Lot, (in equal partnership with Simon Butler, Esq.). Grandchildren, John, Rachel, Jane, and Margaret, children of Simon Morgan. Dau. Margaret Thomas (20 shillings), Simon Butler Jr. (£5) in Trust for use of Baptist Congregation at New Meeting House in New Britain. Son Thomas, residue of estate and exr.
Wit: James Lewis, John Young, Elizabeth Stephens.

Page 282. Samuel Gilbert, of Warminster. June 9, 1755. Proved July 23, 1755. Wife Mary and Bro. John exrs. Son William, 60 acres and Dwelling House. Dau. Margaret, 40 acres.
Wit: Peter Gilbert, Jos. Roberts, John Erwin.

Page 283. William Stockdale of Buckingham Twp. Jan. 29, 1755. Proved July 26, 1755. Wife Sarah and brother John, exrs. Children, Hannah, William, and Thomas. Land in Middletown.
Wit: Jacob Heston, Robert Smith, John Terry.

Page 283. Jeffrey Burges, of Solebury Twp. Wife Mary. Dated 8th mo., 10th day, 1754. Pr. Dec. 23, 1755. Son John and Thomas Ross, exrs. Sons John, Hugh, Joseph, and Thomas. Daus. Ann, Martha, Elizabeth, Mary, and Sarah. Plantation to John.
Wit: Wm. Lee, Wm. Atkinson, John Ross.

Page 283. Eleanor Hart, wife of John Hart of Warminster. Apr. 10, 1750. Proved Aug. 21, 1755. Children, Joseph, Silas, and Oliver Hart, Lucretia Gilbert, and Edith Hough. Joseph Price, son of dau. Susanna, dec'd. each 1 shilling sterling. Husband John Hart, exr. all my interest in estate of my grandfather Thomas Holme late of Lower Dublin, Phila. Co. Gent. dec'd. my mother's father.
Wit: James Wallas, Roger O'Neal, Henry Limboker.

Page 285. Edmond Lovett, of Bristol Twp. Oct. 20, 1752. Proved Dec. 29, 1755. Wife Magdalen. Sons Edmond (5 shillings), Daniel, Plantation bought of John Bown, also Tract bought of John Watson, adj. and swamp,. Son Joseph, Plantation I live on. Dau. Martha Priestly. Sons Daniel and Joseph and Samuel Brown, Enion Williams, Joseph White, Wm. Buckley and John Brown (son of Samuel), exrs.
Wit: John Mitchell, Wm. Large, Thos. Stapler, Jos. Tomlinson.
Deeds of Gift for Real estate and Personal estate from my father, kept from me.

Page 287. John Patterson, of Tinicum Twp., husbandman. Nov. 24, 1755. Proved Jan. 2, 1756. Wife Jean. Bro. Andrew Patterson and John Mains, exrs. Sons James (100 acres), Alexander and Andrew (Plantation bought of Overhold), John and Nicholas (Right in Plantation I live on), Robert (5 shillings), his son John (£6), son-in-law John Mains.
Wit: William Watt and John Dick.

Page 288. Richard Vanhorn, of Middletown, Yeoman. Jan. 19, 1756. Proved Feby. 11, 1756. Mother Elizabeth Vanhorn, extx. Bros. Benjamin, Gabriel. Bro. Benjamin's eldest son Elijah. Sister Mary. Sister Charity's eldest son Isaiah. Bro. Barnard's eldest dau. Elizabeth. Bro. Garret Vanhorn. John Guijant, living at Bristol Twp.
Wit: Andrew Moode, Jos. Wright, and Nathan Breslford.

Page 289. Lawrence Pearson, of Plumstead, Yeoman. July 27, 1752. Proved Mch. 17, 1756. Wife Ann. Samuel Armitage and son-in-law Samuel McKinstry, exrs. Son Joseph. Daus. Hannah Fenton, Martha Shrigley, Mary Jewell and Priscilla McKinstry. Grandchildren, Lawrence Pearson, Lawrence Shrigley, Arthur and Enock Allen and Mary Allen. John Craft. All lands to be sold.
Wit: Jos. Doan, Israel Doan, Esther Doan.

Page 290. Cephas Child, of Plumstead, Yeoman. 3rd mo., Mch. 13, 1756. Pro. Apr. 6, 1756. Wife Mary. Sons John and Isaac, exrs. Sons Henry (interest due on his bond), Chephas (interest due on his bond), John (200 acres on which I live), Isaac, residue of Real estate paying unto John Lloyd, exr. of Adam Harker, £20 I owe on Bond. Kinswoman Margaret Smith.
Wit: Wm. Martin, Isaac Parsons, Jacob Fox.

Page 293. Henry Cherry, of Newtown. May 11, 1756. Proved June 22, 1756. Wife Martha, sole exrs. Bro. James, Overseer. Sons John and Charles. Daus. Sarah and Ruth.

Wit: Jos. Gibson, Saml. Smith.

Page 291. William Spencer, of Northampton, Yeoman. Feby. 29, 1756. Proved Apr. 22, 1756. Wife Elizabeth and son James, exrs. Sons Thomas, Samuel, Enoch, Job, and Abel. Daus. Ann and Sarah, and child unborn. Eldest son James, Plantation formerly my uncle Richard Whitton's in Lower Dublin Twp., Phila. Co. 150 acres when 24. Plantation I live on to be divided between sons Samuel (100 acres in Warminster and 50 acres in Northampton), Thomas (part in Northampton adj. John Beard on which Leonard Kroesen lives), Enoch (remainder adj. Garret and Derrick Kroesen where Elizabeth Dean lives). Jonathan Willet.
Wit: Jos. Hart, Leonard Kroesen, and John Hart.

Page 294. William Hair, of New Britain Twp., Farmer. Jan. 22, 1756. Proved July 6, 1756. Eldest Bro. Joseph Hair and John Davies, exrs. Sister Jean wife of John Robinson, house they live in for life and 2 acres adj. Joseph Barton. Father to be provided for. £8 for support of Gospel Ministry at Neshaminy where Rev. Charles Beatty preaches, Ruling elders to take charge of same. Sister Mary Hair. Bro. Benj. Hair.
Wit: John Mitchell, Mathew Hinds.

Page 296. David Lawell, of Newtown, Merchant. Oct. 18, 1754. Codicil June 26, 1756. Proved Aug. 5, 1756. Wife Sarah and Anthony Teate, exrs. Wife, house and lot in Newtown bought of Thomas Nelson for life. Henry Lawell, house and lot in Newtown where Joseph Winner lives after decease of wife. Bro. John Lawell's 2 children living in Ireland, viz., Margaret and Isabel Lawell. Apprentice girl Elizabeth Gilman. Sarah Teat £10. £5 for use of Pres. Church at Newtown.
Wit: Joseph Kees, John Kees, and Samuel Twining.

Page 297. Abraham Vickers, of Plumstead, Yeoman. Feby. 17, 1756. Proved Aug. 19, 1756. Wife Mary and son Thomas, exrs. Sons Peter, Jacob and Abraham. Daus. Hester Forman, Mary, Rachel, and Leah Vickers. Peter, the place he lives on. Abraham, the 200 acres I live on at 21.
Wit: John Michener, Thos. Ruckman, Jos. Shaw.

Page 298. Mary Hambleton, of Solebury, Widow. Sept. 6, 1756. Proved Sept. 17, 1756. Son Stephen and son-in-law Thomas Paxson, exrs. Dau. Grace Roberts, Jerimet Austin and Mary Paxson. Grandchildren, James and John Hamilton (sons of Stephen), Nicholas, Samuel and Hannah Austin and James and John Armitage.
Wit: Matt. Hughes, Elizabeth Hughes, and George Hughes.

Page 299. Henry Paxson, of Solebury, Yeoman. Mch. 20, 1752. Proved Sept. 18, 1756. Son Thomas, exr. Son Henry. Daus. Elizabeth Hartley, Mary Roberts, Margery Beans, Rebecca Beans, and Ann Paxson. Children of dau. Sarah Duer, dec'd. Children of dau. Jane Preston, dec'd. Dau. Martha Paxson.
Wit: Saml. Eastburn, Jos. Eastburn, Saml. Armitage.

Page 300. Mary Martin (no residence). Son John Martin, exr.

Dated Aug. 23, 1756. Proved Sept. 24, 1756. Dau. Mary Palmer.
Wit: George Oat and Edmund Beakes.

Page 301. Martha Eaton, of Warminster Twp., Widow. Sept. 20,
1756. Proved Oct. 5, 1756. Sons Joseph, Lun, David, and Edward
Eaton. Daus. Mary Jones and Sarah Lewis.
Wit: James Stirling, Jacob Frank and William Hart.

Page 302. Thomas Yeardley, of Makefield. 1st mo. (Jan.) 30th
day, 1754. Proved Nov. 20, 1756. Sons William, Thomas, and
Samuel, exrs. Dau. Sarah and 3 others. Granddau. Elizabeth, wife
of Thomas Lyner. Wm., plantation formerly John Clowes, except for
lot formerly Wm. Janney's. Son Thomas, land purchased of John
Lambert and Nathaniel Hair. latter bounded by Delaware River.
Land of Tunnecliffe, Larzelere, John Winder and John Clowes. Son
Samuel, tract in Solebury with Grist and Saw Mills thereon.
Wit: George Logan, Henry Margerum, F. Parrell.

Page 303. Malachi Jones, of Warminster, Yeoman. Aug. 6, 1750.
Proved Jany. 8, 1757. Wife Mary, extx., all estate including
share of estate of Father Benjamin Jones, late of Northampton,
dec'd. and Grandfather Derrick Kroesen, late of Southampton,
dec'd.
Wit: Isaac Houg, Jacob Cadwallader, and John Hart.

Page 304. Henry Root, of New Britain Twp., Yeoman. Dec. 12,
1753. Proved Jany. 25, 1757. Wife Madlen. Son Christian, exr.
Eldest son Henry, £15. Balance of estate to children by wife
Madlen, viz. Christian, John, Andrew, Abraham, Cornelius, Jacob
and David Root. Friends Christian Swartz and John Root, Trustees.
Wit: John Lapp, Ulrick Brims, Benj. Griffith.

Page 305. John Stackhouse, of Middletown, Yeoman. 12th mo.,
Dec. 23, 1756. Pr. Feby. 22, 1757. Son-in-law John Mitchell and
Friend John Woolston, exrs. Son Thomas and his dau. Rachel. Son
James, 30 acres of plantation on Neshaminy adj. Hayhurst's. Daus.
Sarah Stackhouse, Margaret Mitchel, Grace Stevenson, and
Elizabeth Tomlinson. Lucilla and Abel Stackhouse, children of
John.
Wit: ---.

Page 307. Joseph Carr, of Warminster, Weaver. Feby. 18, 1756.
Proved Mch. 2, 1757. Wife Mary, Wm. Long, and Andrew Long, exrs.
Sons John, William, Joseph, and Andrew. Daus. Margret and Isabel
and Mary.
Wit: James Wallace and Moses Barrol.

Page 308. Eleazer Doan, Junr., of Makefield Upper. Dec. 28,
1756. Proved Mch. 31, 1757. Wife Elizabeth. Thos. Atkinson and
John Terry, both of Wrightstown, exrs. Children, Jonathan,
Susanna, Rachel, and Ruth. Real estate to be sold.
Wit: Bezebel Wiggins, Humphrey Parker, Junr., Grace Doan.

Page 309. John Bradfield, of Buckingham, Yeoman. 4th mo., Apr.
20, 1752. Proved May 5, 1757. Wife Jane and Joseph Fell of

Buckingham, exrs. Son John, plantation 137 1/2 acres purchased of
Robert Sanders. Son William and his dau. Mary. Son Joseph. Dau.
Elizabeth Harman and her children, Jene, Sarah, and Ruth. Son
John's dau. Martha. Benjamin Scrivener's sons James and Thomas.
£3 to the Mtg. toward maintaining Grave Yard.
Wit: Sarah Pennington and Daniel Pennington, Junr.

Page 312. Richard Mitchell, of Wrightstown, Yeoman. 8th mo.,
10th day, 1757. Proved ---. Wife Agnes, sons-in-law Eldad
Roberts and Joseph Watson, exrs. Dau. Margaret, wife of Thomas
Chapman, plantation in Log Town. Son-in-law Miles Shires in
Yorkshire, Great Britain land purchased of John Wilkinson, Daniel
Ashecraft and John Hillbourne. 226 acres to exrs.
Wit: John Wilkinson, Jos. Wilkinson, and Joseph Hamton.

Page 310. Thomas Stradling, Junr., of Newtown, Yeoman. 4th mo.,
Apr. 9, 1757. Proved May 21, 1757. Wife Elizabeth, Bro. Daniel
and Friend Barnet Taylor, exrs. Children, Elizabeth, Sarah, John,
Thomas, Daniel, and child unborn.
Wit: Timo. Smith, Benja. Hamton, Isaac Smith.

Page 311. Thomas Howell, of Warwick Twp. Sept. 26, 1755.
Proved June 4, 1757. Wife Citrian. Son Thomas, exr. All Lands.
Daus. Mary James, Sarah Rowlen, and Citren ---. Granddau. Mary
Howell.
Wit: John Griffith and John Beard.

Page 314. George Logan of Lower Makefield, Blacksmith. Sept. 1,
1756. Proved July 29, 1757. Wife Olive Logan and Friend and Bro.
John Job, exrs. Son-in-law Samuel Lawrence to be put to school
and supported until 14 yrs. of age then to be bound to a Trade.
Son James. Dau. Elizabeth.
Wit: Hezekiah Anderson, Elizabeth Logan.

Page 314. William Marshall of Tenecum, Yeoman. Aug. 18, 1757.
Proved Oct. 1, 1757. Wife Ann. John Watson, Junr., exr. Bro.
Edward title to leased lands and island in Delware call "Tenecum
Island" paying his four sons Peter, William, Moses, and Martin
£50 each at 21. Bro. John Marshall. Bro. Moses Marshall, my
watch. Sis. Rebecca's 2 sons Abner and Benjamin Overfelt.
Wit: Wm. Jeiser and Henry Preston.

Page 322. Hugh Baxter, of Nockamixon, Farmer. Sept. 13, 1757.
Proved Dec. 15, 1757. Wife Margaret and Bro. Thomas Baxter, exrs.
Sons John and Thomas. Daus. Hannah, Elizabeth, and Mary. Mother
Elizabeth Baxter to have use of boys shares during their
minority.
Wit: Daniel Jameson, James Loughrey.

Page 315. William Thomas, of Hilltown, Yeoman. Dec. 11, 1753.
Proved Oct. 13, 1757. "Stricken in years" "To be buried on my own
land in ye Grave Yard by ye Meeting House." Sons Thomas, Ephraim,
John, Manassah, and William, exrs. Dau. Gwenllian, wife of Morris
Morris, her son Cadwaller Morris. Dau. Anna Thomas. "To
Inhabitants of Hilltown forever" the Meeting House erected by ye

Grave Yard together 4 acres and some odd Perches for a Grave Yard
to bury their dead in "and all other far and near" "Whites and
Blacks" "Such as are guilty of self murder, only excepted."
Preachers of all Denominations to hold services for funerals,
"Paptists excepted" Baptists and Presbyterians to use the Meeting
House jointly. My five sons, together with Lewis Evan, Junr.,
Nathaniel Griffith (eldest sons of Evan) and Jonathan Evans of
Hulltown to serve as Trustees of said Meeting House and Grave
Yard, they to name their successors in their wills. Son Ephraim,
150 acres part of 300 acres bought of James Logan; Son Manassah,
150 acres residue of 300 acres bought of James Logan; Son John,
200 acres adj. above bought of James Logan; Son Thomas, 300 acres
bought of Rowland Ellis, Benj. Phillips and Jer. Langhorne. Dau.
Anna, 100 acres adj. Henry Lewis and Evan Griffith; Dau.
Gwenllian, 100 acres adj. Meeting House.
Wit: Benj. Griffith, Benj. Griffith, Junr., and Joseph Griffith.
Acknowledged before Simon Butler, Esq. by Testator as his Last
Will and Testament. Dec. 21, 1753. Codicil dated Oct. 11, 1756.
Letters granted to Thomas, John, Wm., and Mannasseh.

Page 319. Eleazer Doan, Senr., of Upper Makefield, Yeoman.
Sept. 17, 1757. Proved Oct. 24, 1757. Wife Rebeckah, son
Benjamin, Abraham Chapman, and Thos. Ross, exrs. Elizabeth, widow
of son Eleazer, dec'd., and her children. Son David Doan, son
John and his wife Hannah, each 5 shillings. Their children,
plantation he lives on lying on Tohickon Creek near the Haycock,
they are paying such sum for the support of their father as exrs.
direct. Son Benjamin, plantation I live on bought of Widow
Hillbourne con. 15 acres. Dau. Rebekah Doan (£120).
Wit: Humphrey Parker, Junr., John Hayhurst, Grace Doan.

Page 320. Joseph Wells, of Warrington Twp., Yeoman. Oct. 10,
1757. Proved Nov. 7, 1757. Wife Mary. 34 acres where Richard
Stephens lives, for life, Eldest son Samuel, sons Jacob, Thomas.
Children of son Samuel, viz. Joseph, Junr, Henry, and Mary Wells.
Dau. Thamer Thomas and her 4 children, viz., Ann, Joseph,
Susanna, and Benjamin. Dau. Susannah Wells. Granddau. Rachel Van
Winkle (silver snuff box marked "A R." Grandson John Vanwinkle,
granddau. Rebecca Wells and her sisters. Legacy due me by right
of my 1st wife Ann under will of Father-in-law Richard Pugh. Also
Legacy in land which Thomas Meredith holds to his sons, Samuel
and Jacob. 80 acres I live on to be sold. David Stephens, Junr.
and Isaac Evans, exrs. Griffith Owen and William Davis, Senr.,
Trustees.
Wit: Wm. Davis, Junr., Evan Stephens, Junr., and Thomas Batton.

Page 323. John Rea, of Bedminster, "a dying person." Jan. 18,
1753. Proved Sept. 15, 1757. Wife Sidney. Son Joseph Rea, son
James Galbredth and Mathew Rea, Jr., exrs. Son Samuel to be bound
to Tailor, son Moses to a trade. Land to be sold and proceeds
divided among children.
Wit: John Grimes, Ann Galbredth.

Page 324. Derrick Kroesen, of Northampton, "Gentlemen." Dec.
24, 1757. Proved Jan. 14, 1758. Wife Lammity. Bro. John Kroesen

and bro-in-law John Van Asdalen, exrs. Son Garret to have £5 more at age of 21 than the other children, balance to be divided equally "among all my children."
Wit: Henry Lott, Henry Krewsen, Stoffell Van Asdalen.

Page 325. Francis White, of Middletown, Farmer. 4th mo., 7th day, 1752. Proved Feby. 7, 1758. "Stricken in years." Wife Margaret. Son Peter, exr. All lands. Son John (5 shillings). Daus. Elizabeth Stackhouse (5), Mary (5 shillings). Grandchildren, Thomas and Margaret McCape (£10 ea.). Wit: John Deepy, Margaret Deepy, Robert Brodnax.

Page 326. Evan Griffith, of Hilltown Twp., Yeoman. Dec. 15, 1757. Proved Feby. 15, 1758. "Stricken in years." Sons Nathaniel and John, exrs. Wife Mary. Son Nathaniel, 101 acres he lives on bought of John Plumly. Son Abraham, £10 "provided he or his son Edward personally demand it.." Son John, 103, 1/2 acres bought of Jer. Langhorn. Sons Jacob (5 shillings), Howell (5 shillings). "Bond of son Howell;s in consideration of Land conveyed to him to be paid by wife as per my marriage contract with her.." Son Isaac, 103, 1/2 acres he lives on. Gd.son Isaac Lewis. Daus. Catherine, wife of Theophilus Williams and Sarah, wife of Thos. Bate. John Jones, Carpenter of Moungomery, Morris Morris of New Britain, and Thomas and Ephraim Thomas of Hilltown, Trustees. Wit: Jos. Griffith, Mordecai Rowland, Rachel Griffith, Benj. Griffith. Letters to John.

Page 328. John Jones, of Hilltown, Carpenter. Jan. 12, 1758. Proved Feby. 20, 1758. Wife Mary. Bro. Edward Jones and Bro-in-law Thomas West, exrs. Son Edward and John (minors). Daus. Elizabeth, Mary, and Susanna. Latter a minor. Son Edward, my Father's gun.
Wit: Robt. Shannon, Erasmus and John Kelly.

Page 329. James McFarland, of New Britain, Farmer. Dec. 26, 1757. Proved Feby. 24, 1758. Son Arthur and Robert Scott, exrs. Daus. Mary, Elinor and Margret.
Wit: Walter McFarland, Jane McFarland, Mary Scott.

Page 330. John Johnson, of Warminster Twp. Jan. 26, 1758. Proved Feby. 27, 1758. Wife Elizabeth and father-in-law Henry Lot, exrs. Sons Benjamin, Archibald, John and William. Daus. Catharine, Elizabeth, and Mary.
Wit: John McCalla, Henry Shuert, Henry Jones.

Page 331. James Keen, Northampton Twp. Nov. 13, 1757. Proved Mch. 15, 1758. Wife Agnes. Son John, away supposed to have gone out of Province. Son Robert. Dau. Elizabeth.
Wit: Jos. Boyd, Hugh Edams, Gayen Edams.

Page 332. William Miller, Warwick Twp., Yeoman. Feby. 2, 1754. Proved Mch. 5, 1758. Wife Isabel. Children, William, son Robert, dec'd.'s children, son Hugh. Dau. Margaret, wife of John Earle. Dau. Isabel Long. Dau. Mary, wife of James Curry. Grandson(?) John Miller. Archiband McLean of Horsham and John Earle of

Warminster, exrs. Land heretofore granted to Presbyterian
Congregation for Grave Yard confirmed to them forever. Other land
to be sold.
Wit: John Craig, Isabel Craig, Andrew Long. Letters granted to
John Earle. McLean renouncing.
Note: A later will dated Feby. 3, 1756 is on file at Register's
Office against which the eldest son William Miller, Junr. filed a
caveat Feby. 24, 1758 although he was one of the witnesses. It
was "adjudged void both the witnesses being legatees and not
qualified to move it.." It is substantially the same, however, as
the one proved other than it names the children of deceased son
Robert, as follows: William, eldest, Isabel Wallace, Hugh and
Robert. The gd.son John Miller mentioned above is named as
"nephew" in the later one, and is a witness to the will. The
exrs. of the later will were John Earle, Wm. Long, and Francis
McHenry.

Page 333. Mary Mitchell, of Bristol Twp., Widow. Feby. 14,
1758. Proved Apr. 17, 1758. Sons Richard, John and Henry, to be
put to trade at age of 14 years. Dau. Sarah, left to care of her
Aunt Margaret. Relations Thos. Janney and James Bodine, Trustees,
Guardians, exrs.
Wit: Wm. Dye, Jos. Clark, Robt. Brodnax.

Page 334. Richard Sands, of Bensalem Twp. Jan. 7, 1758.
Codicil Feby. 27, 1758. Proved June 5, 1758. Wife Mary. Daus.
Jane, wife of Thomas Bains, and Elizabeth, wife of Ellis Roberts.
Grandchildren, Mary Jones, Richard Sands. Jesse, Phebe, and
Elizabeth Baines, children of dau. Elizabeth Roberts, Stephen
Bains son of dau. Jane, gd. dau. Mary Jones, 11 acres in Tenure
of Peter Jones. Jos. Richardson and Wm. Rodman, exrs.
Wit: Wm. Ridge, Wm. Dunkan, and John Driedrick.

Page 336. Robert Walker, Northampton. Feby. 6, 1757. Proved
June 6, 1758. Bro. Richard Walker, exr. Bro. John Walker and his
eldest son William. Sis. Mary King. Sis. Christine McNaire and
her eldest son Wm. McNaire. Charles Walker. £50 to Presbyterian
Church in care of Rev. Richard Treat, Rev. Charles Beatty and
Bro. Richard Walker.
Wit: James Craig and John Stirling. Friends to join in placing
tombstone over Father.

Page 338. William Briggs, Newtown, Yeoman. 8th mo., Aug. 15,
1758. Proved Sept. 9, 1758. Sons Edmund and James, exrs. Sons
Benjamin, Joseph and Samuel. Son John's children (his son John,
10 shillings more than his sisters). Son William's children.
Daus. Elizabeth Chapman, Jane and Ellen Buckman and Margaret
Briggs. 58 acres in Warwick Twp. lately Abraham Claypoole's to
Edmund and James.
Wit: John Twining, Jos. Hamton and John Story.

Page 340. Eliakim Anderson, Warwick Twp., "Pharmer." Aug. 15,
1758. Proved Sept. 9, 1958. Wife Elizabeth, son John, Bro.
Abraham, and Francis Vannoy, exrs. Sons, Cornelius (eldest, 5
shillings), Richard, Abraham, John, Theophilus, and Eligaah.

Daus. Catharine Howes, Elizabeth, Jemimah, and Sarah Anderson. "Father's Homestead at Hopewell, after Mother's death." "2 Bonds of Andrew Titus to son John to pay Debt to Loan Office on Plantation I live on, bal. toward new house now building.."
Wit: Evan Thomas, Wm. Corbet and Hugh Barr. Letters to Elizabeth and John.

Page 341. Robert Jones, New Britain, "Batcheler." Aug. 7, 1758. Proved Sept. 22, 1758. Bros. Edward and Thomas Jones. Nephew William Williams, Junr., exr.
Wit: Erasmus Kelly, John Wilson and Robert Shewell.

Page 344. Enoch Pearson, Solebury Twp., Yeoman. 8th mo., Aug. 31, 1756. Proved Oct. 2, 1758. Wife Margaret. Son William, exr. "Inventory of Goods in hands of son John for use of dau. Phebe under direction of Buckingham Mo. Mtg." Gd.son Enoch Betts. Have heretofore made provision for my children.
Wit: John Hulme, John Watson, Junr.

Page 342. Benjamin Fell, Buckingham, Yeoman. 9th mo., 6th day, 1758. Proved Sept. 22, 1758. Wife Sarah. Son John and Friend Joseph Watson, exrs. Son John, 50 acres bought of half Bro. Thomas Fell suvyd. by Jno. Watson, Jr. Son Asa, 42 acres bought of Adam Harker and 20 acres bought of Wm. George adj. Thos. Martin. Son Benjamin, land bought of Jonathan Brightwell. Sons Levi and Thomas 125 acres devised by Father Joseph Fell. Son Asa, lots in Phila. bought of Robert Scarborrough and Jos. Houseworth. "Little Son Morrs" 63 acres purchased of Wm. George. Levi to live with his uncle Isaac Cleaver till 21. Daus. Phebe, Deborah, and Hannah, last two left to care of their aunts Mary Good and Rebekah Cleaver. Lots in Northern Liberties bought of Wm. Seiter and Isaac Dawson. John Watson, Junr. and Samuel Foulke, Guardians.
Wit: Nathaniel West, John Brown, Titus Fell.

Page 345. Ann Amos, of Bensalem Twp., Widow. Mch. 27, 1754. Proved Oct. 10, 1758. Friend Edward Hill, who lives at Dunk's Ferry, exr. £2 to Minister at time of my decease at Trinity Church, Oxford Twp. £10 to Poor of said congregation. £5 to Poor of Byberry Twp. £5 to Poor of Bensalem Twp. Residue to Edw. Hill.
Wit: David Thomas, Cornelius Vanosten, Thos. Stammers.

Page 347. Alexander Rickey, Lower Makefield, Weaver. Oct. 1, 1758. Proved Dec. 5, 1758. Wife Ann and son Alexander, exrs. Sons Thomas, John, James, and Kairl Rickey. Daus. Katharine Hutchinson, Ann Kirkbride, Mary and Sarah Rickey.
Wit: Mahlon Kirkbride, Katharine Wilmerton, Rendal Hutchinson.

Page 348. Peter Ashton, of Springfield, Yeoman. Sept. 21, 1758. Proved Dec. 9, 1758. Wife Mary, extx. Sons Robert (lands), John, and Thomas. Dau. Martha wife of Thomas Christy.
Wit: Geo. Vanbuskirk, Thomas Adamson, Ebenezer Walker. Wife being dec'd. Letters to Robert and Thomas.

Page 350. Mary Ashton, of Springfield, Widow of Peter. Oct. 6,

1758. Proved Dec. 9, 1758. Sons Robert, John and Thomas Ashton.
Robert and Thomas, exrs. Dau. Martha Christy.
Wit: Geo. Vanbuskirk, Thos. Adamson, Eben. Walker.

Page 346. Mary Hickst, Widow of Charles Hickst, Buckingham.
Oct. 20, 1758. Proved Nov. 8, 1758. Sons Edward and Kemble
Hickst, Plantation I live on conveyed to my Husband and myself by
my grandfather Richard Murray. also 47 acres adj. conveyed to me
by Abrm. Chapman and survd. by Jno. Watson, Junr. Residue to son
Thomas Hickst. John Thomas and John Wilkinson, exrs.
Wit: Peter Titus, Oliver Titus, and Thos. Chapman.

Page 351. Benjamin Phillips, of Hilltown, Yeoman. Oct. 7, 1758.
Proved Dec. 11, 1758. Wife Catharine. Plantation 40 acres in New
Britain in Tenure of Thos. James. Niece Margaret, wife of John
Williams, Niece Ann, wife of John Wilson. Thos. James, son of
Aaron. Sarah Williams. Isaac C. Jones. John Thomas, Minister.
Abel Griffith. Philip Lewis to dig grave for debt he owes.
Benj. Griffith of New Britain, David Evans or his successor as
Deacon of Moungomery congregation £2 towards mending Grave Yard.
Nephew Henry Harris, exr. 100 acres I live on. Thos. Thomas of
Hilltown and John Williams of New Britain, Trustees.
Wit: Margt. Jones, Jos. Thomas, Jos. Griffith.

Page 353. William Carver, of Buckingham. Feby. 10, 1753.
Proved Jan. 30, 1759. Wife Elizabeth. Sons William and Henry,
exrs. Eldest son Joseph, 80 acres adj. Reynold's Tract "so
called." Residue to sons William and Henry. Daus. Elizabeth, Mary
and Rebecca.
Wit: Samuel Worthington, Nicholas Tucker, Jos. Rickey.

Page 354. Thomas Harvye, of Makefield, Yeoman. Aug. 23, 1758.
Proved Feby. 2, 1759. Wife Tamer, son-in-law Richard Holcombe of
Amwell, Hunterdon Co., N.J. and William Pearson of Buckingham,
exrs. Sons Joseph and Mathias, plantation I live on adj. Benj.
Taylor, John Duer, and Joseph Johnson. Youngest son William,
plantation in Twp. of Plesgrove, Salem Co., West Jersey, when 21.
Daus. Ann Baley, Hannah Milnor, Elizabeth Coryell, Mary Holcombe,
Letitia and Sarah Harvye. Grandson Thomas Harvye, son of
Benjamin, dec'd. Grandson Thomas Milnor, son of John. Granddau.
Ann Harvye, dau. of Thos. Junr.
Wit: Edmund Briggs, Stephen Field, James Dyer.

Page 356. Thomas Dungan, Warminster, Yeoman. Dec. 1, 1758.
Proved Feby. 3, 1759. Wife Esther. Son Thomas and son-in-law
Silas Yerkes, exrs. Son Abel, house where he dwells and 40 acres.
Sons David, Enoch, and Benjamin. Daus. Hannah Yerkes, Elizabeth
and Sarah Dungan.
Wit: Samuel Griffith, Garret Vanbuskirk, and John Hart.

Page 357. Patrick Poe, of Plumstead, Innholder. Sept 7, 1758.
Proved Feby. 9, 1759. Wife Abigail and son Edward, exrs.
Children, Edward, Patrick, John, Sarah, Rich, Abigail Brittain,
Martha and Ann Poe.
Wit: William Jessup, Samuel Simson, John Russell.

Page 357. John Hutchinson, of Northampton. Jan. 8, 1759.
Proved Feby. 27, 1759. Wife Jean and James Hutchinson of
Northampton Co., exrs. Sons Robert and Thomas. Youngest Dau.
Jean.
Wit: Wm. Wear, James Loughrey, Alex. McCamon.

Page 360. Jane Chadwick, of Solebury, Widow of William Chadwick,
late of Solebury, Yeoman. Jany. 11, 1749/50. Proved Mch. 15,
1759. Children of Jonathan Hough, viz., Daniel, Samuel, Thomas
and Letitia Hough. Dau. Mary, wife of Benj. Crips. Dau. Hannah,
wife of Isaac Fell. Granddau. Sarah Hains, dau. of Daniel Hains,
dec'd. Granddaus. Mary and Jane Fell. Son-in-law Isaac Fell,
exr.
Wit: Titus Fell, Geo. Fell, Jno. Watson, Junr. Codicil 11th day
of 3d mo. ---. Wit: to codicil Joseph Duer, John Watson, Junr.

Page 362. Harman Vansant, the Elder, Bensalem, Yeoman. May 8,
1755. Proved May 11, 1759. Wife Judith. Gd. son Harman Vansant
and Gilbert Hicks, exrs. Grandsons Harman and Peter Vansant, sons
of son Garret, dec'd. 4 children of son Harman, dec'd. 9 children
of dau. Elizabeth. Elizabeth and Garret, 2 youngest children of
son Garret. Daus. Gazina, wife of Jacob Titus, and Katharine,
wife of Daniel Severns.
Wit: Hannah Feagas, Richd. Gibbs, Margery Gibbs. Letters granted
to Harman Vansant Junr.

Page 364. John Dawson, of Solebury. 5th mo., 31, 1753. Proved
May 26, 1759. Dau. Anne Brown of Plumstead, granddau. Elizabeth
Brown. Granddau. Martha Harvye of Makefield. Esther, Rachel, and
Sarah, daus. of son Thomas Dawson. Son Thomas, exr.
Wit: Samuel Eastburn, Rees Davis, Henry Paxson, Junr.

Page 365. Thomas Dungan, Northampton, Yeoman. Feby. 9, 1758.
Proved July 4, 1759. Son John, exr. Plantation of 200 acres where
he lives. Sons Thomas, Joseph, and James. Samuel, Jacob, and
Jonathan, sons of son Jonathan, dec'd. Daus. Elizabeth Hellings,
Mary Barton, and Sarah Stephens.
Wit: Nath. Dorland, Jacob Carrell, Jemima Colton, John Hart.

Page 366. Charles Biles, Southampton. Feby. 7, 1754. Proved
Aug. 7, 1759. Wife Ann Mary, lot where I live bought of Harmon
Enoch. Son Samuel "the old Place" 242 acres. Sons William and
Langhorne, minors. Daus. Grace, Mary, and Hannah £50 each when
they marry. Friend Langhorne Biles and Son Samuel, exrs.
Wit: Ezra Croasdale, Thomas Edwards, and John O'Daniel. Letters
granted to Samuel.

Page 367. Elizabeth Vanhorn, Widow of Peter Vanhorn, late of
Middletown. Aug. 27, 1754. Proved Nov. 8, 1759. Son Peter
Peterson Vanhorn and Dau. Charity Van Sant, exrs. 6 sons,
Barnard, Gabriel, Benjamin, Richard, John, and Garret. Daus.
Charity Vansant, Jane Roberts, Elizabeth Praul, Katharine Craven,
and Mary Gosline. Son Peter Peterson's son Gabriel. Son John's
children, Peter and Abigail.
Wit: Thos. Janney, Hannah Janney, Hannah Bates.

Page 364. Jonathan Dye, Bensalem, Laborer. Mch. 20, 1759.
Proved Dec. 11, 1759. Wife Lydia 1 shilling, father William Dye
and Dr. John Denormandie, exrs. Son Josias 1 shilling Residue to
exrs for use and education of Dau. Ann.
Wit: Samuel Woolston, Jos. Kees. Letters granted to Wm. Dye.

Page 369. Samuel Bunting of the Falls Twp. 12th mo., Dec. 1,
1759. Proved Dec. 11, 1759. Wife Priscilla. Son Samuel, exr.
Youngest son Benjamin, other children.
Wit: Samuel Brown, George Brown, Elizabeth Brown.

Page 370. Joseph McFarland, Tenecum Twp. Nov. 4, 1759. Proved
Dec. 12, 1759. Wife Jean and son Robert, exrs. Sons Joseph and
John. Son Robert right of Plantation sold to John Hoperry Lear to
lift my debts. Son-in-law Andrew Booman.
Wit: Wm. Davis, Jos. Davis.

Abstract of Bucks County Wills. Book No. 3.

Page 1. James Rue, Bensalem Twp., Yeoman. Dec. 18, 1759.
Proved Jan. 1, 1760. Wife Mary, "grown in years." Son Richard and
John Gregg of Middletown, Miller, exrs. Sons Richard (eldest),
Mathew, Samuel, and Joseph. Daus. Mary, wife of Timothy Roberts,
Katharine, Elizabeth and Sarah. Son John "so long absent"
"supposed to be dead.."
Wit: Richd. Gibbs, Richard Rue, John Campbell.

Page 3. Edmund Kinsey of Buckingham, Yeoman. 6th mo., 22nd day,
1758. Proved Jan. 31, 1760. Codicil Nov. 26, 1758. Wife Sarah.
Son Benjamin and Bro-in-law Joseph Hamton of Wrightstown, exrs.
Sons Samuel, Benjamin, David, Joseph and Mary and Jonathan,
children of dec'd. son Jonathan. Daus. Mary Fell, Elizabeth
Smith, and Sarah Smith, and Dau-in-law Jemima, widow of Jonathan.
Wit: Wm. Hough, Andrew Ellicott, Samuel Kinsey Taylor, Samuel
Kinsey.

Page 5. Rachel Baker, of Upper Makefield, Widow. 1st mo., 26th
day, 1760. Proved Feby. 16, 1760. Son Henry and son-in-law John
Burroughs, exrs. Eldest son Samuel, sons Henry, Nathan, and
Joseph. Daus. Sarah Janney, Anna Maria Biles, Lydia Burroughs,
and Margaret Tomlinson. Granddau. Hannah Burroughs. Barnet
Taylor, £5 for use of Friends of Makefield Mtg.
Wit: James Rose, Grace Vanhorn, John Beaumont.

Page 6. William Seiser, of Tinnecum Twp., Doctor. Dec. 21,
1759. Proved Feby. 19, 1760. Indexed and filed Yisser but signed
as above. Wife Anna Barbara and George Overback of Nockamixon and
William Nash, exrs. Children, George and Margaret.
Wit: George Sigeman, Ludwick Long. (Letters to widow only.).

Page 7. Joseph Headley of Middletown, Yeoman. 7th mo., July 3,
1756. Proved Feby. 21, 1760. Wife Hannah. Sons John and Solomon,
exrs. Sons David, Joshua, and Joseph. Daus. Lydia, Christian, and
Hannah. Granddau. Elizabeth. Land adj. John Brelsford, purchased
by John Rowland of Phineas Pemberton.

Wit: Joseph Ludlow, Richard Bidgood, William Bidgood. Joseph
Ludlow's signature proven by Thomas Stackhouse.

Page 9. John Sampell, of Bedminster, Weaver. Dec. 1, 1759.
Proved Mch. 31, 1760. Wife Elizabeth and Joseph Brittain of
Plumstead, exrs. Sons Samuel, William, Joseph, James, Nathaniel
and John (last four minors). Daus. Jane Kelly and Ann, Hannah,
and Martha (minors).
Wit: Thos. Erwin, Henry Huddleston, Edward Murphy.

Page 10. John Ketham of Middletown. Feby. 27, 1760. Proved
Apr. 14, 1760. Wife Sarah (sole legatee) and Samll. Allen, exrs.
Wit: Garret Vansant, Mary Vansant, Blackston Ingleduene.

Page 11. Barnard Vanhorn of Northampton Twp. Apr. 14, 1760.
Proved Apr. 22, 1760. Bro. Henry. Bro. John's 3 children.
Sisters Charity Vanduren, Katherine Hagerman and Jane Hagerman.
Garret Wyncoop and Leffert Leffertson, exrs.
Wit: Abram Van Hooren, Patience Vanhorn, Joseph Wildman.

Page 12. John Anderson, of Buckingham Twp. June 5, 1749.
Proved Apr. 28, 1760. Wife Jane. Son James, exr. Sons William and
John. Daus. Barbara Smith and Margery McKeney. Wit: Jos. Sample,
Jos. Arter, Martha Arter.

Page 13. William McDonnell of Warrington Twp. Nov. 11, 1757.
Proved May 24, 1760. Wife Agnes. Sons Michael and William, dau.
Janet. James Weir and John Mitchell, exrs.
Wit: Wm. Oliphant, Robert Weir and John Weir. (Letters granted to
James Weir.).

Page 13. Williamkee Vanhorn, Northampton. Apr. 25, 1760.
Proved May 26, 1760. Daus. Charity Vanduren, Katharine Hagerman,
and Jane Hagerman. Granddau. Mymy Vanhorn and her Bro. and Sis.
Dau-in-law Susanna Vanhorn. Granddau. Mimy Corson. Granddau.
Williamky Vanduren. Daus. Charity and Jane and Garret Wyncoop,
exrs.
Wit: Wm. Hibbs, Patience Vanhorn, Jos. Wildman.

Page 14. John Kelly of Hilltown Twp., Yeoman. Feby. 22, 1760.
Proved May 28, 1760. Wife Eleanor, extx. 27 acres adj. Thomas
Morris, Morris Morris, Wm. Evans, Wm. Williams, Lewis Evans, and
land purchased of Jer. Langhorne. Son Erasmus 223 acres lives on
and to his eldest male heirs forever. Grandson John Kelly, son of
Thomas, dec'd. Mathew Grier and Samuel Ferguson, Trustees.
Wit: Jos. Lunn, Jos. Shannon, John Wilson.

Page 17. Andrew Kelso, of Bedminster. Jun 5, 1760. Proved June
9, 1760. Wife Sarah and Bro. George Kellso, exrs. Children,
Robert, Jane, Mary, John, Allse, Elizabeth and Margaret.
Wit: Charles Stewart, Wm. Nash.

Page 18. Sarah Fitrey of Northampton Twp. Sept. 16, 1759.
Proved May 29, 1760. Husband Nicholas Fitrey, Lands, etc. during
life, then to grandson James Carril, dau. Lidy Tomkins, 3

youngest daus. Cousin John Hellings. John Dungan, exr.
Wit: Peter Vanhorn, Benjamin Vanhorn.

Page 19. John Skelton of Solebury Twp. Mch. 25, 1748. Proved
June 29, 1760. Wife Jane. Son Joseph (Exr.), "Plantation I live
on." Children, Jane, Narey, Robert Skelton, Ann Wilson, William
and Mary Skelton.
Wit: John Watson, Thomas Watson, Thomas Abbott.

Page 20. Deborah Dyer, of Northampton Twp., Widow. Feby. 27,
1759. Proved June 24, 1760. "Aged and weak.." Son Edward and
Friend Evan Jones, exrs. Son James Dyer and his sons Joseph and
Charles. Dau. Elizabeth wife of James Dyer, her son Joseph. Dau.
Sarah, wife of Daniel Done and her dau. Deborah Done. Son Edward
Dyer, Plantation where Manasse Wildman now lives.
Wit: Jacob Suber, Henry Dyer, Silas Watt.

Page 21. Sarah Bates, late of Makefield, but living in Bensalem.
May 16, 1760. Proved July 7, 1760. Sister Hannah, wife of Samuel
Yeardley, extx. Aunt Hannah Janney. Cousins Charles Janney. Betty
Janney, dau. of Abel Janney. Niece Sarah Bates, dau. of Bro.
John. Cousins Ann and Elizabeth Janney. Bro. John and Job Bates.
Wit: Sarah Growden, Margery Hibbs.

Page 22. John Lewis, of Hilltown Twp., Yeoman. June 29, 1760.
Proved July 17, 1760. Wife Anne "£50 engaged to her at the time
of our marriage." she and son John, exrs. Son Richard, 50 acres
of land. John, bal. of Plantation. George, £60 at 19. Thomas £50
at 15. Daus. Elizabeth, Anne, and Martha.
Wit: Thos. Jones, Thos. Morris, Thomas Mathias. Letters granted
to Anne only.

Page 24. Daniel DeNormandie of Burrough of Bristol, Merchant,
Date Apr. 7, 1758. Proved Aug. 6, 1760. Bros., Dr. John, of
Bristol, and Anthony DeNormandie, of Phila., Merchant, exrs. Sis.
Mary, wife of Peter Bard of Phila. Sister Sarah DeNormandie.
Cousin Harriot DeNormandie. Andrew, son of brother John. James,
son of Brother Anthony.
Wit: Wm. Large, Jos. Reese, Ann Higg. Letters to Anthony only.

Page 25. Thomas Atkinson, of Wrightstown, Yeoman. Dec. 18,
1759. Proved Aug. 13, 1760. Wife Mary. extx. Son Thomas, 200
acres I live on at 21. Bros. Ezekiel, William, Cephas and
Christopher. Sister Mary Stockdale.
Wit: John Terry, Abrm. Chapman, Jno. Watson, Junr.

Page 27. Isaac Vanhorne, of Solebury, Yeoman. June 5, 1760.
Proved Aug. 29, 1760. Wife Alice. Daus. Catharine Van Pelt,
Charity and Jane Vanhorne. Sons Barnard and John (exrs.), 200
acres "I live on.." Isaac, £110 when of age.
Wit: Gysbert Bogart, Crispin Blackfan, David Brown. Signed
"Iseeck Van Hooren.."

Page 28. James Johnston, of Wrightstown, "Taylor." Sept. 4,
1760. Proved Sept. 15, 1760. Wife Margaret. Eldest son James.

Dau. Sarah Johnston. Balance to the "rest of the children," one unborn. John Ramsey and Wm. Ramsey, Junr., exrs.
Wit: Ralph Smith, Jos. Smith, and David Nesbitt.

Page 29. Samuel Baker of Upper Makefield, Farmer. June 25, 1758. Proved Sept. 29, 1760. Wife Elizabeth, £12 per year. Bal. to be divided between children when of age. Bro. Joseph Baker and Bro-in-law John Burroughs, exrs.
Wit: John Beaumont, Henry Baker, and Edmund Briggs.

Page 30. Jacobus Swart, of Richland, Yeoman. Sept. 1, 1760. Proved Sept. 29, 1760. Wife Jane. Sons Guisberd and Bernard and son-in-law Rem Hageman, exrs. Sons John and Adrien. Daus. Phebe Hageman and Jane ---.
Wit: Jona Hunt, Wm. Va Vliedt, Junr. and James McKoppenly.

Page 31. Edmund Dunkan, Bensalem Twp., Yeoman. 8th mo., 22nd day, 1758. Proved Oct. 21, 1760. Son Edmund (£20). Six daus. Catharine, Jane, Sarah, Hellen, Ann, and Mary. Residue to son Isaac, exr.
Wit: Wm. Walmsley, John Carver, William Dunkan.

Page 32. Ann Pearson, of Plumstead Twp., Widow. Oct. 30, 1760. Proved Nov. 11, 1760. Son Joseph Pearson, (£40). Gd.son Eleazer Fenton, exr. Daus. Hannah Fenton, Mary Jewell, Priscilla McKinstry. Granddau. Mary Fenton.
Wit: Ursula Fenton, John Brown.

Page 33. James Adair, of the Falls Twp., Yeoman. July 2, 1760. Proved Nov. 19, 1760. Wife Jane, extx. and sole legatee.
Wit: Amos Shaw and Robert Mearns.

Page 37. William Mitchell, of Buckingham, "Taylor." Oct. 24, 1760. Proved Dec. 8, 1760. Wife Elizabeth, extx. 10 acres to be sold to pay mtge. adj. Street Road and Danl. White. Bal. of Est. to wife then to be divided among all children.
Wit: William Bradfield, Joseph Mitchell, and Titus Fell.

Page 34. Susanna Edwards, of New Britain, Widow. Aug. 22, 1758. Proved Nov. 22, 1760. Bro. Richard Clayton and Evan Jones, exrs. Plantation of late husband, Robert Edwards in Lower Makefield Twp. to be sold. Cousins John Booth. Edward Jones and Thomas Jones. Children of Bro. John Clayton, viz, Richard, Stephen, Jonathan, Ezekiel, Elizabeth, and Jane Clayton and Alice, wife of Robert Edwards. Children of cousin John Jones, viz., Elizabeth, Mary, Edward, John, and Susanna. 4 daus. of William Williams, viz., Esther, Elizabeth, Ann and Margaret. Cousins William Williams, Junr., and Ann Williams. Cousin Mary Closon, and her 2 children, William and Zachariah. Cousin William Erwin and James Erwin, his father. Cousin Margaret, wife of John Johnson and all her children, Susanna excepted. Children of sister Jane Duncan. Children of cousin Elizabeth Evans. £50 to Mahlon Kirkbride in Trust for Falls Monthly Meeting.
Wit: George Walker, Thomas Ashton, James Carter. Codicil dated Mch. 31, 1760. Wit: Jaret Erwin, James Irwin. Codicil dated Sept.

20, 1760. Cousin Anne, now wife of Wm. Williams, Senr.
Wit: Jos. Lunn and Erasmus Kelly.

Page 38. Robert Parsons, Senr., of Northampton Twp., Yeoman.
Nov. 26, 1760. Proved Dec. 17, 1760. Son Robert, exr. "Mansion
House and Plantation where I dwell." Daus. Ruth Townsend, Joanna
Shaw, wife of George and Susanna Hall. Grandchildren, Joseph
Shaw, Joseph McAllister, and Mary Parsons, dau. of Wm., dec'd.
Wit: Garet Vanhorn, Thomas McGee, John Evans.

Page 41. Randal Hutchinson of Lower Makefield, Mason. 11th mo.,
8th day, 1760. Proved Jan. 10, 1761. Wife Catharine and son
Mathias, exrs. Sons James and Mahlon.
Wit: Thomas Rickey, Keirll Rickey, Thos. Canby. Letters to widow
only.

Page 39. John Dunkan, Senr., of Bensalem, Yeoman. 7th mo., 13th
day, 1757. Proved Dec. 24, 1760. Bro. Patrick Dunkan, exr.
Plantation conveyed to my dec'd. bro. Edmund Dunkan and myself by
my mother Margaret Duncan.
Wit: Wm. Homer, Jr., William Walmsley.

Page 42. John Watson, of Buckingham, "Practitioner in Physic."
2nd mo., Feby. 23, 1757. Proved Feby. 3, 1761. Wife Sarah. Son
Thomas, exr. Son Joseph 50 acres purchased of Israel Pemberton,
adj. John Beal and Eli Welden. Also 200 acres where he lives
bought of Alex Beal. Dau Elizabeth, wife of John Fell. Son Thomas
200 acres where I live. Grandsons John Watson and Jonathan Fell
and Watson Fell. Granddau Alice Fell 125 acres in occupation of
John Patrick 213 acres in Bedminster on branch of Tohickon Creek.
Granddaus Ann, Sarah, and Elizabeth Fell land purchased of
Claypoole, Kimble and Wilkinson 300 acres.
Wit: John Beal, Junr., Martha Doan, John Poole, Jno. Watson,
Junr.

Page 47. Isaac Hall, of Solebury, Miller. Jan. 19, 1761.
Proved Feby. 16, 1761. Bros. Samuel, Jacob, and Jasper (last two
minors). Sisters Elizabeth and Gardrick. Joseph Paxson, exr.
Wit: John Burges, Oliver Paxson.

Page 48. James Downey, Lower Makefield Twp. 3rd mo., Mar. 5,
1759. Proved Feby. 25, 1761. Wife Hannah and son James, exrs.
Daus. Sarah, wife of Thomas Laramore and Hannah, wife of Thomas
Rickey. Granddau. Mary Wilson.
Wit: John White, Wm. Yeardley. Letters to James only.

Page 52. Thomas Marriott, of Bristol Borough, Sadler. 11th mo.,
28th day, 1760. Pr. Apr.2, 1761. Wife Sarah and Dau. Anna Humber,
exrs. 3 daus. Anna Humber, Martha, and Sarah Marriott.
Wit: En. Williams, Hw. Hartshorne, Wm. Gaiman.

Page 50. Richard Yeardley, of Solebury, Miller. Jan. 5, 1761.
Proved Mch. 4, 1761. Wife Mary and sons Enoch, William and
Benjamin exrs. Sons Thomas and Samuel, plantation in Newtown. Son
Richard. Dau. Mary, wife of Joseph Harvey. Mill and plantation

in Makefield to be sold.
Wit: Geo. Ely, Jos. Burges, John Ely. Letters granted to Mary.

Page 51. John Moland, of Warwick. Nov. 8, 1760. Proved Mch. 17, 1761. Wife ---. 3 daus. and youngest son, viz. Elizabeth, Hannah, Grace and Joseph, exrs. Wife to have £14 out of Rent of Plantation in Northern Liberties "on condiion that she do not converse with her son Thomas, whom I leave 1 shilling only.." Sons Robert, William, John.
Wit: Isaac Lewis and Thomas Howell.

Page 52. Alexander Graydon of Fairview, Co. of Bucks. Mch. 23, 1761. Proved Apr. 2, 1761. Wife Rachel. Children of former marriage Caleb and Elizabeth, wife of David McIlvaine. by 2d. wife Alexander, Janet, Andrew and William. Wife Rachel, son Caleb and son-in-law David McIlvaine and Jos. Biddle, exrs. provide Caleb and Elizabeth agree to release all claim under antenuptial agreement made with their mother Elizabeth, dau. of Caleb Emerson, made in the Kingdom of Ireland June 26, 1730 by which I was to invest £500 in land in this province for her in case of her surviving me, and at the death of the survivor to the issue of sd. marriage.
Wit: Hw. Harkhorn, Joseph Church, Enr. Williams. Letters granted to Rachel Graydon and James Biddle. Caleb and McIlvaine renouncing.

Page 54. John Linton of Wrightstown. 12th mo., Dec. 1, 1759. Proved June 11, 1761. Wife Elizabeth. Sons Jacob and Isaah both of Wrightstown, exrs. Son William land lately bought of Abrm. Chapman. Dau. Rebekah. Son Isaiah land in Wrightstown, adj. Jos. and John Hamton on Road leading from Zebulon Heston's to Wrightstown Meeting House. Daus. Rebecca and Elizabeth Linton. Codicil dated Apr. 15, 1761.
Wit: John Veity, Benj. Hamton, John Heston.

Page 57. Daniel DeNormandie, "Ensign 44th Reg." Mch. 10, 1760. Proved at N.Y. Oct. 7, 1760. Anthony DeNormandie, exr. Sarah DeNormandie and Ann Williams (dau. of Edward Williams, dec'd.) all est. except £50 to Penna. Hospital.
Wit: Gerrard DePuyster, James Daly.

Page 58. John VerKirk of Bensalem Twp., Yeoman. Apr. 7, 1759. Proved July 30, 1761. Wife Mary and sons Jacob and Bernard, exrs. Grandchildren, John, Sarah, and Abraham VerKirk, children of son John, dec'd. Nicholas and John Johnson, sons of Peter Johnson by dau. Sarah. Daus. Rachel, wife of John Wortman and Mary VerKerk.
Wit: Leonard Vandegrift, Folcart Vandegrift, and Thomas Stammers. Letters to Mary and Jacob.

Page 60. John Watson of Buckingham, Surveyor. 11th mo., 8th day, 1760. Proved Sept. 1, 1761. "Being about to set forth on a Journey to New Castle on Delaware to meet commissioners to settles lines between Provinces of Penna and Maryland." Cousin John Watson. Sister Sarah Lewis. Cousin Peter Blaker "Lands and Tenements" to Sister's son John Lewis in "fee tail male." "Money

due me from Grandfather Thomas Watson's estate in hands of
Richard Mitchell Executor of Cousin Joseph Watson." £250 to
Hannah, dau. of William Blackfan of Solebury. Cousin Joseph
Watson, son of John and Crispin Blackfan, exrs.
Wit: Thos. and Mary Tucker.

Page 59. Henry Roberts of Solesbury, Yeoman. Mch. 30, 1761.
Proved Aug. 20, 1761. Wife Mary, extx. Sons Richard (eldest),
William, and Henry. Daus. Mary, Jane, and Margery. Son Thomas.
Wit: Hezekiah Bye and Jacob Dean.

Page 63. Samuel Brelsford of Middletown. Jan. 25, 1748/9.
Proved Sept. 5, 1761. "Far advanced in years." Son Nathan and
Cousin Solomon Headley, exrs. Sons Nathan (plantation I live on),
Benjamin (20 shillings), Joseph (50 shillings), William (£5).
Daus. Rebekah White, Martha Vanhorn, and Esther Harvey each 10
shillings. Sons Samuel and Jacob. Son Benjamin's eldest son.
Dau. Lydia's dau. Lydia and rest of her children.
Wit: Wm. Atkinson, Jos. Atkinson, Saml. Atkinson.

Page 64. John Williamson, of Bensalem. Feby. 29, 1760. Proved
Sept. 21, 1761. Wife Elizabeth, extx. Sons John, Abraham, Jesse,
William, Joseph and David, Jeremiah, and Benjamin. Daus.
Elizabeth Vandegrift and Katharine Watson.
Wit: David Thomas, John Vanhorn, Robert Heaton.

Page 65. Joseph Shaw, Northampton, Yeoman. Dec. 15, 1759.
Proved Sept. 22, 1761. Wife Mary. Son-in-law Henry Harding and
cousin John Brown of Buchinham, exrs. Daus. Mary, wife of Henry
Harding, and Susannah Shaw (a minor). Grandchildren, Anna, Joseph
and Mary Crosedell, children of dau. Sarah, dec'd., late wife of
Ezra Crosedell. John Crosedell, son of dau. Anna, dec'd., late
wife of Eber Crosedell.
Wit: Jacob Randall, James Vansant, Jos. Hart.

Page 68. Isaac Evan, of New Britain, Yeoman. Sept. 11, 1761.
Proved Oct. 10, 1761. Wife Catherin. Son David, exr. Son James,
plantation where he lives bought of Isaac Milnor. Son Daniel,
plantation where he lives bought of Adms. of David Thomas.
Wit: John Williams and William Davies, Junr.

Page 67. Thomas Harvey, of the Falls Twp., Yeoman. May 12,
1761. Proved Oct. 12, 1761. Son Thomas, George Brown, and Mahlon
Kirkbride, exrs. Eldest son Thomas, Lands and Tenements in
Flower, County of Northampton England, also Lands and Tenements
in Burrough of Bristol. Son Samuel, Land in Falls Twp. in
occupation of William Moon. Son William, Land in occupation of
John Scott and Land in Makefield in occupation of John Simmons
and son John's land in occupation of James Jolly in Makefield.
Dau. Elizabeth Harvey.
Wit: John Pursell, James Shaw, Jno. Duncan.

Page 70. Samuel Scott, of Bensalem Twp., Yeoman. 6th mo., 6th
day, 1760. Proved Oct. 20, 1761. Youngest son Samuel, exr. 80
acres "on which I dwell." Son Thomas, 1 acre where he dwells.

Eldest son Jacob, and his sons Jacob and Joseph. Dau. Sarah Lester. Sister-in-law Alice Amos.
Wit: Wm. Walmsley, Thomas Walmsley, and Silas Walmsley.

Page 71. Stephen Wilson, of Middletown. 3rd mo., 25th day, 1761. Proved Nov. 2, 1761. Sons Stephen and John, exrs. Sons Samuel, Francis, Joseph (minor), William (youngest). Gd.son Stephen Wilson, son of Isaac, dec'd. and rest of Isaac's children.
Wit: Joseph Richardson, George Merrick, Benja. Cutler.

Page 72. John Steward, of Warwick, Yeoman. Jan. 13, 1761. Proved Nov. 11, 1761. Sister Margaret Brumfield, Charles Steward, and Wm. Scott, exrs. Sister Hannah Baird and her dau. Hannah Baird. Sis.s Mary Jamison, Jane Brumfield, and Margaret Brumfield. Jane Craig, dau. of Henry Jamison. Henry Davis, son of Tristam. John Scott, son of William.
Wit: John McFarren, Edward Poole, and Robert Scott.

Page 73. John Fricker, of County of Bucks, Merchant. Dec. 1, 1761. Proved Dec. 10, 1761. Wife Salome. Children, Catharine, Theresia, and Joseph. 2 Plantations lately bought. Bro. Anthony Fricker of Reading Town, Berks Co. and bro-in-law Joseph Coole of Bucks Co. exrs. Friend Mr. Theodore Schneider. House and Lot in Easton leased to John Moore, Esq. to be sold, also my mdse. to pay bal. on Plantations, Bills due me in Northampton Co. in hands of John Moore, Esq.
Wit: Anthony Creaser, Jacob Heney, Nicholas Huckey.

Page 74. Henry Vanhorn, of Newtown Twp., Yeoman. May 9, 1791. Proved Dec. 10, 1761. Wife Susanna. Sons Christian and Henry, exrs. Plantation in Newtown. Daus. Jane, eldest, wife of John Johnson, youngest dau. Susanna Longshore.
Wit: George Dunn, Jno. Atkinson, Junr., Wm. Ashburn.

Page 76. Peter Williamson, of Bensalem, Yeoman. Apr. 7, 1760. Proved Dec. 14, 1761. Wife Leah, son Peter Williams, and Jacob Vandegrift, the elder, exrs. Son Jacob Williams. Cornelius Murray to be put to a trade.
Wit: Jean Murray, Jno. Duncan.

Page 77. Thomas Morris of New Britain, Yeoman. Dec. 26, 1761. Proved Feb. 15, 1762. Wife Leyky. Son John, exr. Granddau. Elizabeth Morris.
Wit: Joshua Riale, William Brown, William Davies, Junr.

Page 78. Samuel Willet, of Northampton Twp., Yeoman. June 9, 1757. Proved June 11, 1761. Wife Elizabeth and bro-in-law Joseph Thomas, exrs. Eldest son Augustine (a minor) and youngest son Lawrence. (Plantation). Daus. Catharine and Caroline.
Wit: Thos. Austin, Tho. Rodman, John Gregg, William Rodman.

Page 79. Christophel Hillebrandt, Northampton Twp. Dec. 23, 1761. Proved Mch. 11, 1762. Wife Elizabeth and Neighbor Henry Wynkoop, exrs. Son Christophel "either is or hath been enlisted

in his majesties service.." Dau. Elizabeth, wife of Hendrick
Lymbacker.
Wit: John VanPelt, Johannes Sigmann, Joseph Fenton.

Page 80. William Lacey, of Wrightstown. Jany. 7, 1762. Proved
Mch. 25, 1762. Wife Elizabeth and Bro. Joseph Lacey, exrs. Daus.
Rachel and Hannah.
Wit: Jno. Terry, Jno. Terry, Junr., James Love.

Page 81. John Beal, of Buckingham, Yeoman. July 24, 1760.
Proved Apr. 22, 1762. Wife Martha, extx. Cousin Patrick Malone to
assist her. Son John 200 acres. Dau. Phebe, wife of John Tucker,
100 acres adj. Mathew Hughes, John Watson surveyor and Joseph
Watson. Cousin Jonathan Beal to be under care of sisters
Elizabeth Weldin and Rebecca Rickey. Wife, Log House standing
S.E. of Plantation and 25 acres for life, then to son John.
Wit: Ely Welding, John Fetter, Jos. Watson.

Page 82. John Orr, of Bedminster, Yeoman. Dec. 4, 1761. Proved
June 16, 1762. Wife Jane and Thomas Boy of Buckingham, exrs. Son
Thomas. Dau. Isabella Patterson. Granddaus. Rebekah Orr and
Rebekah Baker.
Wit: Anthony Kennard, John Townsend, Edward Murphy.

Page 83. Evan Jones of Northampton Twp. July 8, 1755. Proved
July 28, 1762. Wife Mary extx and sole legatee.
Wit: Jos. Hart, Garret Wynkoop, and Henry Krewsen.

Page 86. Elizabeth Mitchell, of Solebury. 3rd mo., 8th day,
1762. Proved Sept. 17, 1762. 5 children, Jacob Verity, Deborah,
Samuel, Elizabeth and Enoch Mitchell, minor. Cousins John Ingham
(Exr.) and Mary and Sarah Ingham.
Wit: Jon. Ingham, Jon. Ingham, Junr., John Waterhouse.

Page 84. Nicholas Gilbert, of Warminster Twp. Mch. 23, 1758.
Proved Aug. 13, 1762. Eldest son John, exr. "Land I live on."
Son Joseph. Dau. Mary Jones. Dau-in-law Hannah, widow of son
Jacob and dau. Ann. Abigail, widow of son Peter and his
children, Sarah, Hannah, Elizabeth, and Mary. Mary, widow of son
Benjamin and his dau. Sarah and only son Benjamin. Children of
son Samuel, viz., William and Margaret. Children of son Joseph,
viz. Hannah, Ann, Rachel, and Mary. Land on Bristol Road, adj.
Jno. Radcliffe.
Wit: Isaac Lewis, Mary Eaton, John Hart.

Page 87. Ann Hutchinson of Borough of Bristol, Widow. Jan. 7,
1761. Proved Dec. 13, 1762. "Late husband John Hutchinson."
Children, Phebe, John, Thomas, and Rebecca Hutchinson. Uncle
Mahlon Kirkbride. Bro-in-law Michel Hutchinson and son John
Hutchinson, exrs.
Wit: En. Williams and Joseph Church. Letters granted to Michel
Hutchinson and John Hutchinson, Junr.

Page 88. Charles Wright, of Middletown. Mch. 17, 1763. Proved
Apr. 5, 1763. Dau. Martha Wright and Son-in-law Joseph Smith,

exrs. Dau. Sarah, wife of Wm. Brodnax. Their son Charles.
Gd.son Ira Patterson.
Wit: John Sotcher, Wm. Brodnax, Timothy Wright.

Page 89. John Hart, of Warminster, Yeoman. Jan. 15, 1763.
Proved Apr. 19, 1763. Son Joseph, exr. Cousin Susanna Rush, £6
out of money due from Isaac Hough. Residue to son Joseph he
paying the other children, 5 shillings each.
Wit: Daniel Longstreth, Thomas Handcock, Thos. Griffith.

Page 90. James Shaw, of Plumstead Twp. Dec. 20, 1759. Proved
Apr. 27, 1763. Wife Mary. Sons Jonathan and Alexander, exrs. Sons
Joseph and James. Dau. Elizabeth Dillon.
Wit: William Michener, John Carlile, Isaac Child.

Page 91. Jabus Wood, of the Falls Twp., Yeoman. Nov. 16, 1759.
Proved May 30, 1763. Son Benjamin, exr. Plantation in Falls,
paying his sis. Elizabeth Carman £5. Dau. Susanna Roberts,
Plantation adj. Benj. Linton.
Wit: Thos. Janney, Mary Laramar, Mahlon Kirkbride.

Page 92. Isabel Crawford of Warwick, Widow. Aug. 1, 1763.
Proved Aug. 24, 1763. Son James and Robert Stewart of Warwick,
exrs. Sons Archibald, Robert, Moses, John, Samuel. Daus. Isabel,
Hellen, Ann and Jane.
Wit: James Pook, Eleanor Poak, Robert Scott.

Page 93. John Allen of Burrough of Bristol. 1st mo., 30th day,
1758. Proved Oct. 15, 1763. Wife Rebecca and Friend Jos.
Atkinson, exrs. Dau. Sarah Dickinson, Son William and Dau.
Rebecca, minors.
Wit: John Gilbert, William Board, and William Buckley. Dr. John
DeNormandie being sworn, deposes and says that Wm. Board the last
he heard of him he was at Fort Detroit or Niagara in the Kings
Service. That Wm. Buckley died about 4 yrs ago. That he is
acquainted with their writing, etc.

Page 94. John Hall, of Tinnecome Twp., Yeoman. Jan. 3, 1764.
Proved Feb. 29, 1764. Wife Jean. Dau. Mary (a minor), step dau.
Agnes Cooper. Wm. McIntyre and John Howey, exrs.
Wit: Thomas Yeidler, Mary Cooper.

Page 95. Thomas Stradling of Newtown. June 7, 1761. Proved
Mch. 9, 1764. Wife Lydia. Children, Daniel and Joseph (exrs.),
Elizabeth, Rebecca, Lydia, and Sarah. Children of deceased son
Thomas. Son Joseph, plantation in Newtown between Timothy Smith
and Barnard Taylor.
Wit: Barnard Taylor, Mary Taylor, John Gibson.

Page 96. Josiah Wood of the Falls Twp., Yeoman. Mch. 24, 1764.
Codicil Mch. 24, 1764. Proved May 5, 1764. Wife Elizabeth. Wm.
Yeardley and Henry Baker, exrs. Son Josiah, dau. Sarah Morgan.
Son William, Plantation in Tenure of Chas. Clark. adj. River and
lands of John Roberts and Benjamin Linton. Son John, Plantation
where I live.

Wit: John Anderson, Mahlon Kirkbride, Joshua Linton, Asher
Carter, Margaret Gerton.

Page 98. Abraham Brelsford, of Boro. of Bristol, Butcher. Dec.
13, 1763. Proved May 29, 1764. Wife Joyce and Bro. Isaac, exrs.
Daus. Rachel and Martha. Dau. Mary Johnson. Land adj. Wm.
McIlvaine to be sold.
Wit: Joseph Church, Joseph Tomlinson, and Lawrence Johnson.

Page 99. George Leadley, of Buckingham. Feby. 16, 1764. Proved
---. Wm. Simson and John Wilson, exrs. Son John right of
Plantation in Forks of Delaware. Son George (£60). Daus. Mary,
Jane, Margaret, Agnes, and Sarah. Granddaus. Agnes Miller and
Jane Davis. Gdsons George Miller and James Mickelroy.
Wit: John Sherer, Christopher Carter, John O'Daniel.

Page 100. James McAllister, of New Britain. July 11, 1764.
Proved July 20, 1764. Wife Mary. Son Robert, Jos. Griffith and
James Lewis, exrs. Son Robert, lands he lives on in County of
Baltimore, Maryland. Dau. Mary Brooks, 100 acres purchased of Lux
Mat in Baltimore, Maryland. Sons James and Joseph, residue bought
of Lux Mat in Baltimore, Maryland. Sons Eligah and Elisagh. Dau.
Rachel. Philip Martz, Henry Lewis, and David Davis, Guardians.
Wit: James Thomas, Benj. Thomas, Wm. James.

Page 105. John Scott of Southampton Twp. Apr. 21, 1762. Proved
Aug. 18, 1764. Mother Jane Scott. Bro. Benjamin, his sons
Jonathan and Eman. Benjamin and John States, sons of Edmund and
Rebekah States. Ezra Croasdale and Edmund Staats, exrs.
Wit: John Bennett, Harman Vandegrift.

Page 102. William Thomas of Hilltown Twp., Yeoman. Jan. 20,
1763. Proved July 26, 1764. Wife Abigail and Bro. Mannasse,
exrs. Wife use of Plantation to my Sister Anna Thomas, by will
of my father William Thomas. Sons William (eldest), Joseph (2d.),
and William, and dau. Martha. James Lewis to succeed me as
Trustee of Mtg. House as directed by Father's will. Bros. John,
Thomas, and Ephraim, James Lewis and Joseph Griffith of New
Britain, Overseers. Land in Tenure of Jaob Fry adj. County line.
Wit: Robert Evans, James Lewis, Benj. Thomas.

Page 104. Benjamin Scott, of Southampton, Carpenter. Apr. 30,
1764. Proved July 31, 1764. Wife Grace. Goods, etc. she took
from me when separating from me. together with money belonging
to me in right of her in the hands of the Admr.'s of Joseph
Walker, dec'd. late of Middletown. Gilbert Hicks and John Gregg,
Esgrs. both of Middletown, exrs. Sons Jonathan, Eman, Benjamin,
and Joseph.
Wit: Edmund Stats, Christian Vanhorn.

Page 106. Thomas Morgan, Junr., of Middletown, Yeoman. July 12,
1764. Proved Aug. 17, 1764. Wife Martha and Jonathan Carlile,
exrs. Son Thomas, Grist Mill at 21 . Dau. Magdalene and Pamela.
Wit: Richd. Lanning, Martha Lanning, George Suber.

Page 108. Simon Butler, Esq., New Britain, Yeoman. July 30, 1764. Proved Aug. 30, 1764. Son Simon, 1/2 of Grist Mill and Lot. Grandson Abiah Butler, exr., land adj. Mill bought of James Steel, dec'd., adj. Thomas Mathews and Henry Kelso. Also, 50 acres bought of Son Simon, exr. of Benj. Butler, dec'd. Gd.son Benj. Butler, Land on Road leading from Mill to Montgomery adj. David John and Wm. Thomas. Granddau. Margaret Butler.
Wit: John Mathew, Benj. Thomas, Benj. Mathew, Wm. Davies, Junr.

Page 109. Elijah Leedom, Southampton, Yeoman. Sept. 6, 1764. Proved Sept. 21, 1764. Bro. Samuel and John Thornton, exrs. Bro. John, Benj., and William.
Wit: John Hoff, James Reed.

Page 110. Agnes Miller, of New Britain, Widow, (Spinster). Aug. 30, 1764. Proved Oct. 1, 1764. Gd.sons William and Philip Miller, £5 each immediately after marriage of only Dau. Susanna, Residue to Susanna immediately after her marriage. John Lap, exr.
Wit: Henry Wireman, Richd. Hay, and Cadwallader Morris.

Page 111. Euclides Longshore, Middletown, Yeoman. 11th mo., 8th day, 1760. Proved Oct. 8, 1764. Wife Alice and Friend Thomas Jenks, exr. Sons Euclides, Robert, and Thomas. Daus. Margaret Atkinson and Alice Lamb. Gd.son Isaac Pearson. House near Four-Lane-End adj. Geo. Walker's Lot to be sold.
Wit: Samuel Sykes, Saml. Smith, and Saml. Cary.

Page 112. John Fowler, of Bensalem. Aug. 13, 1764. Proved Oct. 10, 1764. Edward Hill of Bensalem, Ex. and sole legatee.
Wit: Jno. Lamb, Leod. Morrey. "Wallet at John Mitchell's."

Page 113. Joseph Kinsey of Buckingham, Yeoman. 9th mo., 14th day, 1764. Proved Oct. 16, 1764. Wife Hannah. Bro-in-law Thos. Smith and Friend Jos. Watson, exrs. "Girl Margaret Stackhouse who lives with us." Lands to be sold and proceeds divided among all the children.
Wit: Paul Preston, Benj. Kinsey, Agnes Yates.

Page 114. Griffith Owen, of Hilltown, Yeoman. Mch. 11, 1763. Proved Oct. 29, 1764. 2 Eldest Sons, Owen and Ebenezer, exrs. Son Levy, 14 acres in Hilltown bought of Thomas Phillips. Gd.son Griffith Owens, son of Owen. Only dau. Rachel Erwin. Jason Thomas, son of David Thomas, late of New Britain, Glover, Bro. Nicholas Owen.
Wit: Henry Lewis, Lawrence Swink, Benjamin Griffith.

Page 115. Thomas Tomlinson, of Bensalem, Yeoman. June 9, 1759. Proved Nov. 24, 1764. Wife Joan and son Thomas, exrs. Sons Joseph, Henry, and Francis. Daus. Elizabeth Shearman and Mary. Bro-in-law Thos. Walmsley.
Wit: Thomas Townsend, John Townsend, William Dunkan.

Page 116. John Watson, of Middletown, Yeoman. 9th mo., 21st day, 1764. Proved Dec. 11, 1764. Wife Ruth. Son John, exr.

House and Lands. Dau. Ruth.
Wit: Benj. Cutler, David Barton, John Woolston.

Page 117. John Vastine, of Hilltown, Yeoman. Dec. 25, 1764.
Proved Feby. 1, 1765. Nephew Benj. Vastine and Erasmus Kelly,
exrs. Bro. Abraham's children, viz., Rebecca, wife of Andrew
Armstrong; Rachel, wife of Hugh Mearns; Mary, wife of Robert
Jamison; Ruth, wife of James Armstrong; and Sarah, wife of Saml.
Wilson. Bro. Jeremiah's children, viz., Jeremiah, Junr.; Martha,
wife of Jno. Lowther; Hannah, wife of Samuel Grimes; and Ezra
Vastine. Nephews John, Abraham, Benjamin, Jonathan, and Amos
Vastine and Niece Hannah, wife of Erasmus Kelly. Nephew Isaac
Vastine.
Wit: Jos. Lunn, Davis Heaton, Jemima Heaton.

Page 119. James Wallace, of Tinnecom. Jan. 4, 1765. Proved
Mch. 12, 1765. Wife Hannah and Son Robert, exrs. Dau. Jean
Hutchinson and her son John Hutchinson. Children, Robert, Elinor,
William, Samuel, Hannah, Elizabeth, and Mary.
Wit: Thomas Hutchinson, Robt. Patterson, John Howey.

Page 120. David Spear, of Northampton Twp., Yeoman. July 7,
1761. Proved Mch. 13, 1765. Wife Elizabeth and Son David, exrs.
"Ancient Mother-in-law Janet Craig." Son David all Lands 200
acres. Son John. Dau. Jane Burley. Daus. Elizabeth and Mary.
Debt due Evan Jones. Horse I have of Alexander McMasters. John
Wilkinson and Thomas Chapman, Overseers.
Wit: Jos. Smith, Ralph Smith, Tho. Chapman.

Page 122. John Fisher of Buckingham. 12th mo., 15th day, 1756.
Proved Mch. 13, 1765. Son Robert (Exr.), Lands in Buckingham and
Plumstead. Sons Robert, Joseph, Barak and Samuel. Daus. Mary
Butler, Sarah Michener, Elizabeth Stradling. Hannah Preston and
Deborah and Katharine Fisher.
Wit: Mathew Beans, Jos. Skelton, Paul Preston.

Page 123. Mary Beakes, of Middletown, Dated. 10th mo., 9th day,
1764. Proved Mch. 23, 1765. Daus. Ruth Walker and Lydia Beakes,
exrs. Son Stacy Beakes.
Wit: Benj. Cutler, Richard Mitchell, Esther Beckerdike.

Page 124. Andrew Overpeck, of Nockamixon, Dated. Apr. 26, 1758.
Proved Apr. 10, 1765. Wife Elizabeth. Sons George and Jacob,
exrs. Daus. Mary Oelah (?) and Ann Mary Herble.
Wit: John Henery, John Dennis.

Page 125. Henry Baker, of Upper Makefield, Whellwright. Nov.
16, 1764. Proved May 4, 1765. Wife Mary and Bro-in-law John
Burroughs, exrs. Dau-in-law Hannah Mathias. 5 daus.
Wit: Jos. Baker, John Burroughs and John Beaumont.

Page 126. Jonathan Palmer of Lower Makefield. 4th mo., 24th
day, 1763. Proved Oct. 2, 1765. Wife Jael, money due from estate
of her late husband, Wm. Blakely, dec'd. Sons Jonathan and
Joseph, exrs. Son-in-law Samuel Woolston. Dau. Hannah Woolston.

Dau. Elizabeth, wife of Jeremiah Woolston land bought of Richard Hough. Son Joseph to have a Road and Land he bought of Thomas Davis.
Wit: Wm. Blakey, Sarah Blakey, Jr., Jonathan Kirkbride.

Page 131. William McLeroy of Nockamixon Twp., Yeoman. May 6, 1765. Proved Oct. 31, 1765. Wife Joan, extx. Son Alexander, Land in Manor of Moorland. Dau. Jean, wife of Samuel Joans. Children of sons Alexander and George. Dau. Agnes Scott. Bond due from John and Jonathan Joans. £5 towards repairing Tohickon Church.
Wit: John McKey, John Howey.

Page 128. John Merrick, of Middletown. Oct. 2, 1765. Proved Oct. 23, 1765. Sons George and John, exrs. Son George, 3 Lots purchased of Jos. Bennet, Christian and Henry Vanhorn and Jos. Stackhouse. Son John, 2 Lots in Bristol purchased of Mary Shaw and Jas. Downey and Lot in Middletown purchased of Jeremiah Woolston. Son Joseph, 3 Lots in Bristol purchased of John DeNormandie. Son Timothy, Part of Plantation in Upper Makefield adj. Land of Heirs of John Harvey, on Road leading from Newtown to Baker's Ferry. Son Robert, residue of Makefield Plantation adj. Joseph Johnson. Dau. Hannah.
Wit: John DeNormandie, Jos. Stackhouse, John Woolston.

Page 130. John Vandegrift, of Bensalem, Yeoman. June 25, 1765. Proved Oct. 29, 1765. Wife Anna and Son Joseph, exrs. Son Nicholas, part of Plantation he lives on. Son Jacob, part of Plantation. Son John, part lying next Wm. Allen, adj. Land late Henry Fisher now Lawrence Johnson. Son Joseph, residue of Plantation. Daus. Catharine Sands, Esther Houton and Rebekah Vanseiver.
Wit: Thomas Dunbar, Philip McGlaughin and John Evans.

Page 133. Samuel Jones, Senr., of Plumstead, Yeoman. Oct. 28, 1765. Proved Feby. 20, 1766. Wife Margaret and Son Samuel, exrs. Son John (a minor). Daus. Rachel Brittain and Dau. Mary. Grandson Samuel Brittain. Son Samuel.
Wit: Edwd. Murphy, Alex. Metlan, Agnes Metlan.

Page 135. Joseph Burroughs, of Newtown Twp., Farmer. Feby. 9, 1760. Proved Mch. 4, 1766. Bro. John Burroughs and his children. Bro. Jeremiah's son Abraham and his other children. Mary Headly and her bros. and sisters. Jospeh Burroughs, son of Bro. James, Elizabeth Doughty, dau. of Thomas and Ann Doughty, 20 acres lately bought of John Story "if she dye to her Sister Martha." Lands and tenements to Thomas Doughty, exr.
Wit: Samuel Sykes, Wm. Sykes, Saml. Smith.

Page 136. William Preston, of Buckingham, Mason. Feby. 28, 1766. Proved Mch. 4, 1766. Son Joseph and Friend Paul Preston, exrs. Son Joseph "All Lands," etc. Daus. Martha Wilson and Sarah Preston, children of dau. Mary, dec'd. late wife of Joseph Brown.
Wit: Jos. Fell, Jos. Fell, Junr., and John Brown.

Page 137. Jacob Shup, of Nockamixon Twp. Jan. 11, 1766. Proved

Apr. 11, 1766. Wife Franey, all estate until youngest child is 14
yrs. of age. Sons Jacob, Henry, John, Larrance, and Michel (a
cripple). Daus. Margaret Hocus, Ann and Franey. Wife and eldest
son Jacob, exrs.
Wit: James Loughrey and Jacob Frelich.

Page 138.   Jacob Heston, of Upper Makefield, Yeoman.   5th mo.,
9th day, 1765.   Proved Apr. 12, 1766. Wife Mary and Sons Jesse
and Edward, exrs. Son Jesse, Land bought of Richard Parsons and
George Newburn. Son Edward, Land in Blockley Twp., Phila. Co.
formerly his grandfather, John Warner's. Sons Isaac and Jacob,
residue of land in Wrightstown. Son Thomas, 52 acres bought of
Samuel Merrick, Makefield. Daus. Mary Paxson and Rachel Heston.
Wit: Jos. Hamton, Isaiah Linton, and Elizabeth Linton. Codicil
Dec. 1, 1765. Wit: Geo. Newburn and Benj. Hamton.

Page 141.   Zachariah Drake of Upper Makefield, Yeoman.   Jan. 28,
1766.   Proved Apr. 12, 1766. Wife Elizabeth.   Bro. Daniel of
Hopewell, N.J. and Jos. Hamton of Wrightstown, exrs. Children,
Jacob, Jaon, Benjamin, Robert, Elizabeth, Mary, Ann, and Hannah.
Wit: Samuel Merrick, Robert Comfort, and James McNaire.

Page 142.   Henry Jamison, Senr., of Warwick Twp.   Apr. 18, 1765.
Proved Apr. 4, 1766. Wife Mary, and Son Alexander, exrs. Son
Robert, Plantation. Son John (£100). Son William. Daus. Isabel
Davis. Jean Craig.   Ann Darroch, Margaret Scott, and Mary
Jamison.
Wit: Robert Jamison, Daniel Aston.

Page 143.   Jeremiah Williams, of Nockamixon, Yeoman.   1st mo.,
Jan. 23, 1760.   Proved June 6, 1766. Wife Mary and Son Benjamin,
exrs. Daus. Hannah Doughty.   Anne Woods, Martha Hill, and Dau.
Mary.
Wit: Christian Weaver, John Moore, and Henry Heite. Letters
granted to Benjamin.

Page 144.   John Cowley, of Middletown, Yeoman.   Dec. 16, 1765.
Proved June 9, 1766. Dau. Elizabeth Bratt and John Gregg, exrs.
Granddau. Sarah Cowley. Dau. Elizabeth, Land where I live adj.
Jona. Carlile, Amos Palmer, and School House on Road leading from
Richard Yeardley's Mill to Phila. Son John "Now in England" all
lands except above tract.
Wit: Jonathan Carlile, Marcy Carlile, Wm. Yeardley. Codicil Feby.
12, 1766 gives another Tract to Elizabeth adj. Patrick Gregg and
"now in tenure of John Sickman." Wit: Rebecca Carter, Wm. Carter.

Page 146.   Samuel Cary, of Newtown.   4th mo., 2d. 1764.   Proved
June 16, 1766. Wife Sarah, use of all lands purchased of Anthony
Wilson "until 3d son Thomas arrive at lawful age.." Son Samson.
Son Samuel, Land adj. Geo. Dunn and Est. of Jos. Poole bought of
Jas. Yates. Son Thomas, 48 acres adj. John Watson, Wm.
Satterthwaite and Euclides Longshore, purchase of Christian
Vanhorn and Patrick Gregg. Son Joshua, Lot in possession of
Samuel Stackhouse, also Lot purchased of James Yates and Tract
purchased of James Arbuckle. Son Asa, Lot in Bristol which Uncle

Samson Cary bought of Wm. Hope. Son Phineas, Lot in Bristol mortgaged to me by William Heaton. Daus. Sarah, wife of Joshua Blakey; Ann, wife of Amanuel Walker; Hannahmeal, wife of Jonathan Gilbert; and Bethula, Bula and Hepsibah. Wife Sarah, son Samuel and Jos. Hamton and David Twining, exrs.
Wit: Wm. Satterthwaite, Sr. and Jr. and James Moon.

Page 152. Robert Craft, of Buckingham, Labourer. Apr. 11, 1766. Proved July 28, 1766. Father and Mother, William and Elizabeth Craft, all Est. Saml. Kinsey, exr.
Wit: Saml. Kinsey, Saml. Kinsey, Junr., Sarah Kinsey, and John Ross.

Page 150. William Eaken, of Nockamixon Twp., Yeoman. Dec. 9, 1765. Proved July 2, 1766. Wife Isabel and son Redmon, exrs. 7 sons, Thomas, Joseph, Redmon, William, Nathan, Samuel, and Robert. Daus. Jean, Ishabel (minors). Sister-in-law Rebecca Morrison.
Wit: Robert Wilson, John Howey.

Page 153. John McCarty, of Haycock Twp., Farmer. Apr. 24, 1766. Proved Aug. 22, 1766. Wife Ann and Bro. Nicholas, exrs. Daus. £30 each. Real estate to sons. Rents to be used for schooling and maintaining children until son Nicholas is of age.
Wit: Alexander McLeroy, George McLeroy.

Page 154. Matthew Hughes, of Buckingham. Apr. 17, 1762. Proved Sept. 3, 1766. Son Uriah and Grandson George Hughes, exrs. Sons Uriah and George 1/2 Personal estate, the other 1/2 to surviving grandchildren, John Hughes excepted. Son Elias, 1/2 Plantation whereon John Craft lives next to Moses Marshall. To his two children, Elizabeth and Uriah at his death. Grandson Mathew Hughes the other 1/2. Grandson George Hughes, Land near mouth of Tohickson. Grandson, John Hughes, 10 acres N. side Phila. Road adj. Joseph Large. Jane Roberts, 10 acres where she lives. Granddau. Hannah Hughes, 50 acres of Tract I live on adj. Jos. Watson and John Beal. Son George, all residue of land on S. side Phila. Road. Son Uriah, all residue, Contiquos to Phila. Road for life then to children of son Mathew, dec'd.
Wit: Adrien Dawes, William Hill, Francis Dawes.

Page 155. Jesimah Vansant, of Middletown, Spinster. Feby. 5, 1761. Proved Nov. 5, 1766. Sister Rachel Rue and Relation John Praul, exrs. Sis. Alshea Rue. Jesinah, Anne and Catharine and Christopher Rue, children of sister Rachel Rue.
Wit: Richd. Rue, Wm. Dye, Robert Brodnax.

Page 157. David Morgan of New Britain Twp., Yeoman. July 2, 1760. Proved Nov. 20, 1766. Wife Catharine, formerly Catharine James, payments set forth in Ante nuptial contract dated Mch. 17, 1742/3. only child Martha Dungan, and her son David Dungan. Son-in-law Wm. Dungan, exr.
Wit: Wm. Davis, Elizabeth Sole, Benj. Griffith.

Page 156. Edward Hill, of Bensalem Twp. Oct. 5, 1766. Proved

Nov. 17, 1766. Wife Sarah, John Kidd, Dr. John DeNormandie and
Richard Gibbs, exrs. Ann Mankin £50. Ralph Williamson and his
sister Hannah and John Wilkinson, son of Widow Williamson £50
each. Leonard Murray £150. Sarah Fennemore £5. Stephen Sands £10.
John Sands, the elder, wearing apparel. Mary Rue £50. Penna
Hospital £100. £50 for a new Episcopal Church at Four Lanes End.
£50 toward enlarging Church at Bristol; residue to wife Sarah.
Wit: Jos. Vandegrift, Seth Lucas, Jos. Fenimore.

Page 158. John Strickland, of Southampton, Yeoman. 9th mo, 8th
day, 1766. Proved Nov. 20, 1766. Wife Margery, Corn and Grist
Mill for life toward bringing up my four children, viz., John,
Elizabeth, Joseph, and Miles. Dau. Mary Ashton and her son Jacob
Thomas. Dau. Margaret Thomas, Lot of land bought of Thomas
Hillborn. Dau. Rachel Comly. Dau. Frances Strickland. Dau. Mary,
son Amos and son-in-law Thomas Ashton, exrs.
Wit: Nicholas Vansant, Jacob Vansant, Thos. Groom.

Page 161. Eleanor Stackhouse, wife of Samuel Stackhouse of
Bristol Boro. Dec. 15, 1766. Proved Jan. 13, 1767. "Formerly
Eleanor Clark, dau. of James Clark, late of Bristol, dec'd., who
died intestate leaving four daus., all at that time minors,
youngest yet a minor, and leaving Real estate yet undivided."
Husband Samuel Stackhouse, exr. and sole legatee.
Wit: Philip Streaker, Jacob Holloman, Phebe Ashton.

Page 162. Thomas Paxson, Junr., of Solebury, Yeoman. 12th mo.
(Dec.) 29, 1765. Proved Jan. 27, 1767. Wife Hannah. Sons
Abraham, Aaron and Moses. Dau. Ann Paxson. Abraham Harvey of
Makefield and William Blackfan, Junr. of Solebury and son
Abraham, exrs. Abraham, 300 acres on which I live (Deed from
father Henry Paxson, Apr. 26, 1748). Aaron, 2 Lots, 99 acres
conveyed to me by Charles Norris atty. for the Pikes. Moses,
Plantation where Wm. Daniels lives devised to me by Will of
Father. Ann, £150 and Household Goods "that were her mother's"
"in care of her Aunt Jane Brown." If wife have a son, Plantation
bought of Wm. Paxson.
Wit: Jon. Ingham, Isaac Pickering, and Joseph Eastburn.

Page 164. John Wilson of Buckingham. Jan. 15, 1767. Proved
Feb. 27, 1767. Wife Jannet, son John and Friend Timothy Smith,
exrs. Son John, right of Plantation I live on both improvement
and by Deed. £100 in hands of Titus De Witt to Daus. Janet
Dougherty, Elizabeth, Ann, Isabel, and Sarah. Son Robert, £64 in
hands of John Sloan, when 21. Grandsons Samuel McGrady and John
Miller. Granddaus. Jannet and Margaret McGrady.
Wit: William Simpson, John Sample, Jas. Alexander.

Page 166. Jane Hough, of Solebury, Spinster. Mch. 17, 1767.
Proved Apr. 15, 1767. Bro. John Hough, exr. his son Jonathan and
his dau. Martha Hough.
Wit: John Brown and John Mires.

Page 169. James Dougherty of Northampton. Apr. 15, 1767.
Proved July 28, 1767. Wife Lettie, extx. 1/2 Est. the other half

to granddau. Gartery Dougherty.
Wit: Ezra Croasdale and Michel Dowd.

Page 167. Garret Kroesen, of Northampton Twp., Weaver. Jan. 4, 1758. Proved June 11, 1767. Wife Ariatie. Son John and son-in-law John VanArsdalen, exrs. 4 children of son Derrick, dec'd., viz., Ariatie, Gerret, Janitie, and Derrick. Ariatie, dau. of son Cornelius. Dau. Ariantie. Grandson Gerret, son of John Huff. Daus. Elizabeth, Affe, and Ariantee and Heirs of son Derrick, Plantation. Dau-in-law Lammetie, Land cleared by son Derrick. Wit: Henry Lott, Henry Jones, Henry Krewsen.

Page 168. William George, of Buckingham, Yeoman. Jan. 25, 1765. Proved July 24, 1767. Sons Philip (1 shilling if demanded). Son Thomas. Daus. Jane Kerrel, Martha Hylyard, Ann West, and Susanna Heyferlin. Granddau.s. Martha George and Anne Hyly. Baptist congregation at New Britain £5 John Mathews Trustee thereof. Sons-in-law John West and Cornelius Hylyard, exrs. David Stephens, Trustee.
Wit: Simon Mathew, John Boyd, David Evans.

Page 170. Amos Poole of Bucks Co., Wheelwright. July 28, 1767. Proved Aug. 8, 1767. Mother Rebecca Poole and Friend Amos Palmer, exrs. Bro. Thomas Poole. Bro-in-law Paul Pennington. Money in hand of Amos Strickland.
Wit: Marcy Carlile, Kate Hunter.

Page 170. Jacob Bennett, of Northampton, Yeoman. July 18, 1767. Proved Aug. 8, 1767. Wife Moyke and sons Simon and Jacob, exrs. Daus. Hellena Ranasey (?), Charity, Moyke, and Angenite Bennett. Son Simon, Plantation on which I live. Jacob, that on which he lives.
Wit: Thomas Wilson, Andrew Copland, Henry Wynkoop.

Page 171. Andrew Wright, of Bristol Twp., Yeoman. Apr. 19, 1761. Proved Sept. 28, 1767. Wife Rachel and Son Antony, exrs. Son Aaron, land at death of wife. Daus. Mary, Rachel, Sarah, and Plesent. Son Moses (£50 at 24).
Wit: Benjamin Swain, Daniel Hooper, and William Bidgood.

Page 172. Isaac Hodgson, of the Falls Twp. 8th mo., 31, 1767. Proved Oct. 17, 1767. Bros. David and John Hodgson. James Moon of Middletown, exr. James Moon, Junr. £5. Mark Watson £5. Bro. John Hodgson £30. Pleasant Satterthwaite £5. Land bought of Edward Bayley in Falls Twp.
Wit: William Satterthwaite, John Bayley, James Neele.

Page 173. Joseph Hamton, of Wrightstown, Yeoman. 9th mo., 15th day, 1767. Proved Nov. 19, 1767. Wife Mary. sons Benjamin and John, exrs. Daus. Sarah Wilson, Jane and Mary Hamton (each £100). Grandchildren, each £30. Son John, Land adj. Isaiah Linton, Joseph Tomlinson and London Co. on Road leading from Zebulon Heston's to Wrightstown Mtg. House. Son Benj., residue of land.
Wit: John Long, James Stokes, Andrew Horner.

Page 175. Lettice Dougherty, of Northampton. Sept. 2, 1767. Proved Dec. 9, 1767. Widow of James Dougherty, late of Northampton, dec'd. "Advanced in Years" Sons John and William Mills, exrs. Dau. Sarah Mills.
Wit: Michael Dowd and Ezra Croasdale.

Page 176. Eleanor Thomas, of Hilltown Twp., Widow. Jan. 11, 1768. Proved Feby. 26, 1768. Sons Thomas and John Thomas. Daus. Elizabeth, Mary, Pegey, Sarah, Ketren Thomas and Nealy Thomas. Grandchild, Nancy, dau. of Ketren. Land adj. Jared Erwin, William Dorroch and others. Jared Erwin and Dau. Ketren Thomas, exrs.
Wit: Robert Robinson, Henry Wismer.

Page 177. John Worman of Tinicum Twp., Yeoman. Mch. 16, 1765. Proved Apr. 5, 1768. Son Michel, exr. All Lands "in Tinicum and elsewhere." Son-in-law John Cooper of Tinicum (£20), John Heney of Bedminster, near Deep Run (10 shillings). Granddaus., children of said Heney, viz., Susannah Heney (£20 in 2 yrs.), Catharine Heney (£20 in 3 yrs.), Barbara Heney (£20 in 4 yrs.).
Wit: Edwd. Murphy, Ludwick Long, George Long.

Page 178. Daniel Tolwick of Tinicum Twp., Yeoman. Apr. 16, 1768. Proved May 4, 1768. Wife Margaret, Nicholas Wiker and John Neese, exrs. Step-son Lodowick --- (deaf and dumb), all estate for life then to children of dec'd. brother and sister, supposed to be residing in some part of America.
Wit: Edwd. Murphy, Balser Keeler, and John Hopry Lear.

Page 179. David Wilson, of Southampton, Mason. May 16, 1768. Proved June 6, 1768. Wife Grace and Sons, Thomas, Jonathan and Asaph, exrs. Sons Robert and David and Jesse. Daus. Elizabeth Baker, Dinah Besor, and Rachel Harding. Granddau. Sarah Scattergood.
Wit: Joseph Carter, Deborah Willet and William Carter.

Page 181. Ezekiel Atkinson, Weaver, Upper Makefield. 5th mo., 4th day, 1768. Proved June 23, 1768. Wife Rachel, Bro. William and Cousin Samuel Smith, exrs. Children, Benjamin, Thomas, Watson, Rachel, and child unborn (all minors).
Wit: Christopher Atkinson, Cephas Atkinson, and John Stockdale.

Page 184. Thomas Rossel, of Hilltown Twp., Yeoman. Nov. 18, 1763. Proved Oct. 22, 1768. Wife Sarah and Thomas Jones, Junr. exrs. Bro. John Rossell 1 English Crown. Residue to wife.
Wit: Jno. Phillips, Jenkin Jones, Nathaniel Jones.

Page 182. Anthony Siddon, of Newtown, Inn Keeper. July 1, 1768. Proved Aug. 19, 1768. Wife Deborah and Eldest son John, exrs. Lot in Phila. adj. Dr. Benjamin Franklin and Richard Brockden, on Market St. to be sold to pay debts. Residue to wife until dau. Martha arrive at age of 18 yrs. Then Real estate to be sold and proceeds to two daus. and rest of children.
Wit: Samuel Smith, George Campbell, and Gilbert Hicks.

Page 183. Sarah Walker, of Middletown, Widow. July 31, 1768. Proved Aug. 26, 1768. Son Joseph, dau. Sarah Thornton and son-in-law John Thornton, exrs. Sisters Elizabeth Noble and Grace Croasdale. Son George Walker. Dau. Grace Scott, Bond of £60 agt. son George with Mtge. on Lott in Attleborough which Robert Croasdale and Margery his wife conveyed to son George. Dau. Sarah, Bond £80 agt. her husband John Thornton, with Mtge. on Lot in Attleborough, which representatives of John Briggs conveyed to him. Dau. Margaret, wife of Samson Cary. Son Emanuel Walker. Granddau. Sarah Palmer.
Wit: Gilbert Hicks, Sarah Brittain, Abrm. Brittain.

Page 185. Christian Eyedam, of Nockamixon Twp. Sept. 2, 1768. Proved Nov. 17, 1768. Wife Catharine and Son Philip, exrs. Son Peter. Dau. Elizabeth. Land to Philip.
Wit: Peter Young and Henry Shieveler.

Page 188. Langhorne Biles, of the Falls Twp. Feby. 18, 1769. Proved Mch. 20, 1769. Wife Hannah and six daus. Sarah, Jonipher, Molly, Becky, Charlotte, and Nancy. When they come of age all estate. John DeNormandie and Gilbert Hicks and Thos. Yeardley, "Gentlemen" exrs. Wit: Rebecca Godly, Thos. Janney, Jr., and Richd. Gibbs.

Page 186. Joshua Glass, of Hilltown Twp. May 3, 1764. Proved Mch. 13, 1769. Oldest Bro. Daniel Glass, 2d. Bro. Samuel, 3d. Isaac, Sis. Anne and Sister's son James Kerr, all of Parish of Seapatrick, County Downs, Kingdom of Ireland. James and Daniel McCally of Fredericks Co., Virginia. Cousin Robert Glass to obtain deed for Tract of land in Frederick Co., Virginia, purchased of Arthur McConnell, which said Tract I bequeath to Thomas Glass, son of Bro. Samuel and to sister's son James Kerr both of Ireland. Cousin Robert Glass' son Samuel. Cousin Elizabeth Vance's son William. Robert Glass of Frederick Co., Va. and Matthew Grier of Plumstead Twp., Bucks Co., exrs.
Wit: Geo. Kelso, Mark Kerr, and Hugh Boden.

Griffith Davis of Solebury Twp., Bucks Co. Mar. 19, 1767. Proved Mar. 3, 1769. This will omitted from our abstracts but listed in the Index to Bucks Co. Wills. Correction made April 3, 1928. Signed Mary Hose Headman.

Page 194. John Kevill of Bristol Twp., Yeoman. Aug. 24, 1764. Proved July 4, 1769. Plantation where I live to be sold, proceeds to Kinsmen and Kinswomen Thomas, John, Alexander, James, Kevill, Rachel, and Mary Rickey, Catharine Hutchinson, and Ann Kirkbride, children of Alexander and Ann Rickey. Kinsman Kairl Rickey, Plantation adj. Wm. Bidgood, Thos. Stanaland, John Brown and John Pemberton. Bro. Joseph Kevill's children. Sister Mary Dungan's children. Sister Catharine Wilmerton. Kinsmen Kairl Rickey and Mahlon Kirkbride, exrs.
Wit: Anthony Wright, Aaron Wright, Martha Wright.

Page 195. George Hair, of Warwick, Weaver. Jan. 2, 1768. Proved July 29, 1769. Son Benjamin, exr. Son Joseph (£50). Daus.

Jean Robinson and Mary MacFarland. £21 for support of Gospel at New Pres. Mtg. House at Neshaminy. Benj. all Real Est.
Wit: David Caldwell, Tho. Barton, Wm. Davis.

Page 196. Jane Roberts, Widow of Wm. Roberts of Buckingham. May 12, 1769. Proved Sept. 2, 1769. Samuel Harrold, exr. All estate except wearing apparell. Hannah Hughes, da. of Matthew, dec'd. and Rebecca, wife of Hezekiah Guy apparel.
Wit: Samuel Fisher and John Kerr.

Page 197. Jeremiah Vastine, Senr., Hilltown, Yeoman. Aug. 30, 1769. Proved Nov. 9, 1769. Wife Deborah and son Jeremiah, exrs. Jeremiah 170 acres "where I live." Dau. Martha, wife of John Louder, 68 acres in Plumstead bought of Edward Poe. Dau. Hannah, wife of Samuel Graham.
Wit: John Thomas, Evan Pugh, David Evans.

Page 199. Mary Rue, Widow of James Rue of Bensalem. Sept. 20, 1768. Proved Nov. 29, 1769. Son Richard Rue and Friend Richard Gibbs, exrs. Son Mathew Rue. Daus. Mary Roberts, Katharine Rankins, Elizabeth Yerkes, and Sarah Kidd. Grandchildren, Joshua, Richard, Mary, and Rachel Rue, children of son Samuel, dec'd. Son Joseph Rue.
Wit: Sarah Growden, Margery Gibbs.

Page 199. Nicholas Tucker, of Buckingham, Yeoman. 11th mo., 4th day, 1769. Proved Dec. 18, 1769. Son John, exr. 140 acres I live on. Nephew Isaac Worthington, Goods purchased of Thomas Pugh and 1/2 of Pers. Est. in Trust for use of Dau. Margaret wife of Thomas Pugh for life then to her children. Dau. Sarah, wife of John Bradfield, balance of personal estate. Sons Thomas and Abraham £140 each. John. Grandchildren, Mary Tucker, William John, and Sarah Preston.
Wit: Sarah Carver, William Carver, and Sarah Thomas.

Page 201. Samuel Brown, of the Falls Twp., Yeoman. 4th mo., 15th day, 1761. Proved Dec. 25, 1769. Son George, exr., All Lands. Dau. Mary Baldwin. Dau. Esther, Bed and furniture bought of vendue of Goods of Jos. Hutchinson, dec'd. and yearly sum of £20. Samuel Bunting and Joseph White, Trustees for her under direction of Falls Mo. Mtg. Granddau. Martha Lovet and Gd.son Joseph Lovet, children of Daniel Lovet.
Wit: Jonathan Palmer, Jas. Moon, Benja. Linton, Junr.

Page 203. Isaac Piller, of Solebury Twp., Carpenter. Dec. 1, 1768. Proved Jan. 16, 1770. Wife Sarah. Son James, exr. Son Isaac, 400 acres "whereon I live.." Daus. Sarah Cowgill and Tamer Burley and Mary Elwell.
Wit: Benjamin Paxson and Mary Davis.

Page 204. Eleanor Neeld of Lower Makefield. Feb. 1, 1769. Proved Feb. 19, 1770. Son John Neeld, exr. Daus. Mary Watson and Judith ---. Grandson Amos Watson.
Wit: William Murdaugh, Benj. Palmer, Esther Palmer.

Page 205. Abram Vanhorn, of Northampton, Yeoman. Feby. 7, 1770.
Proved Apr. 2, 1773. Wife Mary. Sons Abram and Isaac, exrs. Sons
Barnet and David. Plantation to sons Abram, David, and Isaak, 85
acres adj. Saml. Palmer, dec'd. John Feaster, Samuel Dyer, Benj.
Dyer. 65 acres to David. Residue to Isaak Profits of 1/2
thereof to son Jacob for life. Daus. Mary Krewsen, Charity, and
Martha Vanschive.
Wit: Gerrardus Wynkoop, Mary Brodnax.

Page 207. Robert Stockdale, of Northampton, Yeoman. Jan. 24,
1769. Proved Aug. 10, 1772. Wife Mary, exr. Son Robert,
Plantation when 21. Sons William, George, and David. "Little
Dau. Mercy.." Wife and John Plumly, exrs. Wits.

Page 209. Lawrence Growdon, of Trevose, Bucks Co., No Date.
Proved May 1, 1770. "Aged and infirm." Wife Sarah, annuity of
£200 and use of Larger House on Arch St., Phila. where Thomas
Lawrence Esq. now lives. Ann Janney and Rebecca Godly, each £50.
Richard Gibbs "my clerk," £100, his wife Margery, £100. Their 4
children, Samuel, Mary, Sarah, and Elizabeth, £100 each at 21.
Cousin Mary Smith of Trenton and her sister Bessonett each £50.
Lawrence Growden of St. Wen or elsewhere in England, annuity of
£5 sterling. Grandchildren by daus. Elizabeth Nickleson and
Grace Galloway £1000 each, "residue of estate Personal I have or
ought to have in Great Britain" and son-in-law Thomas Nickleson,
"agreeable to what I wrote him my estate there called "Trevose"
being formerly settled by marriage articles with my first wife."
Residue of estate, real and personal, to Daus. Elizabeth
Nichleson and Grace Galloway. Wife and sons-in-law Thomas
Nickleson and Joseph Galloway, exrs.
Wit: Gilbert Hicks, John DeNormandie.

Page 210. John Baldwin, of Neshaminy Ferry. Oct. 30, 1765.
Proved May 11, 1770. Sons John and Joseph, exrs. John, 50 acres
of Tract I dwell on in Bristol Twp. adj. Charles Edgar, Joseph
Tomlinson, and William Sturgeon. Son Joseph, 150 acres of sd.
Tract on East side of Neshaminy, also Flats, Utensils, and
Vessels belonging to Ferry. Residue to children John, Rachel
Gilbert, Sarah Gilbert, Rebecca Lancaster, and son Joseph. Daus.
each 1/2 acre Lot and House in Bristol Boro. adj. each other and
adj. land late Wm. Large, dec'd. where Davis Davis, Thos. Brown,
and Rees Meredith live.
Wit: Edmund Sands, Charles Lovett, Wm. Davis.

Page 211. James Price, of Middletown, Date. Apr. 16, 1770.
Proved June 26, 1770. Wife Sarah and William Satterthwaite the
elder, exrs. Son James. Daus. Pamelia and Rebecca Price, £200
each at age of 18 yrs.
Wit: William Huddleston and Joseph Huddleston.

Page 213. John Porter, of Northampton Twp., "Road Maker." July
8, 1770. Pr. July 23, 1770. Grandson Robert Porter and James
Dungan, exrs. Son Thomas, 5 shillings. Grandchildren, Robert,
John, and Margaret Porter residue of est. Jacob Myers "with whom
I live" £3.

Wit: Jacob Myers, Garret Dungan, James Dungan.

Page 214. Jane Scott of Southampton, Widow of Benjamin Scott, the Elder. Apr. 23, 1770. Proved Aug. 8, 1770. "Advanced in Years." Dower in Land of husband (Lee Rolls Office Bucks Co. Book D. Vol. 3 p. 98). Dau. Rebecca States and son-in-law, Ezra Croasdale, exrs. Benjamin Croasdale and Hannah Croasdale issue of dau. Hannah Croasdale, dec'd. Granddau.s. Martha Willet and Rachel Harding issue of dau. Jane Harding, dec'd. Grandsons Benjamin and Joseph Scott, sons of Benjamin, dec'd.
Wit: Mercy Comfort and Mary Eastburn.

Page 215. John Winder, of Lower Makefield. Aug. 6, 1770. Proved Sept. 5, 1770. Wife Rebecca and Son John, exrs. Son Thomas, Plantation where he lives adj. Benj. Canby and Lamb Torbert. Son Aaron. Sons James and Moses, Plantation "where I live.." Daus. Elizabeth Linton, Sarah Whitacre. Hannah Brooks, Rebecca, Mary, and Ann Winder.
Wit: Jane Slack, John Chapman, Wm. Yeardley.

Page 217. Deborah Johnson, of Bensalem, "Spinstress." Dated Aug. 5, 1770. Proved Sept. 8, 1770. Codicil same date. Bros. Peter and Benjamin Johnson, exrs. and sole legatees. Mary, wife of Lawrence Johnson. Sister Wilmoth, wife of Jacob Vandegrift. Cousin Deborah Johnson, dau. of Benj.
Wit: Aaron Lovett, John Evans, Adam Weaver.

Page 218. Mathew Rice, of Middletown, Date July 2, 1770. Proved Nov. 15, 1770. Wife Mary. Son Richard Rue and John Bessonett, exrs. Dau. Mary Case and her dau. Mary, house in Trenton where she lives. her sons each £40. Dau. Catharine (100 acres). Grandsons Benjamin and Lewis Rue, sons of son Mathew, dec'd. Also widow of son Mathew and residue of land. Grandson Mathew, son of Richard. Children of son Lewis, dec'd. Granddaus. Mary Ramsey and Rebecca, eldest dau. of Benjamin Gown.
Wit: John DeNormandie and Charles Bessonett.

Page 220. William Wood, of the Falls, Blacksmith. July 17, 1770. Proved Nov. 19, 1770. Mother Elizabeth Wood, Rents of Plantation in Falls for Life then to Bro. John Wood. Mahlon Kirkbride and Wm. Yeardley, exrs.
Wit: John Roberts, Daniel Linton, Charles Clark.

Page 221. Samuel Harvey, of Falls, "Practitioner in Physic." July 29, 1770. Proved Nov. 19, 1770. Wife Catharine, extx., pregnant, Plantation to child if it survive, if it dye to Bros. Thomas, William, and John Harvey, and Sister Elizabeth Gillingham, wifes Bros. and Sister's viz. Mary, Jane, John, and Peter Vansiller and Samuel Timbrook. Wife and Wm. Yeardley, exrs.
Wit: Joseph Gillingham, Jona. Kirkbride, Jos. Milnor.

Page 223. Peter Ceveler of Nockamixon Twp., Husbandman. Aug. 17, 1770. Proved Nov. 30, 1770. Wife Katrin, extx. Sisters son Adam Osterday.
Wit: Peter Michael, Adam Black.

Page 224. Simon VanArsdalen, of Southampton, Yeoman. Sept. 29, 1766. Proved Dec. 5, 1770. Sons John and Nicholas, exrs. Nicholas, Plantation. Son John, dau. Lamety Wycoff. Children of son Stophell, dec'd. Margaret Krewsen, son Simon Junr. Jacobus and Nicholas. Dau. Lamety's late husband's exrs. Wit: Jacob Vansant, Daniel Hogeland, and Jos. Davenport. Signed Syme VanArdalen.

Page 226. Mary Barr, of Warwick, Widow. July 8, 1770. Proved Dec. 12, 1770. Son Adam Barr, exr. Son George and Thomas Barr under 16. Dau. Martha Hirst. Wit: William Corbet, John Thomas, Thos. Chapman.

Page 227. Susanna Heaton, Northampton Twp., "Antient." Jan. 15, 1766. Proved Jan. 24, 1771. Son Joseph Carter, exr. Entitled Annuity as per Bond given by son William Carter, dec'd. to late husband, Robert Heaton, dec'd., dated Mch. 2, 1731/2, bequeath same to son-in-law John Plumb to be recovered of son Robert Heaton's, exrs. Grandsons Richard and William Carter, son of Joseph. Katharine Hayhurst, dau. of Sarah Hayhurst. Granddau. Mary Plumly. Ann Carter dau. of Rachel and Joseph. Residue to grandchildren, Isabel, Susanna, and John Heaton at 21. Wit: Jas. Cooper, Ezra Croasdale, and Sarah Hayhurst (dau. Ann Hibbs, granddau. Susanna Hebbs).

Page 229. Jacob Vandegrift, of Bensalem Twp. Oct. 4, 1770. Proved May 11, 1771. Sons John and Bernard, exrs. John £20 beside Plantation already given him. Bernard, Plantation in Lower Dublin Twp. late belonging to Peter Keen, 210 acres also 5 acres of Meadow late Neels Boon's. Son Jacob, Plantation "whereon I dwell." Daus. Charity and Hellen. Bro. Abraham. Wit: Wm. Baker, James Horn, Anne Foster.

Page 230. William Dungan, of Warminster Twp., Yeoman. Apr. 11, 1770. Proved June 6, 1771. Wife Catharine. Son-in-law Isaac Hill and Thomas Barton, exrs. Son Nathan, 7 acres 140 P. bought of John Crawford, where I live. Son John, Plantation where he lives. Sons William, Joseph, Jeremiah, and Joshua. Daus. Mary Shaw, Ann Stephens, and Elizabeth Hill. Granddau. Rachel Eaton. Wit: Joseph Barton, James Evans, David Evans.

Page 232. Ely Welding, of Buckingham, Blacksmith. 4-13-1763. Proved June 11, 1771. Wife Elizabeth, extx., all personal estate, except £10 to Ely Carver, and plantation of 172 acres purchased of Humphrey Murray, 172, 1/2 acres adj. John Beal, Joseph Watson, William Corbet and Patrick Malone also 17 perches of land adj. Jos. Watson and Nicholas Tucker, purchased of Alex Beal - during life then to grandson Watson Welding. Granddau.s. Elizabeth, Hannah, and Ann Welding. Wit: Patrick Malone. John Beal and John Malone.

Page 233. William Taylor, of Newtown, Yeoman. 8th mo., 13th day, 1770. Proved June 18, 1771. Wife Hannah, all Est., Friend Bernard Taylor, exr. Wit: Robert Hillborn and Samuel Hillborn.

Page 235. Thomasin Hollingshead, of Co. of Somerset, N.J. Jan.
3, 1757. Proved Aug. 20, 1771. Sons Francis and William each 1
shilling. Residue to Dau. Elizabeth Hollingshead, extx.
Wit: Wm. Hollingshead and Benjamin Hunt.

Page 237. Agnes Mitchel, of Middletown Twp., Widow. Apr. 29,
1768. Proved Aug. 30, 1771. Son Thomas Warner and son-in-law
James Wildman, exrs. Children, John, Joseph Croasdale, Abraham,
Isaac and Thomas Warner, Mary Wildman, Ruth Warner and Sarah
Wigons. Granddau.s. Agnes Wigons.
Wit: John Thornton, Sarah Thornton.

Page 238. Deborah Town, of Bristol Twp. July 20, 1771. Proved
Sept. 6, 1771. Bro. Benjamin Town, exr. Bro. Thomas Town. Two
Brothers wives Catharine and Elizabeth Town. Sisters Mary Rue and
Rebecca Tawser. Aunt Joyce Johnson. Catharine Rue, dau. of
sister Mary. Rebecca, wife of Joseph Belford.
Wit: Gilbt. Rodman, Norris Carr.

Page 239. Elizabeth Beans, of Southampton, Widow. Dec. 27,
1768. Proved Sept. 16, 1771. Dau. Elinor and Son Joseph Beans,
exrs. Sons Joseph, Mathew, Thomas, Timothy, Jacob, and William.
Dau. Elizabeth Sands and Elinor Beans. Grandson Jesse Beans, son
of James dec'd.
Wit: Abel Morgan, Mary Morgan, Daniel Longstreth. Letters to
Elinor.

Page 240. John Lacey, of Buckingham, Yeoman. Aug. 8th mo., 1st
day, 1766. Proved Sept. 11, 1771. Son John and Son-in-law John
Wilkinson, exrs. Son John land of S. side of line drawn from
Great Gate on Road leading from Mill to Wrightstown to Mill Race.
Residue of Real estate to dau-in-law Hester Lacey so long as she
remains widow of son Joseph, dec'd. Grandsons Joseph and Isaac
and other children of son Joseph. Dau. Mary Wilkinson and Sarah
Lacey. Grandsons John Lacey, John Wilkinson. Granddaus. Hannah
and Mary Lacey.
Wit: Jos. Hamton, John Terry, Jesse Heston.

Page 242. Rudolf Drach, of Rockhill Twp., Yeoman. Jan. 5, 1770.
Proved Oct. 1, 1771. Wife Marelas, all estate for life, except £5
to son Henry. at her death to "our surviving children." Sons
Henry and Adam and 6 daus. named in agreement bearing even date
herewith. Peter Drak and Philip Shrias, exr. Codicil dated
April 1, 1771. Dau. Susanna having died leaving husband Lodrick
Siple and child Henry Madlenah.
Wit: Abraham Landis, Johan Philip DyerWynr and John Jamison.

Page 244. Thomas Morris, of Hilltown Twp., Yeoman. July 5,
1771. Proved Oct. 12, 1771. Wife Ann. Sons Isaac and Thomas,
exrs. Plantation. Daus. Phebe Griffith and Mary, wife of Robert
Dorroch. Grandchildren. Howell and Ann James. Jos. Griffith and
Thos. James, Junr., Trustees.
Wit: James Armstrong, John Lewis, Adam Frowlan.

Page 246. William Blackfan, of Solebury Twp. 8th mo., 12th day,

1765. Proved Oct. 17, 1771. "Ancient and infirm" Wife Elinor. Eldest son Crispin, exr. Son William, 4 acres 100 P. adj. 153 acres 134 P. already conveyed to him adj. Pidkcocks Creek. Eldest Dau. Elizabeth Ely. Daus. Sarah Wood, Hannah Paxson, and Rebekah Bye. Twin Granddaus. Rebekah and Sarah, dau. of Crispin. Residue of land 200 acres as per Patent dated 11th mo., 1st day, 1733 to son Crispin.
Wit: Cephas Atkinson, Thos. Smith, Wm. Lee, Junr.

Page 248. Elinor Blackfan, of Solebury Twp. 10th mo., 4th day, 1771. Proved Oct. 17, 1771. Son William Blackfan, exr. Dau. Elizabeth Ely, all Est. except looking glass to granddau. Elizabeth Blackfan, dau. of Wm.
Wit: Thos. Ross, Thos. Smith.

Page 249. John Anderson of Saulsbury Twp., Cordwainer. Nov. 1, 1771. Proved Nov. 25, 1771. Wife Sarah and Robert Henderson, of Buckingham, exrs. Son James, Father James Anderson. Bros. Israel, Joseph, David and Joshua. Nephew John Brooks, son of Thos. and Hannah.
Wit: Richard Vandike and John Kerr.

Page 252. Hugh Ely of Buckingham Twp., Yeoman. 8th mo., 22nd day, 1764. Proved Jan. 29, 1772. Wife Phebe. Sons Thomas and Hugh, exrs. Thomas' son Hugh, dau. Ann wife of Peter Matson. Children of dau. Anna, late wife of John Wilkinson son Hugh Plantation 250 acres.
Wit: Isaac Pickering, Joseph Watson, Paul Preston.

Page 250. Joseph Beans, of Southampton Twp., Yeoman. Aug. 4, 1771. Proved Dec. 9, 1771. Wife Hester. Sons Seth and James and Jos. Hart, exrs. Son John and his children, John, James, Hester, Mary. Wife use of House Garden and 3 acres of Meadow in Tenure of Joseph Van Pelt for life then to son Mathew. Residue to Seth and James.
Wit: John Brooks, Jesse Banes, Thos. Folwell.

Page 254. Mary Shaw of Northampton Twp., Widow. 5th mo., 18, 1771. Proved Feby. 11, 1772. Son-in-law Phineas Paxson and Daniel Longstreth, exrs. Daus. Mary Strickland and Susanna Paxson. Grandsons John Croasdale, Thomas, Jonathan, Isaac and Abraham Harding and Joseph Shaw Paxson. Granddau.s. Sarah Harding and Anna, Mary and Susanna Strickland. Grandchildren, Anna, Joseph, Mary and John Croasdale. Having brought up grandson John Croasdale from 2 yrs. of age until apprenticed to Isaac Longstreth, his father Eber Croasdale to be charged £88 being £8 pr. yr. for 11 yrs.
Wit: James Vansant, Joseph Longstreth, and Rebecca Worthington. Codicil 1-1-1772. Wit: Hannah Gumry.

Page 256. Jean McLeroy, of Nockamixon, Widow. June 21, 1770. Proved Feby. 18, 1772. George McLeroy and Nicholas McCarty, exrs. Son Alexander. Daus. Agnes, wife of John Scott; Gean Goans, wife of --- Goans; Dau. Sarah Goans. Sons in law Samuel and Derrick Goans. Grandchildren, Wm. and Gean Scott. Gean Jones dau. of

Gean, Wm. Goans son Samuel. William Goans son of Derrick. Wm.
McLeroy son of Alexander and Jean, James McLeroy son of Alex and
Jean.
Wit: Margaret Baxter, Edward McCarty. Letters granted to Geo.
McLeroy.

Page 258. Elizabeth Carver, of Warwick Twp., Widow. 2nd mo.,
9th day, 1771. Proved Mch. 2, 1772. Son-in-law Isaac
Worthington, exr. Son Joseph Carver. Wm. Carver. Henry Carver.
Late husband William Carver, of Buckingham. Daus. Elizabeth
Buckman, Mary Wilkinson, Rebecca Schofield, and Martha
Worthington. Grandchildren, William, John and Mary Worthington.
Wit: Wm. Worthington, Thos. Tomlinson, Tho. Chapman.

Page 260. Amos Shaw, of the Falls Twp., Yeoman. 2nd mo., 4th
day, 1772. Proved Mch. 10, 1772. Codicil 2nd mo., 12th day,
1772. Wife Catharine and George Brown, exrs. 6 children, Anne,
Robert, Elizabeth, Amos, Thomas, and Margaret. "Relation Margaret
Shaw."
Wit: James Darraygh, Michael Stackhouse, John Brown.

Page 261. Joanna Tomlinson, of Bensalem Twp. 3rd mo., 6th day,
1772. Proved Mch. 23, 1772. Widow of Thomas Tomlinson of same
place, dec'd. Sons Joseph and Francis, exrs. Son Joseph. Daus.
Elizabeth Shearman and Mary Hommer. Granddaus. Rebecca and Joanna
Tomlinson and Joanna Hommer.
Wit: Rynear Hallowell, Elizabeth Ashton, and Thos. Tomlinson.
Letters granted to Francis only.

Page 263. Clement Doyle, of New Britain Twp., Yeoman. Sept. 8,
1771. Proved Apr. 11, 1772. Wife Margaret. Son Richard, exr.
Sons John and Jonathan. Daus. Rebecca Byle and Margaret Evans.
Wit: Thos. Fell and George Fell.

Page 264. Thomas James, of New Britain Twp., Yeoman. Mch. 14,
1772. Proved Apr. 13, 1772. Son John, exr. Sons Samuel, James,
and Thomas. Daus. Elizabeth, Aaron and Rachel Shewell. Margaret
and Benj. James, children of son John. £5 to New Britain Baptist
Church. John Williams and James Evans, Trustees.
Wit: John James, Wm. James, David Evans.

Page 266. Lambert Vandyke, of Southampton, Yeoman. Mch. 13,
1770. Proved Apr. 13, 1772. Wife Mary. Son Jacob and Friend
Henry Kroesen, exrs. Sons Jacob, Richard, Adrian, Henry (his bond
date June 11, 1755), John, Cornelius and Hezekiah. Daus. Jane
Rue, Elizabeth Bartley. Land bought of Samuel Swift, deed dated
Apr. 19, 1733 of Jeremiah Langhorne Dated Sept. 23, 1736.
Wit: Wilhelmus Cornell, John Leedom, and John Watts.

Page 268. Joseph Richardson, of Attleboro, Gent. Sept. 20,
1770. Proved Apr. 29, 1772. Wife Mary and Sons Joshua and
William, exrs. Daus. Rebecca, wife of Thomas Jenks, Junr. (112
acres); Ruth Richardson (Land in Southampton formerly Philip
Dracords); Mary Richardson (150 acres bought of Edwd. Glover). 4
children of Son Joshua, viz., Joseph, Sarah, Mary, and Jane. 4

children of son William, viz., Rachel, Marcy, Ann and Elizabeth.
4 children of dau. Rebecca Jenks, viz., Jus. Richardson Jenks,
Rachel, Marcy and Mary Jenks. Land bought of John Parsons (200
acres) of Wm. Huddleston (60 acres) of Wm. Shreeve. of Heirs of
Joseph Walker (319 acres).
Wit: William Blakey, Stephen Comfort, Gilbert Hicks.

Page 271. Daniel Bratt, of Middletown Twp., Yeoman. Mch. 28,
1772. Proved May 8, 1772. Son Samuel land devised to wife
Elizabeth by father-in-law John Cowley adj. Thos. Jenks, Junr.,
Patrick Gregg, and late Amos Palmer. Daus. Martha Ashton. Dau.
Margaret Johnston, land where she lives adj. Jonathan Carlile and
others. Granddaus. Elizabeth Twining and Letitia, Pleasant,
Silence, and Margaret Ashton. William Yeardley, exr.
Wit: Hw. Thompson, Andrew McMinn, and Patrick Gregg.

Page 273. Titus Dewitt of Salisbury Twp., Bucks Co. Mch. 24,
1772. Proved May 16, 1772. Wife Elizabeth. Son Peter, exr.
Plantation, etc. 3 daus. Ann and two others.
Wit: William Roberts, John Hutchinson.

Page 274. Simeon Pownall, of Solebury, Yeoman. 2nd mo., 14th
day, 1772. Proved May 16, 1772. Wife Catharine and Friend Joseph
Eastburn, exrs. 3 sons, Simeon, Levi and Moses. 5 daus. Ann,
Mary, Hannah, Margaret, and Katharine.
Wit: Aaron Phillips, Mary Phillips, Paul Preston.

Page 277. Stephen Twining, of Wrightstown, Yeoman. 8th mo., 8th
day, 1771. Proved July 31, 1772. Wife Margaret. Son Stephen,
exr. Dau. Abigail Hillborn's children, viz., Samuel, Joseph,
Mary, Elizabeth Hillborn, 50 acres of land in Springfield Twp.
adj. land late Casper Wistars and James Logan. Her other
children, John, Thomas, William and David Hillborn. Dau. Mary
Chapman, widow of John Chapman, 50 acres in Springfield afsd.
adj. Jacob Hooker, Abrm. Funk and John Moffit. Son Stephen, 100
acres in Wrightstown adj. Richard Mitchell, late Hugh Young and
late John Chapman. Son-in-law Samuel Hillborn, dau. Margaret,
wife of Thomas Hamilton and her children, grandsons Stephen,
William and Joseph Kirk. Thomas Kirk son of Isaac and Rachel.
Wit: James Briggs, Junr., John Story, Junr., John Story.

Page 284. Oliver O'Haighan of Warminster, Yeoman. July 29,
1772. Proved Oct. 26, 1772. Wife Catharine, extx. and sole
legatee.
Wit: James Wallace, Willm. Man and Samuel McRafferty.

Page 279. Jonathan Abbett, of Northampton, Cordwainer. Feby.
17, 1772. Proved Aug. 24, 1772. Son William. Grandsons
Jonathan, son of Jonathan Abbett, dec'd., William, Henry and
Dennis sons of son William. Bro. Richard Abbett, living in
Government of Virginia (if living). Richard Leedom and Jacob
Twining, exrs. £5 to overseers of Wrightstown Friends Mtg. £10
to overseers of Southampton Baptist Mtg.
Wit: John Addis and Phineas Paxson.

Page 281. Rev. Charles Beatty, of Warminster. Apr. 13, 1772.
Proved Sept. 14, 1772. Son John and Friends Henry Wynkoop, Esq.
of Northampton and Samuel Erwin of Moreland, exrs. Estate, real
and personal to be sold. Land in Hardwick Twp., Sussex Co. West
Jersey. sold to Thomas Fleming of Bethlehem, W. Jersey to be
confirmed to him by executors. Son John £100, residue to sons and
daus., when of age. Dau. Mary Green. Sons Charles, Clinton, and
Reading to attend College of N.J. Bro-in-law Rev. William Mills
of Jamaica, overseer, also Rev. Richard Treat of Abington.
Wit: Adam Kerr, Nathl. Ellicott, Willm. Man.

Page 283. James Evans, of New Britain, Yeoman. Sept. 3, 1772.
Proved Oct. 20, 1772. Wife Margaret and Bro. David Evans, exrs.
Bro. Daniel Evans, Eldest son Isaac and Brother David's Eldest
son James. £6 to John Mathew, and David Stephens, Deacons of New
Britain Baptist Church, for support of minister at said Church.
Wit: Thos. Jones, Thos. Jones, Junr., Richard Riale. Letters to
Margaret.

Page 285. Abraham Vastine, of Hilltown, Gent. Dated May 9, 1770.
Proved Oct. 31, 1772. Codicil Dated May 9, 1772. Wife Sarah 1/2
of Grist Mill and Land in Bedminster Twp. in Tenure of John
Clymer. Dau. Ruth wife of James Armstrong. Daus. Abigail wife
of Andrew Armstrong. Rachel Mearns wife of Hugh Mearns, her 4
children, viz., Robert, Abraham, William, and Sarah Mearns. Dau.
Sarah, wife of Samuel Wilson. Mary, wife of Robert Jamison.
Grandson Abraham son of James and Ruth Armstrong. Wife and son-
in-law James Armstrong exrs.
Wit: Benjamin Mathias, Adam Fowler, Rachel Berry.

Page 288. Joseph Wilson, of Lower Makefield, Wheelwright. 10th
mo., 24th day, 1772. Proved Nov. 16, 1772. Wife Rachel and Uncle
James Moon, exrs. 3 children, Achilles, Mary, and Latitia Wilson.
Land bought of Patrick Gregg.
Wit: John Winner, Rachel Neeld, Richard Neeld.

Page 289. Michael Eberhard, of Lower Milford Twp., Yeoman. Oct.
15, 1768. Proved Nov. 21, 1772. "Advanced in life" "To be buried
in Church Yard near Reformed Calvinish Church in Upper Milford
not far distant from my Plantation." Wife Anna. Eldest son
Michael. Youngest son John. Daus. Elizabeth and Anne . Eldest
dau. Margaret, wife of Peter Wetzel. Wife Anna and John Heany,
exrs. 230 acres adj. upper County line and Lands Christian
Wollawer, Andrew Beyer and Lawrence Eberhard 25 acres in Richland
Manor adj. Jacob Beider and Ulrich Spinner.
Wit: Andrew Keithline, John Keller, and Dave Shultze.

Page 308. Richard Margerum, of Lower Makefield, Blacksmith.
Feby. 17, 1773. Proved Mch. 6, 1773. Wife Rebecca and John
White, Senr., exrs. 2 children, Henry and Fankey Margerum.
Benjamin Margerum, coate etc.
Wit: Herman Margerum, Benj. Margerum, Edwd. Margerum.

Page 299. Stephen Comfort, of Middletown. 9th mo., 20th day,
1772. Proved Dec. 9, 1772. Wife Mary and Jeremiah Comfort, exrs.

Sons John, Ezra, Jeremiah, Stephen, Moses and Robert. Dau. Grace and Marcy. Son John and Mary his wife "all that estate of John Woolman lying in the Jerseys or anywhere else.."
Wit: Robert Croasdale, Macre Wilson.

Page 302. Sarah Watson of Upper Makefield, "Spinster." Mch. 27, 1770. Proved Jan. 15, 1773. Dau. Mary Harvey, her son Jonathan Harvey. Son John Brown yearly income due and to become due from my 1st husband's Est. and Bond mentioned in Will of last husband. Grandchildren, George, Jonathan, Susanna, and Lucresia Kinsey.
Wit: Jonathan Kirkbride, Elizabeth Kirkbride and Mahlon Kirkbride. Letters granted to Mary, wife of Henry Harvey.

Page 303. Jonathan Knight, of Southampton. 3rd mo., 25th day, 1772. Proved Jan. 18, 1773. Wife Grace, and Son John, exrs. Land bought of John Eastburn. Sons John, Abraham, Absalom, David, Samuel, and English. David Buckman, Giles Knight and James Thornton, Trustees.
Wit: Joseph Knight, Samuel Biles, and Ezra Croasdale.

Page 300. Titus Fell, of Buckingham, Yeoman. June 11, 1772. Proved Dec. 14, 1772. Wife Elizabeth (Exr.) and Mother, use of Plantation for life, then to son Zenas. 2 dau. Charity and Joyce. Dau. Rachel, Christian Freise's time to son Zenas.
Wit: Jonathan Fell, John Fell.

Page 306. John Earles, of Warminster, Yeoman. Nov. 13, 1772. Proved Jan. 21, 1773. Wife Margaret and Friend James Wallace, exrs. Grandsons John Vanhorn and Earles Barnes. Daus. Mary, wife of John Barnes; Isabella, wife of Barnard Vanhorn; and Margaret, late wife of William Erwin, dec'd.
Wit: Nathl. Ellicot, Willm. Man, John Carr.

Page 309. Elinor Jones, of New Britain, Widow. Feby. 17, 1773. Proved Mch. 9, 1773. "Stricken in years." Kinswoman Margaret, wife of Wm. Davis with whom I reside. Their children, Abednego, Ann Brown, Rebecca Rowland, and Sarah Foster. Ann Brown's dau. Mary Evans. Rebecca Rowland's dau. Margaret Rowland. Hester Truby wife of John living in Virginia. John Thomas, Baptist Minister in Hilltown. Rachel Davis, widow of Rev. William Davis formerly Minister at New Britain. Mathew Adams of New Britain and Twin children, Mathew and Richard. Hannah, wife of David Lewellyn. Ezekiel Wilson of Hilltown. Stepson Benjamin Jones and his wife Elizabeth. Mathew Adams and Cadwallader Morris of Hilltown, exrs.
Wit: Gwen Morris and John Wisler.

Page 313. John Sebring of "Salisbury" Twp. Feby. 16, 1773. Proved Mch. 13, 1773. Wife Elinor. Eldest son Roeloff. Sons John, Fulkerd, Thomas. Daus. Elizabeth, Christine, Agnes and Elinor. 1/8 part of undivided right where widow Hart keeps Tavern in Plumstead. Sons Roeloff and Thomas, exrs.
Wit: John Tasman, Derrick Kroesen, John Hutchinson.

Page 315. George Emig of Springfield Twp., Farmer. Mch. 2,

1773. Proved Mch. 15, 1773. Wife Mary. Son George, exrs. All Lands and Est. at death of wife. Bible to Dutch Reformed Church of Springfield.
Wit: Peter Seen, Michael Smell, Peter Hest.

Page 316. Daniel Palmer, of Lower Makefield, Yeoman. 9th mo., 12th day, 1771. Proved Mch. 23, 1773. Codicil 11-7-1772. Wife Mary and sons Daniel and Joshua, exrs. Son Caleb. Dau. Hannah, widow of son Amos 50 acres bought of Margery Kirkbride and 68 acres formerly Amos Palmer's. her son Abner and daus. Letitia and Theodosia. Son Daniel 50 acres bought of Richard Hough. Dau. Margery Hutchinson.
wits. Jas. Thackray, Junr., Benjamin Palmer, Mahlon Kirkbride.

Page 320. Lewis Lanoir, of Bristol Twp., Yeoman. 9th mo., 1771. Proved Mch 12, 1773. Wife Mary and Friend Joseph Atkinson, exrs. Dau. Ann, all Lands etc at death of wife. 40 shillings to use of Friends Mtg. at Bristol, Samuel Bunting, present overseer.
Wit: Joseph Hall, Jos. Brown, Mary Lowry.

Page 322. Benjamin Linton to Lower Makefield, Weaver. 4th mo., 9th day, 1772. Proved May 11, 1773. Wife Jane and sons Benjamin and Samuel, exrs. Sons Samuel, Daniel, Hezekiah, John and Joshua. Daus. Jane Satterthwaite, Lucia and Martha Linton.
Wit: Jona. Kirkbride, Elizabeth Kirkbride and Joseph Taylor.

Page 323. Elinor Baines of Warminster. Mch. 1, 1773. Proved May 14, 1773. Daniel Longstreth, exr. Richard Sands and his Dau. Elinor Sands. Anna White, dau. of Bro. Mathew. Jesse, Phebe and Elizabeth Baines, children of Bro. James, dec'd. Martha and Rachel Longstreth. Thos. Spicer Jones, son of Rev. Samuel Jones. Sarah Harding, dau. of Henry Harding. Residue to Hester and Mary Baines daus. of Cousin John Baines, their bros. Joseph and James Baines.
Wit: John Folwell, Arthur Watt, and John Longstreth.

Page 325. Elizabeth Welding, widow of Ely Welding, Buckingham. 10th mo., 1771. Proved May 22, 1773. Grandson Watson Welding exr. and granddau. Hannah Welding. Cousin Sarah Beal. Granddau. Elizabeth Platerer.
Wit: Patrick Malone, John Malone, Thos. Watson.

Page 327. Edmund Sands, of Bensalem, Farmer. 5th mo., 2nd day, 1773. Proved May 25, 1773. Wife Mary and cousin John Mitchell, exrs. Bros. Thomas, William, Abraham, Benjamin Sands. Sis. Jennet Clauson and Mary ---.
Wit: James How, John Vandegrift, John Evans.

Page 328. Anna Paxson of Middletown, Widow. 1st mo., 1st day, 1773. Proved June 1, 1773. Bro. Joseph Marriott of Phila. and Relation Joshua Richardson of Middletown, exrs. Daus. Mary and Ann. Sons William, Isaac, Joshua, Joseph, Phineas, Thomas, Mahlon, Samuel, Israel.
Wit: John Woolston, Mary Richardson, Elizabeth Woolston.

Page 330. Louisa Knowles, of Upper Makefield. Mch. 12, 1773. Proved June 11, 1773. Mother Catharine Knowles, extx. John Beaumont to assist her. Dau. Louisa. Nephews Joseph Holcombe and James Hartley. Sister Sarah's children, viz., Rebecca, Hannah, and Joseph Phillips.
Wit: James McMasters, James Mathew, John Beaumont.

Page 332. Rachel Dawson, of Solebury Twp. 6th mo., 19th day, 1773. Proved July 26, 1773. Father Thomas Dawson and Mother, exrs. Jonathan Smith, son of Edmund Smith and Sarah his wife, my sister dec'd. Rachel, Elizabeth, Hannah, and Agnes Blackfan. Dau. of my.(?) Esther, wife of William Blackfan of Solebury.
Wit: Henry Paxson, Aaron Paxson and William Blackfan.

Page 333. Nicholas Dillon, of Bedminster Twp. 7th mo., 2nd day, 1773. Proved Sept. 23, 1773. Wife Mary and Anthony Kennard of Bedminster, exrs. Daus. Bridget Dillon, Mary Shaw, Rebecca Vickers, Esther Doan, and Elizabeth Townsend. Son Thomas and his children, Amos, Isaiah and Thomas Dillon, Junr.
Wit: Jonathan Shaw, John Carlile and Benjamin Cutler.

Page 335. Robert Davis, of Warrington, Yeoman. Oct. 17, 1772. Proved Sept. 27, 1773. John Crawford, Senr. of Warrington, exr. Sons Jonathan and Robert. Daus. Leah Patorius and Rachel, wife of Thomas Jones of New Britain. Grandson William Pastorius. Granddaus. Sarah, eldest dau. of son Robert and Rachel Jones. Land adj. James Dunlap, George Shoemaker and Thomas Rickey.
Wit: Joseph Wallace, John Wallace, and Thos. Lusk.

Page 339. Mary Linton, of Northampton Twp. 1st mo., 10th day, 1765. Proved Oct. 1, 1773. Son Joseph Linton and Son-in-law Thomas Winder, exrs. Sons Joseph, Isaac, Jonathan. Daus. Elizabeth Winder, Mary Walker, and Phebe. Grandson Nehemiah Linton son of Joseph, Land purchased of Robert Walker and wife.
Wit: Joseph Walker, James Wildman, John Woolston.

Page 341. Eleanor Kelly of Hilltown, Widow. Sept. 18, 1773. Proved Oct. 20, 1773. David Stephens of New Britain and Thos. Jones of Hilltown, exrs. Son Erasmus Kelly. Gdsons John Kelly and Rachel his wife and Erasmus Kelly. Granddaus. Catharine, Sidney, Mary, Hannah, Eleanor, and Rachel Kelly and Eleanor Thompson. Eleanor Thompson, dau. of sd. Eleanor. Niece Sidney George, Schoolmistress. Grandson Benjamin Kelly, Mathew Grier, of Plumstead, Trustee. Land adj. Abraham Kratts and Abraham Dursten.
Wit: Edwd. Jones, Abrm. Krats, and Barbara Krats.

Page 346. Leffert Leffertse of Northampton. Oct. 6, 1773. Proved Nov. 20, 1773. Wife Anna and sons Peter and Arthur, exrs. Other sons Leffert, John, Abraham, and Jacobus. Daus. Sylvee and Ida. Land in Newtown lately bought of Wm. Abbett.
Wit: Rem Cornell and Henry Wynkoop.

Page 348. Esther Hoskins, of Town and County of Chester. 7th mo., 11th day, 1773. Proved Jan. 3, 1774. Nephews Joshua and Wm.

Blakey and Niece Lydia Smith, exrs. Sister Hannah King living near Skipton in Yorkshire "Old England" and her 3 children. Nephew Joshua Blakey and his dau. Esther. Niece Ruth Walker. Nephew Wm. Blakey and wife Sarah. Nephew Stacy Beaks.
Wit: John Woolston, John Woolston, Junr., James Wildman.

Page 350. Thomas Simpson of Newtown, Yeoman. Dec. 23, 1773. Proved Jan. 11, 1774. Wife Sarah and Francis Murray, Merchant of Newtown, exrs. Bro. William Simpson, Yeoman, and cousin William Simpson, Blacksmith.
Wit: Jane McCoy, Thos. Janney, Andrew McMinn.

Page 352. Nicholas Grougher, of Tinicum Twp. May 15, 1772. Proved Feby. 1, 1774. Wife Ulifronica. Son Nicholas and Jacob Beidleman, exrs. 5 children, Nicholas, Philip, Mary, Barbara and Anna Elizabeth.
Wit: John Huber and John Scott.

Page 354. Deborah Mitchell of Solebury, Spinster. 3rd mo., 13th day, 1766. Proved Mch. 8, 1774. John Pickering of Solebury, exr. Hannah, his wife. Sister Elizabeth Mitchell. Bros. Samuel and Enoch Mitchell.
Wit: Wm. Scarbrough and Paul Preston.

Page 355. Robert Parsons, of Northampton, Blacksmith. Sept. 12, 1772. Proved Mch. 24, 1774. Wife Elizabeth and son George, exrs. Sons Robert and William. Daus. Susanna and Mary. Grandsons William Short and George Parsons.
Wit: Hugh Tomb, Thomas Hellings, Thomas Worthington.

Page 357. Mary Williams of Nockamixon Twp. 6-12-1766. Proved Mch 28, 1774. Widow of Jeremiah Williams. Son Benjamin, exr. Daus. Hannah, wife of Benjamin Doughty, Ann Carter, and Mary Williams. Granddau. Mary, Margaret, Lydia, Anne, and Susanna Williams, Elizabeth and Frances Woods and grandson Benj. Woods, children of Fortunatus Woods. Grandchildren, Mary, Hannah and Sarah Hill, children of Benjamin Hill.
Wit: John Iliff, Henry Weaver and John Williams.

Page 359. Benjamin Courson of Northampton, Yeoman. Mch. 3, 1774. Proved May 23, 1774. Wife Mary and son Benjamin, exrs. Sons Ryck, Cornelius, Henry, John, and Abraham. Daus. Janitie, wife of John Kroesen, and Mary Courson.
Wit: Richard Leedom, Robert McDowell and Gilliam Cornell.

Page 361. Abraham Staats, of Bensalem, Yeoman. Feby. 24, 1774. Proved Apr. 23, 1774. Wife Elizabeth and sons Edmund and Daniel, exrs. Son Abraham. Dau. Hannah. Son Peter.
Wit: John Carr, Abrm. Lerew, Mahlon Carver.

Page 363. Thomas Steegleets, of Warwick, Miller. Apr. 26, 1774. Proved May 12, 1774. Nathaniel Ellicott, Innholder, and Adam Carr, Storekeeper, both of Warwick, exrs. Eldest son of sister Sarah Arthur of Springfield Twp., Chester Co., Penna. Congregation of Church of England, at White Marsh. Alex Jamison

of Warwick, Miller. Elizabeth, wife of David Fulton of Manor of
Moreland. Residue to committee of Pres. Congregation at
Neshaminey.
Wit: William Scott, Thos. Lusk, Robert Jamison.

Page 364. John Wilson, of Nockamixon, Blacksmith. Dated Oct.
23, 1773. Proved June 9, 1774. Wife Elizabeth and Bro. David and
Rev. Alexander Mitchell, exrs. Son John and Dau. Mary both
minors.
Wit: John Bailey, Saml. Wilson.

Page 366. Thomas Brown, of Bristol Twp., Yeoman. Dated Feby.
18, 1761. Proved June 20, 1774. "Relation" George Brown, exr.
Sons John, Joseph, Clark and Christian. Daus. Mary Thompson and
Rachel Mitchell.
Wit: Joseph Hough, Wheeler Clark, Samuel Brown.

Page 367. George Dunn, of Newtown Twp., Yeoman. June 2, 1774.
Proved July 29, 1774. Wife Margaret and Son Joseph and Richard
Gibbs, Esq. exrs. Sons Joseph and Ralph.
Wit: Timothy Taylor and Richard Yeardley.

Page 368. Andrew Moode, of Middletown, Weaver. 9th mo., 4th
day, 1773. Proved Aug. 3, 1774. Wife Hannah and son William,
exrs. Sons Andrew and Alexander to live with William. Son Joseph.
Daus. Hannah, Sarah, Eleanor, and Lydia.
Wit: Nathan Brelsford, Margaret Brelsford, Benj. Palmer.

Page 370. Philip Angel of New Britain, Mason. Nov. 19, 1769.
Proved Aug. 16, 1774. Wife Margaret, extx. Sister Margaret.
Wit: John Mathew, James James, and David Evans.

Page 371. Joseph Bye, of Buckingham. July 7, 1769. Proved Oct.
1, 1774. Wife Rebecca, all Est for life. Nephew Joseph Ellicott
and Hugh Ely, Jr. exrs. Children of bro. Thomas, viz., Thomas
Bye, Junr. Elizabeth Hutchinson, Martha and Lydia Bye. Children
of sister Ann, viz., Joseph, Andrew, Nathaniel, Thomas and John
Ellicott and George Wall, Junr. and Mary Wall. Children of
sister Margaret, viz. Martha Blackfan, Sarah Corgell and Mary
Davis.
Wit: Michael Harker, John Heaton, and Samuel Godfrey.

Page 372. Cornelius Courson of Northampton, Yeoman. Sept. 10,
1774. Proved Oct. 13, 1774. Wife Charity. son Christian and
John Kroesen, Senr., exrs. Sons Christian, Cornelius, Daniel,
John and Benjamin. Daus. Jemima, Mary, Ann (her unworthy husband
Wm. Maynard), her children, Cornelius, Ann, and Elizabeth
Maynard.
Wit: Isaac Bennett, John Rankins.

Page 374. Thomas Biles, of Penna., Farmer. Oct. 1, 1774.
Proved Oct. 19, 1774. Wife Abigail, sole legatee. Edmund
Bainbridge of Maidenhead and his Bro. Absalom of Princeton, exrs.
Wit: Jane Biles and William Vasey.

Page 375. Henry Carver of Buckingham, Yeoman. 9-10-1774.
Proved Oct. 25, 1774. Wife Rachel and Joseph and William Carver,
exrs. Sons Thomas, John, Joseph, and Benjamin. Daus. Rachel and
Elizabeth.
Wit: Thomas Dougherty, Isaac Kirk and John Tucker.

Page 376. Barbara Deal, of Nockamixon, Widow. June 5, 1774.
Proved Dec. 7, 1774. Son Felix, exr. 2 eldest sons, John and
Daniel Deal, sons Peter and Felix. Daus. Ammie and Barbary.
Wit: Nicholas McCarty and Henry McIntyre.

Page 377. William Yeardley of Lower Makefield, Yeoman. July 29,
1774. Proved Dec. 4, 1774. Wife Sarah and Bro. Thomas and
Father-in-law Mahlon Kirkbride, exrs. Sons Thomas, Daniel,
Mahlon, and William. Daus. Ann Warner, Sarah Taylor, Margaretta
Potts, Mary, Hannah, Achsah, and Letitia. Land bought of Saml.
Burgess.
Wit: Richard Plumer, John Robbins, Thos. Canby.

Page 381. Jacob Linton of Wrightstown. Mch. 19, 1769. Proved
Jan. 23, 1775. Mother Elizabeth Linton. Sis. Rebecca Linton.
Bros. Isaiah, William, Sister Elizabeth Linton. Bro. William,
exrs.
Wit: Wm. Reece, Saml. Chapman, Cuthbert Warner.

Page 382. Thomas Morgan of Newtown, Yeoman. Sept. 8, 1774.
Proved Feby. 11, 1775. "Advanced in Age" Wife Magdalen. Dau.
Magdalen, wife of Thomas Bulger. Grandson John Morgan, son of son
Charles, dec'd. Granddau. Elinor wife of John Simpson,
Grandchildren, Thomas, Josiah, and Magdalen Morgan, children of
son Peter, dec'd. Grandson Thomas Morgan, and granddau. Magdalen
Morgan, children of son Thomas, dec'd. Grandchildren, Moses, John
and Elizabeth Neeld, children of dau. Elizabeth dec'd., late wife
of John Neeld. Grandson Joseph Dyer, granddau. Ann, wife of Mark
Hall. Wife and son-in-law Wheeler Clark, exrs. Wit: Jos. Jenks,
James Gregg, Hu. Thompson.

Page 385. William Biles, of the Falls Twp. Apr. 11, 1770.
Proved Feby. 11, 1775. Codicil dated Nov. 20, 1773. Son William,
Island called "Great Island." Wife Jane. Son Thomas. Daus.
Susanna Thorn and Ann Mott and granddau. Sarah Baker. gdson
William Douglass. Son William, Thomas Thorn, and Edward
Pennington, exrs.
Wit: Isaac Smith and Sarah Stevenson.

Page 388. Isaac Bolton of Southampton, Yeoman. 7th mo., 1st
day, 1771. Proved Feby. 11, 1775. Codicil dated 2-9-1774. Wife
Sarah and son Isaac, exrs. Sons Everard and Joseph. Daus. Sarah
Rigby, Jemima Tomlinson, Margaret and Rachel Bolton. Lot on
Front St. Phila. in possession of son Joseph. 228 3/4 acres in
Southampton to son Isaac.
Wit: Danl. Longstreth and Jona. Clayton.

Page 394. Elizabeth Oberbeck, of Bedminster Twp. Apr. 22, 1772.
Proved Feby. 11, 1775. Daus. Anna Maria and Maria Magdalena. 4

children. Jacob Beidleman, exr.
Wit: Jacob Yearling, John Lear.

Page 395. James Meredith, of Warwick. Feby. 3, 1774. Proved
Feby 16, 1775. "Well stricken in years" son John, Plantation in
New Britain. Son Simon, Tract he lives on in Warwick, bought of
Joseph Wells. Son Thomas (Tract he lives on). Grandchildren,
James, Joseph, John and Elizabeth Meredith, children of son
Simon. Grandchildren, John and Mary, children of son Thomas. Son
Hugh and his dau. Elizabeth. Plantation in Lower Merion to be
sold. Son Thomas, exr.
Wit: David Stephens, Elizabeth Stephens, and Joseph Hair.

Page 399. William Baker, of Bensalem Twp., Cordwainer. Dec. 8,
1774. Proved Mch. 1, 1775 "Friend" Giles Knight, exr. and
residuary legatee. Sister Elizabeth Jones. Kinswoman Hannah
Shields (late Baker). Kinsman John Baker (if living), 3
relations Henry, Samuel, and John Bennett, sons of Charity
Bennett (late Baker) Mary Bennett, dau. of Charity. Abel and
Israel Knight. Elizabeth Knight, dau. of Giles.
Wit: Jos. Mitchell, Mary Mitchell, Evan Thomas.

Page 400. Thomas Jones, Senior, of Hilltown Twp. June 8, 1774.
Proved Mch. 14, 1775. Wife Rosannah. Son Thomas and son-in-law
Thomas Mathias, exrs. Oldest son Thomas. sons Jenkins,
Nathaniel, youngest son William. gd.son Thomas Jones, son of
Thomas. Daus. Letitia, wife of John Leedom, Elizabeth, wife of
Thomas Mathias, Martha, Sarah, and Mary Jones. £5 to managers of
Baptist Meeting House and Grave Yard at Kelly's in Hilltown. Land
adj. Richard Williams, Abraham Derstine, John Kelly, Abram
Cratts, and "where Ezekiel Wilson lives." Mathew Grier, Senr and
Mathew Grier, Junr., Overseers and Guardians.
Wit: Henry Wismer, Wm. Morris, Jared Erwin, James Irwin and James
Armstrong.

Page 406. Samuel Worthington, of New Britain, Yeoman. Jan. 29,
1775. Proved Mch. 20, 1775. Wife Mary and Sons Jonathan and
David, exrs. Daus. Sarah and Hester Kimble, Rachel Rue, Pleasant
Lap. Nephew Isaac Worthington. Sons Samuel, Jonathan, and David.
Wit: Joseph Carver, William Worthington, David Evans.

Page 409. Alexander McCamon of Nockamixon. May 18, 1776.
Proved Apr. 4, 1777. Wife Margaret. Sons Samuel and John, exrs.
Daus. Mary Johnston, Elizabeth wife of John McCamon, Rachel wife
of Abraham Johnston, and Catharine.
Wit: George Merkleroy, Thomas Lytle.

Page 441 or 411. John Feaster, of Northampton Twp., Yeoman.
Dec. 18, 1775. Proved Dec. 27, 1775. Sons Henry and David, exrs.
Children, Henry, David, Dorothy wife of Jacob Brant, Elizabeth
wife of Richard Smith.
Wit: Henry Wynkoop, Jesse Palmer, Robert Richmont.

Page 412. Henry Shoup, of Rockhill Twp., Yeoman. Apr. 2, 1774.
Proved Apr. 17, 1777. Sons Conrad and John, exrs. Sons, Conrad

(eldest), Ludwig (or Lewis) Lewis, John. Children of dau. Hannah, dec'd., late wife of Peter Linch. Children of dau. Susanna, dec'd., late wife of Jacob Bennett. Elizabeth, wife of McHell; Catharine, wife of Jacob Bender.
Wit: Jacob Rei, John Keller, Michael Grosman.

Page 414. Philip Jacob Wolf of Haycock Twp., Yeoman. Oct. 6, 1775. Proved Apr. 17, 1777. Wife Christina and John Keller of Haycock, exrs. Eldest son John Nicholas, his children. --- first born Christina.
Wit: Philip Pearson, John Fostbinder.

Page 415. Derrick Kroesen of Northampton Twp. Mch. 6, 1777. Proved Apr. 22, 1777. Uncle John Kroesen and cousin Simon Vanartsdalen, exrs. Bro. Garret and his son Derrick. "Este Underdunk, my intended spouse." Sisers Ariantie Vandeventer, Jane Whitlock, and half sister. Catharine Wycoff.
Wit: Arthur Lefferts, John Bennet, Abraham Lefferts.

Page 417. Daniel Craig, of Warrington Twp., Yeoman. July 6, 1775. Proved Apr. 22, 1777. "Far advanced in years" Wife Margaret. sons Thomas (Exr.), John and William, his children, Mary, Sarah, Hugh, and Daniel. Daus. Margaret, wife of James Barckley; Sarah, wife of John Barnhill; Jane, wife of Samuel Barnhill; Mary Lewis and Rebecca, wife of Hugh Stephenson. Plantation in Tenure of Wm. Robinson, Junr. to son Thomas. Bro-in-law Richard Walker and son Thomas, exrs.
Wit: Thos. Lusk (Scrivener), Wm. Dean and John Rickey, certify that they guided testators hand in making mark he having been blind for many years. Letters granted to Thomas.

Page 410. Barnard Vanhorn, of Northampton, Yeoman. Jan. 27, 1775. Proved Sept. 21, 1776. Wife Elizabeth. Sons Benjamin and Garret, exrs. Sons Peter, Garret, Benjamin, William, and John. Daus. Jane Williamson and Rachel Bankson. Children of dau. Yanica Duboias. Children of dec'd. dau. Charity Booskirk. Children of dec'd. son Richard. Son Christian. Children of dec'd. dau. Elizabeth Slack. Son Barnard's (dec'd.) sons and daus. Granddau. Elizabeth Williams. Land adj. Jos. Fenton and Paul Blaker.
Wit: Arthur Leffertson, John Rankin.

Page 423. John Shaw, of Northampton, Yeoman. Feby 28, 1771. Proved Dec. 7, 1776. Wife Sarah. Dau. Elizabeth, wife of John Beans and her 4 children by her 1st husband, viz., George, Elizabeth, John and Sarah Randall. Sons James, John and Jonathan, exrs.
Wit: Arthur Watts, Abel Morgan, and John Hart. Letters granted to Jonathan only.

Page 426. John Emerick, Nunnemacker of Rockhill, "Joiner." Jan. 16, 1776. Proved May 20, 1777. Wife Judith. Plantation she was possessed of before our marriage, adj. Ulrich Sholler and Ludwick Benner. Sons Johannes, Daniel, Henry, Jacob, and Solomon. Daus. Barbara, widow of Mathias Sheetz; Mary, wife of Valentine Kramer.

Grandchildren, George, Mathias, Godfrey and Henry Wilkeel and their two sisters. Son Henry and Friend George Nase, Blacksmith, exrs.
Wit: Geo. Nase and Abrm. Stout.

Page 427. Elizabeth Hutchinson of Bristol Twp., Widow. 8th mo., 19th day, 1776. Proved May 21, 1777. 4 daus. Mary Worstall, Elizabeth Higgs, Jane Hall, and Ann Brown. 2 sons James Higgs and Joseph Hutchinson. Son Joseph and son-in-law Joseph Brown, exrs.
Wit: Joseph Fell and Henry Wilson.

Page 429. Zebulon Heston, of Upper Makefield, Yeoman. 6-26-1773. Proved Apr. 4, 1776. Wife Elizabeth, extx. Son Zebulon, land inherited from father. Sons William, David, John and Isaiah. Bro. John Heston, 4 daus. Elizabeth Fell, Jemima Done, Rachel Merick and Mary Hirst.
Wit: John Story, Rachel Dean, William Linton.

Page 431. Mahlon Kirkbride of Lower Makefield. 5-18-1774. Proved Nov. 30, 1776. Wife Mary and sons Mahlon, Robert and Jonathan, exrs. Son Stacy, and his children, Joseph, Mary, Prudence and Sarah. Daus. Mary Taylor, Sarah Yardley. Grandchildren, Joseph Taylor, Stacy Taylor, and Mahlon Taylor, Timothy, David, and Jonathan Taylor, children of dau. Latitia. Grandson Barnard Taylor. Granddaus. Hannah and Mary and grandson Mahlon, Mary's children. Land in Morris Co., New Jersey in tenure of David and Thomas Logan and Daniel Kelsey and Saml. Hiblock.
Wit: Samuel Linton, Daniel Linton, Hezekiah Linton.

Page 435. John Praul, of Middletown, Yeoman. Aug. 13, 1777. Proved June 27, 1777. Wife Jane. Son John and son-in-law John Vandegrift, exrs. Sons John and Peter. Daus. Mary, wife of John Vandegrift and Jane Praul. Plantation in Southampton bought of Thomas Tomlinson to son Peter.
Wit: Daniel Larew, Junr., Elizabeth Larew, Jane Vansant.

PAge 437. Felix Leig of Rockhill Twp. Apr. 17, 1777. Proved June 17, 1777. Wife Margaret. Son Henry and son-in-law Valentine Bergstresser, exr. Sons John and Henry and stepsons Gasper and Alexander Nagle. Step.dau. Elizabeth, wife of Valentine Bergstresser. Dau. Christina, wife of Peter Shipe. Granddau. Catharine Stiner. Hanadam Movehard.
Wit: Thos. Armstrong, John Burgstresser, Michael Smith.

Page 438. Adam Lautenslager, of Haycock Twp. Feby. 10, 1777. Proved June 27, 1777. Wife Margaret, Bro. Peter and Bro-in-law Leonard Hunkle, exrs. Eldest son John Adam. Son Peter. Daus. Margaret, Elizabeth, Ann, and Mary.
Wit: Philip Stiter, Nicholas Smith (6 children now living).

Page 440. Adrian Cornell of Northampton, Yeoman. Feby. 16, 1774. Proved Aug. 18, 1777. Wife Neltye. Sons Gilliam and Rem, exrs. Grandson Adrian Cornell. Land purchased of Isaac Pennington and Godfrey Vanduren.

Wit: Direk Hogeland and Henry Wynkoop.

Page 441. Rachel Hamilton, of Warwick Twp., Widow. July 9, 1777. Proved Aug. 2, 1777. Bro. James Smith's daus. Mary Atchison and Elizabeth Scott, his 3 sons John, James, and David. Jean Smith, dau. of sister Margaret. Friends Jane Williams. Ann Flack. Ann Swelzer. Mary McKinstry. Martha Dungan. Mary and Benjamin Snotgrass. Robert Kirkbride and Benj. Snotgrass, exrs. Wit: Jacob Antre, Ludwick Sweizer.

Page 443. Samuel Torbert, of Upper Makefield. Feby. 12, 1777. Proved July 28, 1778. Sons William and Lamb, exrs. Son-in-law Anthony Teate, on behalf of dau. Elizabeth, dec'd. 7 children, William, Samuel, James, Lamb, Thomas, Benjamin, and Ann, wife of John Henderson. Wit: John Hayhurst, James Kennedy, William Atkinson.

Page 445. Dirck Hogeland, of Southampton, Yeoman. Dec. 7, 1775. Proved Aug. 1, 1778. Wife Mary. Sons Daniel and Benjamin, exrs. Dau. Mary, wife of Giles Craven, Land purchased of Blaithwaite Jones adj. John Blackledge and Francis Titus. Sons John, Dirck, land bought of John Swift, Thos. Duffield and Jeremiah Langhorne. 6 daus. Jane Dorsius, Mary Craven, Catharine Vansant, Ann Bennett, Sarah and Elizabeth Hogeland. Son Benjamin. Granddau. Phebe Hogeland, dau. of son George, dec'd. Dirck and George, sons of George. Wit: Walter Willet, Mathias Fenton, John Watts.

Page 449. Thomas Longshore, of Middletown. Jan. 11, 1777. Proved Feby. 13, 1777. Wife Joanna. Sons Cyrus and Thomas, exrs. Sons Thos. Cyrus and Euclides. Daus. Elizabeth Hunter and Margaret Wiley. Wit: Euclides Longshore, James Hibbs, Joseph Wildman.

Page 451. John Hornecker, of Rockhill Twp., Yeoman, Jan. 13, 1777. Proved Aug. 10, 1778. Bro-in-law Peter Hillegas, exr. John Hornecker and his 3 sisters, children of dec'd. Bro. Ulrick Hornecker by his third and last wife. Joseph Hornecker eldest son of sd. Ulrick, dec'd. Children of Peter Hillegas by my sister Barbara. Sisters Catharine, wife of David Hottenstein and Elizabeth, wife of Richard Klein. Bro. Isaac Hornecker. Margaret eldest dau. of Bro. Ulrick. Wit: Yost Sleigher, David Schultze and Frederick Pannebacker. (John Loh a legatee).

Page 455. Michael Kapleberger, of Rockhill, Farmer. Feby. 7, 1778. Proved Aug. 13, 1778. Wife Margaret. Stepson Andrew Kachlin, exr. Son-in-law Peter Shepherd. 3 step children, Charles, Andrew, and Peter Kachlin. Wit: Samuel Smith and Henry Shlesman.

Page 456. Joseph Barton of New Britain Twp., Yeoman. June 17, 1777. Proved Aug. 19, 1778. Wife Elizabeth, money and effects she had before our marriage. Son Job Barton, exr. Daus. Hannah, Mary Stuart, Susannah Evans, Ann Weaver, and Amey Barton. 3

grandchildren, Mary and Rebecca daus. of dau. Elizabeth Ewers and Joseph Gorely.
Wit: John Dungan, Wm. Dungan, David Evans.

Page 456. Michael Good, of Nockamixon, Weaver. Feby. 16, 1777.
Proved Aug. 24, 1778. Wife Elizabeth and Philip Pearson, exrs.
Sons Henry and George, Est to be divided among all children when youngest, Elizabeth, is 14.
Wit: Nicholas Gruver, Michael Shick.

Page 457. William James, of New Britain Twp. Jan. 17, 1776.
Proved Aug. 26, 1778. Dau. Rebecca Butler and David Evans, exr.
Bro. Isaac James and Peter Evans, of Twp. of Montgomery, £10 for support of Ministry at Baptist Church at Montgomery. David and Daniel Evans of New Britain £70 for support of Ministry at New Britain Baptist Church. £5 for use Burying Ground at New Britain. £5 to Joshua Jones Minister of the Gospel. Son John James, dau. Margaret Lewis. Dau-in-law Sarah James, widow of Isaac. Granddau. Oswald James by son Isaac, dec'd. Granddau. Catharine and grandson William and Abel James by son Abel, dec'd. Grandchildren, Daniel, Isaiah, John, Margaret, and Martha James. Tacy James granddau. of Bro. Isaac. Grandson Abiah Butler house in Tenure of Wm. Pastorius. Niece Elizabeth Pawling. Granddau Mary Kerr. David Evans, Peter Evans and Thomas Harris, both of Montgomery Twp., exrs. after death of wife.
Wit: Henry Harris, Amos Griffith, James Giffon.

Bucks County Wills. Book No. 4.

Page 1. David John of New Britain Twp., Joiner. Aug. 1, 1771.
Proved Aug. 26, 1778. "Friend" Amos Griffith, exr. Nephew Benjamin John. Nephew William Thomas. Baptist Church of New Britain. Residue of personal estate, present Deacons of sd. Church, viz. John Mathew and David Stephen. Plantation to Amos Griffith.
Wit: William Stephens, Evan Stephens, Elizabeth Stephens.

Page 2. Robert Henderson, yeoman, of Warminster. Apr. 12, 1775.
Proved April 25, 1775. Wife Margaret, plantation in Warwick Twp. bought of Henry Jamison. 8 daus. Elizabeth, Margaret, Jane, Agnes, Mary, Elinor, Martha, and Rachel. Son-in-law John Carr and Friend John Ramsey, Exs.
Wit: William Carr, John Peterson, Janet Grimes.

Page 4. Thomas Stanaland, Bristol Twp., yeoman. Mch. 12, 1771.
Proved Aug. 12, 1778. Bro. John Stanaland, exr. Plantation in Mansfield Twp., Burlington Co., N.J. "directly opposite the place I live on." "Relation" John Hutchinson of Bristol, Joiner, Plantation in Tenure of Wm. Dilworth and Tract adj. Aaron Wright, John Dowdney, John Pemberton and Thomas Stackhouse.
Wit: William Bidgood and John Hutchinson.

Page 6. William Main of Tinicum, Yeoman. July 25, 1776. Proved Sept. 28, 1778. Youngest son William and son-in-law William

Davis, exrs. Son John.   Daus. Jane Hart, Margaret Beatty, Isabel Roger.   Elizabeth McCalla and Mary Davis.   Dau. Ann.
Wit: William Marshall, James Ruckman, Sarah Carrell. Caveat filed by son John May 25, 1778.

Page 9.   John George Wildonger of ---.   Dec. 2, 1777.   Proved Sept. 1, 1778. Wife. ---. Son George and other children.   John Wildonger, exr.
Wit: George Koder and Godfried Premauer.

Page 10.   Alban Thomas of Plumstead Twp., Yeoman.   Apr. 22, 1776. Proved June 8, 1776. Wife Jane.   Son Isaac, exr.   Sons Joseph, Daniel and Isaac.
Wit: Daniel Evans and David Evans.

Page 11.   Benjamin Snodgrass Senior, New Britain.   Dec. 18, 1772. Proved Oct. 13, 1778. "Far advaned in years." Wife Jane.   Sons Benjamin and James, exrs. James Watson and Ann his wife, dau. and son-in-law of wife Jane. John Boreland, son of wife Jane.   Jean Grier and Elinor McCoy, daus. of my dau. Mary Stewart, by my 1st wife "long since dec'd.." Sons Benjamin and James, both of Warwick Twp.   Daus. Rebecca Watson and Margaret Law.   Children of dau. Jane Harvey, viz. Rebecca, John and Jane Harvey.
Wit: John Garvin and Wm. Roberts.

Page 14.   Christian Keiser, of Northampton Twp., Yeoman.   Mch. 28, 1778. Pr. Oct. 20, 1778. Wife Jean.   Son Gasper and dau. Margrit. Gilliam Cornell and John Kroeson, exrs.
Wit: Hugh Edams, Daniel Corson, Sarah Gardner.

Page 15.   John Twining of Newtown.   Mch. 31, 1773.   Proved Sept. 5, 1775. Wife Elizabeth.   Sons David and Jacob, exrs.   Land in Warwick where grandson Joseph Twining lives, adj. Thomas West and Saml. McGrandy.   sons John, Eleazer, William, Jacob, Stephen, and David.   Granddau. Mary Twining, dau. of son John.
Wit: John Story, John Story, Junr., John Cutler.

Page 17.   John Balderston Senr., of Solebury, Weaver.   4th mo., 29th day, 1773.   Proved Nov. 22, 1778. Wife Hannah and Son John, exrs.   Sons John, Jonathan, Bartholomew, Timothy, Jacob, Isaiah and Mordecai.   Daus. Hannah, Sarah, Lydia, and Mary.   Legacy bequeathed to children by Bartholomew Balderston of Great Britain, dec'd.
Wit: Saml. Armitage, James Armitage and John Armitage. Caveat filed by son Bartholomew Nov. 16, 1778 on ground of failure of Testator to take oath of allegiance. John debarred from executorship for same reason.

Page 19.   Dr. Robert Mitchell.   Aug. 10, 1776.   Proved Nov. 3, 1778. Wife Rebecca Mitchel, alias Newtown, alias, Kennedy, extx. "In case I should not return from the present excursion against the natural foes of our country."   Dau. Jean and possibly child unborn.
Wit: Edward Murphy and Catharine Murphy.

Page 21. Henry Huber of Lower Milford, Shoemaker. Dec. 16, 1777
Proved Dec. 8, 1778. "Present wife Ann." Bros. Henry and Jacob
Huber. Friends Adam Willower and Vallentin Huber, exrs.
Wit: Johannes Klein, Frdk. Limback. Signed Huber Henrich.

Page 23. John Wilkinson Junr. of Warwick, Cooper. Aug. 7, 1777.
Proved Dec. 8, 1778. Wife Jane. Father John Wilkinson and Cousin
John Chapman, exrs. 4 children, John, Abraham, Elias, and Amos.
Plantation of 133 acres .
Wit: Thomas Ross Senr., Josiah Dawes, Margaret Chapman.

Page 24. James Melvin of Lower Milford, yeoman. Dated Sept. 24,
1777. Proved Dec. 8, 1778. Son Samuel, exr. Sons Thomas, John,
and Joseph. Daus. Susanna Dungworth and Jane Barnes.
Wit: William Edwards, Charles Dungworth, Samuel Foulke.

Page 25. John Blaker, of Northampton Twp. May 15, 1778. Proved
Jan. 4, 1779. Sons Peter and Paul, exrs. Sons John and Achilles.
Grandson Peter Blaker son of John. 5 daus. Ruth Hibbs, Sarah
Hibbs, Phebe Wiggons, Catharine Weisner, and Mary Hampton.
Plantation adj. John Cooper "where Elizabeth Routledge lived."
Plantation that was "my uncle Paul Blakers."
Wit: John Story, Henry Cooper, Paul Blaker.

Page 28. Robert Burr of Richland, Yeoman. 6th mo., 20th day,
1777. Proved Jan. 4, 1779. Wife Christiana. Thos. Foulke and
Thos. Roberts, of Lower Milford, exrs. "If I die without issue
by my present wife." Son Joseph, all lands etc. Bro. William
Burr and Sister Rebecca Chapman. Nieces Jane Deacon, dau. of
brother-in-law, George Deacon and Abigail and Rachel Ridgeway,
daus. of Bro-in-law David Ridgeway.
Wit: John Lester, Saml. Foulke, Thos. Foulke, Junr.

Page 30. John Bessonett, of Bristol Borough. Mch. 4, 1774.
Proved Oct. 26, 1778. Wife Joyce. Son John of City of N.Y. and
son Charles, of Bristol, exrs. Son John's son John. Daus.
Catharine Goheen, Anne Boucher, and Martha Johnson. Children of
late dau. Elizabeth Larzeler, dec'd. Children of dec'd. dau.
Mary Mitchell. Children of dec'd. dau. Sarah Bodine, Martha
Brelsford dau. of wife Joyce.
Wit: Sims Betts, Jos. Brown.

Page 33. John Seabring of Solebury Twp. Dec. 2, 1777. Proved
Jan. 3, 1779. Wife Ann, son Henry, Bro-in-law John Smith and Geo.
Wall, Jr., exrs. 6 children, Henry, John, Thomas, Ann, Mary, and
Catharine Seabring. Letter to Ann and John Smith, Wall renounces
and Henry, a minor about 14.
Wit: John Seesman, Jonathan Stout, and Mary Johnson.

Page 34. John Vandegrift of Neshaminey, Bensalem Twp. Jan. 13,
1777. Proved Jan. 16, 1779. Wife Ann, her Bro. Jonathan Walton
and my Bro. Jos. Vandegrift, exrs. "Aged Mother." Wife
Plantation "to raise up the children."
Wit: James How, Wm. Lindsay. Letters granted to Ann Fetters late
Vandegrift and Jos. Vandegrift. Walton renouncing.

Page 35. Edward Eaton of Hilltown, Yeoman. May 6, 1776. Proved
Feby. 24, 1779. Wife Mary and son-in-law John Boize, exrs. Dau.
Mary. Daus. Ann, wife of Thomas Howell and Martha, wife of James
Shannon. Grandson William Boize. John Davis of New Britain,
Trustee.
Wit: Philip High, Michael Snyder, and Thos. Jones. Letters to
Boize "extx" not appearing on account of her great age.

Page 38. Joseph Harvye of Upper Makefield, Yeoman. June 20,
1778. Proved Mch. 3, 1779. Wife Margaret, son Thomas and Samuel
Yardley, exrs. Sons Thomas, Joseph, William, Enoch, Joshua, and
John. Daus. Mary and Latitia.
Wit: John Duer, Jr., Benjm. Hickman, John Mathews.

Page 41. Daniel Bartholomew, of Haycock Twp., Blacksmith. Jan.
5, 1777. Proved Dec. 15, 1778. Wife Hannah and John Ludwick,
exrs. Children, minors.
Wit: Jacob Strawn and Alexander Hughes.

Page 42. John James of New Britain Twp., Yeoman. Feby. 10,
1779. Proved Mch. 10, 1779. Cousin William James, Cordwainer,
and nephew Moses Aaron, exrs. Sons Benjamin and James. Daus.
Margaret and Catharine James, Bro. James James. Cousins John and
Wm. James. 300 acres in Chestnut Hill Twp. Northampton Co. as
per Propr. Warrant dated Dec. 8, 1773. Friend Alex Gray.
Wit: Hugh Edmund, David Evans.

Page 44. Alexander Finley of New Britain, Weaver. Apr. 19,
1777. Proved Mch. 10, 1779. Wife Mary and bro-in-law Henry Kelso
and Samuel Weir, exrs. Children, Jane, James, Mary, Martha, and
Sarah. Bro. John Mehelm of New Jersey, trustee.
Wit: Aaron Boorom, John Weir, Thos. Lusk.

Page 47. Rudolf Huber of Milford Twp. Jan. 6, 1779. Proved
Apr. 30, 1779. Wife Annah and Bro. Jacob Huber, exrs. 5
children, Jacob, Henry, John, Adelhite, wife of Stephen Ott, and
Annah Huber.
Wit: Henry Huber and Benjamin Seigle.

Page 50. David Walton of Bensalem Twp. May 12, 1777. Proved
Apr. 30, 1779. Wife Rebecca. Bro. William and bro-in-law Benj.
Severns, son of Daniel, exrs. Daus. Elizabeth, Rebecca, and
Catharine. Rebecca Cooper.
Wit: Mary Hellings and Sarah Cox.

Page 51. Hugh Hartshorne, of Borough of Bristol. Feby. 11,
1777. Proved May 22, 1779. Wife Hannah and sons William,
Pattison, Richard, and John, exrs. Daus. Elizabeth, Sarah, and
Rachel. Land purchased of Joseph Merrick and Resse Meredith.
Milford Mills purchased of Attny. of Stephen Williams.
Wit: Ebenezer Large and John Green. Large testifies that John
Green is a "prisoner or otherwise with the English.."

Page 53. Mary Jackson, of Borough of Bristol, Widow. 2-6-1774.
Proved Nov. 5, 1775. Kinsman Hugh Hartshorne and Phineas

Buckley, exrs. Son Ebenezer Robinson and his daus. Mary, Elizabeth, and Sarah. Granddau. Margaret and Sarah Green. Dau. Mary Green.
Wit: Pattison Hartshorne and Enion Williams.

Page 54. Christopher Hughes, of Twp. of Bedminster. July 23, 1777. Proved Aug. 17, 1779. Wife Jean and Sons Alexander and Thomas, exrs. Son-in-law Wm. Wilson and his son John. Daus. Elizabeth, Jean, Susanna, and Agnes.
Wit: Henry Eckel, James Grier, Clerk, and Robert Darroch.

Page 56. Andrew Shibling, Lower Saucon Twp., Northampton Co. Dated Apr. 1, 1773. Proved Sept. 13, 1779. Wife Anna Margaret. Eldest son Frederick S.
Wit: Melchior Edinger and Conrad Fogelman. Translated from German by Lewis Weiss, Phila.

Page 57. Edward Bayly, of Falls Twp., Yeoman. 7th mo., 25th day, 1778. Proved Nov. 15, 1779. Wife Ann and bro-in-law Wm. Satterthwaite, exrs. Sons, Edward, William, and Thomas. Daus. Ann, Edith, Susanna, Mercy and Tace Bayly. Land adj. Bro. John Bayly, Mark Watson, late Isaac Hodgson, Wm. White and Thos. Cornish.
Wit: James Moon, Richard Neeld, and Eli Neeld.

Page 60. Philip Henry Rapp, of Nockamixon, Minister. July 12, 1779. Proved Nov. 8, 1779. Wife Mary and son Philip Henry, exrs. Sons Frederick and Christian. Daus. --- wife of Joseph Yoest and Catharine wife of John Rohrback.
Wit: Godfrey Miller.

Page 62. Amos Strickland, of Newtown, Gent. Mch. 31, 1779. Proved Dec. 24, 1779. Wife Margaret and Samuel Yardley, of Newtown, exrs. Son Amos. Daus. Rachel, Elizabeth, and Frances.
Wit: Thos. Buckman, George Campbell, Isaac Hicks, Wm. King. John Story, Junr. Codicil Aug. 7, 1779.

Page 65. Thomas Mitchell, of Newtown, Farmer. Dec. 11, 1779. Proved Dec. 30, 1779. Wife Elizabeth, John Heath, and Thomas Buckman, exrs. Thomas, son of cousin Thomas Mitchell. Ann Heath. Saml. Yardley and Thos. Yardley.
Wit: Archd. McCorkel, Thos. Buckman, Junr., Benj. Buckman.

Page 65. Jacob Kuckert of the County of Bucks, Yeoman. May 2, 1776. Proved Feby. 7, 1780. Wife Susanna, exrs. Bro. Adam Kuckert. Children of Sister Christina, Jacob Weidneght and other children. Sister Mary Catharine. Ch. of sister Mary Elizabeth. Wit: Lewis Gordon, Robert Traill, John Mashall. Plantation partly in Lower Saucon, Northampton Co. and partly in Springfield Twp., Bucks Co., bought of John Chapman. Land in tenure of Michael Lightcap. Letters granted to Susanna Brackenridge, the widow and her husband Saml. Brackenridge.

Page 68. Abiah Butler, of New Britain, Yeoman. Feby. 23, 1778. Proved Mch. 14, 1780. Wife Elizabeth and Friend Amos Griffith,

exrs. Bro. Benjamin and his daus. Rebecca and Mary Butler.
Sister Margaret, wife of Nathan Mathews, now living in Virginia.
Elie Mathews and 3 other children of Nathan. £10 to Baptist
Church at New Britain. John James, Jr. and Benjamin Mathews,
Yeomen of New Britain, Guardians of minor legatees.
Wit: Henry Harrie, Wm. Dungan, George Congle.

Page 67. Ralph Trough, of Nockamixon, Cordwainer. Nov. 22,
1779. Proved Feby. 14, 1780. Wife Susanna and Jacob Stealey,
exrs. Son Peter and 3 daus.
Wit: Michael Kohl and Nicholas McCarty.

Page 69. Henry Huddleston of Plumstead, Yeoman. Feby. 21, 1780.
Proved Mch. 14, 1780. Wife Mary and son Nathan, exrs. Sons
William, Daniel and Abraham. Daus. Rachel Clymer, Huldah
Montgomery and Martha Fox. Grandchildren, Samuel and Mary,
children of son Daniel. Land adj. saw mill of Jas. Buckman.
Wit: Abraham Swartz, Edw. Murphy, Allen Rice.

Page 72. Jacob Suber of Northampton, Yeoman. Jan. 20, 1777.
Proved Apr. 7, 1780. Wife Anna and son Amos, exrs. Dau. Mary,
wife of Wm. Paxton.
Wit: Henry Wynkoop, Edward Dyre, Jonathan Willett.

Page 72. Thomas Thomas, of Hilltown, Yeoman. May 27, 1778.
Proved Mch. 15, 1780. Wife Mary and sons Job and Amos, exrs.
Sons Job, Amos, Jonah, Asa and Abel. Daus. Ann, wife of John
Custard; Alice, wife of John Mathias; Catharine, wife of Charles
Miller; Sarah and Anna Thomas. Granddau. Elizabeth, dau. of John
Mathias. Revd. Bro. John Thomas. John Jenkins of "Gwinnedin,"
trustee of minor children. Land adj. Jacob Cope, Henry Lewis,
Peter Bother and John Thomas.
Wit: Daniel Pugh, Peter Boder, Cadwaller Morris.

Page 76. Thomas Warrant of Lower Milford, Farmer. May 2, 1780.
Proved June 10, 1780. Wife Elizabeth. James Ellison, exr.
Wit: Israel Barge, Priscilla Roberts, Catharine Allison.

Page 77. Philip Fluck of Hilltown. Jan. 10, 1780. Proved June
13, 1780. Wife Barbara and Eldest son John, exrs. Children,
John, Christian, Ludwick, Casper, Frederick, Philip and
Elizabeth.
Wit: Christian Kern, Mathias Hartman.

Page 79. Josiah Dyer of Plumstead Twp., Yeoman. 4 mo 12, 1780.
Proved June 21, 1780. Wife Esther. Sons Joseph, Josiah, and John
and son-in-law John Bradshaw, exrs. 9 children, Joseph, Josiah,
Thomas, John, Mary, Esther, Elizabeth, Phebe, and Rachel.
Wit: Wm. Doyle, John Carlile and Isaac Rich.

Page 80. James Hughes Senr. of Bedminster. Oct. 10, 1779.
Proved Dec. 21, 1779. Wife Rebecca. Grandsons Alexander and
Thomas Hughes, exrs. Daus. Abigail Thomas, Elizabeth Mathews,
and Anne Olipant. children of dau. Martha Burk, dec'd. Sons James
and Joshua. Grandsons Alexander and Thomas, sons of son

Christopher, dec'd. Gtgdson James Hughes, son of grandson
Alexander Hughes. "Meeting House at Deep Run, where I have and
my children belong" Plantation "over or near the Blew Mountains."
Wit: James Irvine, Samuel Wallace.

Page 82. James Bradshaw, of Buckingham, Weaver. Oct. 3, 1774.
Proved Apr. 8, 1776. Wife Ruth. Eldest sons John and William,
exrs. Sons James, David, Amos, Joel, and George. Daus. Rachel,
Sarah, Ruth, Mary and Martha. Grandson Israel Child.
Wit: Jos. Preston, Thos. Gilbert, Junr., Joshua Anderson.

Page 83. John Davids of Middletown. Jan. 12, 1776. Proved Jan.
30, 1776. Wife Sarah, and Son Linter, exrs. Sons John and
Joseph. Daus. Mary, wife of Cyrus Longshore and Sarah, wife of
John Roney. Thomas Harper. Martha Morris.
Wit: Thos. Jenks, Thos. Jenks, Junr., and Euclides Longshore.

Page 84. Stephen Wright, of Bristol Twp. May 24, 1780. Proved
Aug. 8, 1780. Bro. John Wright, exr. Mother Mary Harrison.
Kinsman Stephen Wright, son of John and Jane. Wife Catharine.
Bro. Thomas Wright's children. Land adj. Michael Hillegas, Aaron
Wright, Christian Merick and Benj. McDonald.
Wit: Keirll Rickey, Sarah Rickey and Francis Anderson.

Page 85. Henry Sheveler of Nockamixon Twp., Farmer. July 24,
1780. Proved Aug. 28, 1780. Son Rudie, exr. Wife Freeney. Sons
Henry, Rudie, and Jacob. Daus. Catharine, Franey, Christina,
Mary and Magdalenah.
Wit: Jacob Shory and Nicholas McCarty.

Page 88. Cornelius Clauson of Solebury Twp., Cooper. 12th mo.,
29th day, 1773. Proved May 19, 1775. Wife Jennet. Only son
John. Daus. Ann, Mary, Elizabeth, and Susanna. Bro-in-law Aaron
Phillips, exr.
Wit: Jos. Paxson, Rebecca Phillips.

PAge 89. Thomas Thomas, of Richland, Yeoman. 8th mo., 8th day,
1773. Proved Nov. 24, 1780. Bro. John Thomas and Nephew James
Green, exrs. Bro. William Thomas. Sisters Eleanor Samuel, Sarah
Ashton, and Margaret Foulke. Nephews Benjamin, Samuel, Joseph,
Ezekiel, Thomas, and James Green. Thomas and Samuel Thomas.
Samuel and Joseph Lester. Nieces Tabitha and Peninah Evans,
Eleanor Sachervil and Mary Lester.
Wit: Samuel Foulke, Thomas Foulke, Junr., Amelia Foulke.

Page 91. Rachel Prichard, of Southampton, Widow. Oct. 26, 1780.
Proved Nov. 27, 1780. Daus. Rebecca Hellings and Sarah Pritchard,
extxs. Dau. Hannah West. Son Joseph Pritchard. Son James
Pritchard "if living" and "if he return." Mary Feaster, dau. of
Henry.
Wit: Wm. Carter, Henry Feaster, John Bennett.

Page 92. Thomas Cornish of Falls Twp., yeoman. Oct 22, 1780.
Proved Nov 30, 1780. Wife Catharine and dau. Elizabeth Palmer,
exrs. 5 daus. Elizabeth Palmer, Catharine Margerum, Mary

Vansant, Rebekah Welch and Ann Cornish. Grandsons Cornish Margerum and John Burton.
Wit: Daniel Larue, Joshua Anderson, Nathaniel Price.

Page 94. David Larrew, of Bensalem Twp. 9th mo., 6th day, 1780. Proved Jan. 12, 1781. Wife Grace and Friend Thomas Townsend, exrs. Dau. Rebecca.
Wit: Henry Tomlinson, John Townsend, Ezra Townsend.

Page 95. Joseph Dilworth, of Warminster Twp., Yeoman. 5th mo., 19th day, 1775. Proved Jan. 13, 1781. Wife Alice. Son William and son-in-law William Buckman, exrs. 3 children, William Dilworth, Hannah Buckman, and Amos Dilworth.
Wit: Isaac Hough, Jacob Cadwallader, Junr., Charles Deane.

Page 96. Jacob Overpeck, of Springfield Twp. July 9, 1779. Proved Jan. 22, 1781. Wife Sarah. Sons Andrew, George, Philip, and Henry. Daus. Elizabeth and Anna Maria Overpeck. Servant Sarah Rice. £50 to "German Presbyterian Meeting House and Grave Yard in Springfield" Philip Conyell and Thomas Long, exrs. and Trustees.
Wit: Philip Hess and Michael Root.

Page 99. Joseph Eastburn of Solebury, Yeoman. 9th mo., 1st day, 1780. Proved Feby. 28, 1781. Wife Mary. Son Joseph and Friend Oliver Paxson, exrs. Sons Benjamin, Samuel, David, John, Thomas, James and Amos. Daus. Rebecca and Mary. Land bought of Euclides Scarborough, Richard Pike and Samuel Wilson. Land in Bedminster Twp.
Wit: Aaron Phillips, Joseph Paxson, Abraham Paxson.

Page 101. Peter Hanse of Nockamixon Twp., Yeoman. Feby. 14, 1781. Proved Mch. 13, 1781. Dau. Elizabeth wife of Frederick Eberhard and her children, Christian Traugher (the youngest) and Elizabeth Sumstine. Frederick Eberhard and Christian Trauger, exrs.
Wit: Nicholas McCarty and Jacob Shaub.

Page 103. Samuel Shaw, of Richland, Yeoman. Sept. 11, 1780. Proved Mch. 13, 1781. Wife Mary. Sons John and William and Friend Saml. Foulke, exrs. Sons Samuel and Moses. Son-in-law Robert Miller and his children by dau. Mary, dec'd. Dau. Hannah Hicks. Son Joseph. Land adj. Nathan Roberts and Samuel Nixon.
Wit: Saml. Foulke, John Foulke, James Green.

Page 104. David Whitson of Solebury, Yeoman. 3rd mo., 24th day, 1777. Proved Mch. 22, 1781. Sons Solomon and David and Friend Oliver Paxson, exrs. Daus. Ruth, Ami, Mary and Clement (helpless) Buckingham Mo. Mtg. to appoint Trustees to care for dau. Clement. Land at Oyster Bay, Queen's County, New York.
Wit: William Pettit, Grace Huet, Thomas Ross, Junr.

Page 106. Jacob Beidler of Hilltown Twp., Yeoman. Oct. 5, 1780. Proved Mch. 26, 1781. Wife Anne. Sons Henry and Jacob. Dau. Anne (minors) Henry Oberholtzer and Henry Rickert, exrs.

Wit: Henry Lyse, Johannes Lyse, Abrm. Stout.

Page 107. Peter Taylor of Newtown Twp., Yeoman. Jan. 28, 1777.
Proved Apr. 9, 1781. Wife Elizabeth. Children, John, William,
Peter, Jemima, Sarah, and Mary. Father-in-law John Scott.
"Brethen" John Knowles and Jacob Buckman, exrs.
Wit: David Johnson, William Tomlinson.

Page 108. William Keish of Upper Makefield. June 20, 1780.
Proved Apr. 27, 1781. Wife Elizabeth. Sons Isaiah and John and
Friend Wm. Neeley, exrs. Sons John, Noble, Robert, Isaac,
Isaiah, and Samuel. Daus. Sarah Keish, Martha McNair, Margaret
Mann and Elizabeth Torbert. "Sum due wife before marriage by
Thos. Dougherty.."
Wit: James Stokes, Jno. Chapman.

Page 110. Abraham Vandegrift, the elder, Bensalem, Farmer. Dec.
16, 1775. Codicil Sept. 26, 1776. Proved Mch. 14, 1781. Wife
Charity, Nephew Jacob Vandegrift (son of Bro. Jacob) and John
Harrison ("who now lives with me"), exrs. Abraham Foster, son of
Joseph, late of Byberry.
Wit: Mary Paulin, Mary Kettler, Jacob Jackson.

Page 113. John William of New Britain, Yeoman. Aug. 12, 1780.
Proved May 18, 1781. Wife Margaret and sons-in-law Thomas Jones
and David Worthington, exrs. Son Isaac. Daus. Hannah Jones,
Sarah Worthington, Mary Eders, and Rachel James. Son-in-law
Christopher Wells, his dau. Sarah and other chiildren of dau.
Elizabeth, dec'd. Son-in-law William Cornell and his children by
dau. Ann Cornell, dec'd. Son-in-law Paul McCarty, his dau.
Margaret and other children of dau. Cazzandra, dec'd. Gdson Loy
Barton.
Wit: Robert Shewell, Benjamin Griffith and David Evans.

Page 112. Joseph Atkinson of Bristol. 11th mo., 6th day, 1780.
Proved May 4, 1781. Wife Sarah and Bro-in-law Thomas Stapler,
exrs. Children, Mary, Elizabeth, Anne, Joseph, Archable, James
and Abigail.
Wit: Henry Wilson, William Bidgood, Junr. Letters granted to
Sarah only.

Page 116. George Newburn of Buckingham. Mch. 13, 1781. Proved
May 28, 1781. Codicil Mch. 18, 1781. Sons William and David.
Grandchildren, Margaret and George Newburn, children of son
George, dec'd. Jonathan Newburn, son of son William. Daus.
Hannah Nelson and Mary Curry. Dau. Hannah Nelson's children by
her late husband George Ewers, viz., Mary, Pleasant, and Dorothy
Ewers. Land bought of Benjamin Chapman, Richard Parsons and
Robert Strettle. Land in possession of Jesse Heston and Heirs of
John Sample adj. John Terry.
Wit: John Terry, William Waters and Benj. Clarke. Wm. Linton exr
(renounced).

Page 119. Sebastian Stiger of Richland, Yeoman. Apr. 18, 1781.
Proved June 12, 1781. Wife Agnes and son-in-law Yost Weaver,

exrs. Dau. Catharine Weaver. Wife's grandchildren, Catharine and Stephen Horn, Junr.
Wit: Philip Stahl, Jacob Bergy.

Page 120. Samuel Blaker of Warwick Twp., Millwright. Mch. 9, 1776. Proved June 18, 1781. Wife Catharine and Andrew McMicken of Warwick, exrs. Son Peter. Daus. Mary Timms, Lydia ---, Sarah Hough, Judith Ellicott, and Hannah Foster. Son-in-law Joseph Ellicott, late sheriff. Bond agt. Jacob Miers and Henry Stover.
Wit: Thos. West, Wm. Heston, Edwd. Murphy.

page 122. William Huston, of Warminster, Weaver. May 5, 1781. Proved June 28, 1781. Wife Mary. Son John, exr. Sons Alexander, John and Mathew. Daus. Margaret and Sarah Huston.
Wit: John Ramsey, Jno. Horner, James Horner.

Page 123. Robert Collison, of Middletown, Weaver. 4 mo 4, 1771. Proved Aug. 10, 1781. Wife Jane, extx. Cousin Daniel Longstreth to assist her. Cousins Dorothy Collison, dau. of Bro. George and George Collison son of Bro. Richard. Friends James Thackeray and Jasper Terry.
Wit: Henry Simmons, Wm. Blakey, Joshua Blakey.

Page 124. Jacob Fissler, of Lower Makefield, Brickmaker. Mch. 6, 1781. Proved Aug. 14, 1781. Wife Barbara. Sons Michael and Jacob. Daus. Anna Mary, wife of Philip Fether; Christina, wife of Frederick Heiler; Elizabeth, wife of Michael Shuppert; Eva, wife of Francis Taylor; and Dordea, wife of George Prouse "laiquais" children of second wife Barbara, Mary wife of Conrad Heninger and Susanna wife of Philip Singmaster.
Wit: Peter Buck and Edward Roberts. Michael Shuppert and Frederick Heiler of Phila., exrs.

PAge 126. Clement Dungan of Northampton Twp. Mch. 8, 1780. Proved Sept. 11, 1781. Wife Eleanor. Sons Jaremy, James and Elias, exrs. Granddaus. Ann, dau. of Ann and Elizabeth Dungan.
Wit: Hugh Edams and Sarah Crossley.

Page 127. Elizabeth Aaron of Hilltown, Widow. Feby 15, 1781. Proved Sept 11, 1781. Son-in-law John Kelly, exr. Sons Moses and Obed Aaron. Daus. Ann, wife of Thomas Morris; Rachel Kelly; and Hannah Jones, wife of Jonathan.
Wit: John Lap, Isaac Lap, David Evans.

Page 129. Andrew Emerick, of Tinnecum, Yeoman. Nov. 2, 1779. Proved Sept. 14, 1781. Wife Mary and son Peter, exrs. 7 children, Peter, Lorance, Andrew, Cathren, Mary, Elizabeth and Eve.
Wit: John Thompson, John Miller, Elizabeth Bowman.

Page 130. Andrew Keichline of Rockhill. Sept. 4, 1781. Proved Sept. 24, 1781. Wife ---. Bro. Charles and son Abraham, exrs. Sons Jacob, Peter, and John. Daus. Elizabeth and Susanna. Land bought of John Shoup, adj. Samuel Smith and Wm. Armstrong.
Wit: Thos. Armstrong, Peter Weaver.

Page 133. Jane Huston of Warwick. May 18, 1779. Proved Sept. 25, 1781. Son Robert Mearns and Dau. Mary Mearns, exrs. Sons Hugh Mearns, William and John Thompson and Thomas Huston. Son William Smith and Dau. Agnes.
Wit: Wm. Ramsey, John Huston.

Page 134. Henry Wireman of Buckingham, husbandman. Aug. 25, 1781. Proved Oct. 2, 1781. Wife Catharine and son Christian, exrs. 5 children, Ann Roat, Mary, wife of Cornelius Ruth, John, Christian and Catharine, wife of John Fritzinger.
Wit: Jonathan Fell, John Fell, John Kerr.

Page 136. William Croasdale, of Middletown. 4th mo., 18th day, 1769. Proved Oct. 10, 1781. "Considerably advanced in years" Wife Deliverance. Cousin Ezra Croasdale, exr. Daus. Mary Blaker, Sarah Lucas, Ann Briggs, Grace Knight, Rebecca Huff, Rachel and Phealy Watson. Sons-in-law Henry Huff and Joseph Watson. Jael Palmer, Wm. Blakey, John Cutler. Letters of Admn. granted to James Briggs, son-in-law.

Page 137. John Cummings of Northampton Twp., Yeoman. Jan. 15, 1776. Proved Oct. 11, 1781. Son James and Friend Yayne Edams, exrs. Children of son James, viz. James, Margaret, and Jane. Son Hugh and his dau. Jane. Son John. Son Robert and his dau. Jeane. Dau. Grizel and her children, Alexander, William, Jean, and Catharine Lindsay. Dau. Ann. Margaret. Agnes, Jean. Granddaus Margret and Agnes Marshal, Jean Whitford and Jean Johnston. Granddau Elizabeth Colman's child Jean. Land adj. David Dungan and Christian Kiser.
Wit: Hugh Edams, John Rankin.

Page 137. Thomas Stackhouse of Bristol Twp., Yeoman. 7th mo., 14th day, 1781. Proved Oct. 13, 1781. Son William and Kinsman John Brown, exrs. Sons Joseph, William, John, George, James. Daus. Rachel Thompson, Margaret Sotcher, Elizabeth Wright, Esther Emley, Ruth Green and Mary Stackhouse. Grandsons Joseph Hutchinson and John Green. Niece Agnes Stackhouse, dau. of Bro. James. Grandchildren, Hannah, Marcy, Robert Silas, Sarah, Ann and Abigail Sotcher. Grace Strickland, Luezar Bolton, John and Charles Hill. 2 children of dau. Ruth Green.
Wit: Wm. Bidgood, Jos. Merrick, and Kevill Rickey.

Page 141. Nicholas Pope of Bedminster Twp. Apr. 18, 1781. Proved Nov. 15, 1781. Wife Mary Catharine and Friend John Keller, exrs. Eldest son George "5 shillings more than rest of children." Heirs of dau. Donty, late wife of John Fry to share equally with children.
Wit: John Ott, Thos. Armstrong.

Page 143. Valentine Renner of Bedminster, Weaver. Apr. 5, 1775. Proved Nov. 5, 1781. Wife Magdalena and Friend Jacob Ott, exrs. Sons Jacob, Peter, Henry, Adam, and Michael. Daus. Clara, Catharine, Magdalena and Ellisabeth.
Wit: Henry Ott and Michael Ott.

Page 144. Peter Stats of Bensalem, Yeoman. 9th mo., 15th day, 1776. Proved Nov. 23, 1781. Wife Mary and Sons James and Abraham, exrs. Sons Andrew and Isaac. Son Peter's six children. Daus. Martha Wright, Jemima Shaw, and Mary Stats. Granddau. Mary Shaw.
Wit: John Carver, Samuel Scott, John Townsend. Letters to Mary and James. Abrm. being dead.

Page 145. Abraham Stats of Bensalem, Wheelwright. 7th mo., 17th day, 1779. Proved Nov. 23, 1781. Bro. James and Friend Henry Tomlinson, exrs. Mother. Sisters Mary Sitah, Martha Wright. Sister Jemima Shaw's dau. Mary. Bros. James, Andrew, Isaac. Isaac and Peter sons of Bro. Peter, dec'd. Land formerly Uncle Abraham Stats'.
Wit: John Townsend, Thos. Ridge, Henry Walmsley.

Page 150. Joseph Carter, of Northampton Twp., Miller. June 6, 1781. Proved Dec. 20, 1781 "Aged and infirm." Wife Rachel. Son William, exr. Mill and Land in Northampton Twp., sons James, Benjamin, Joseph and Richard, land they live on in Frederick Co., Va. in accordance with division made between them Oct. 20, 1778 by Jos. Day, Surveyor, Grandson Joseph Carter, son of John. Granddau. Katharine Carter, dau. of son Edmund, dec'd. Daus. Sarah (late wife of Wm. Hayhurst) and Rachel Carter.
Wit: Ezra Croasdale, Thomas Wilson, Joseph Croasdale.

Page 148. Benjamin Taylor of Upper Makefield, Blacksmith. 3-4-1780. Codicil 8-12-1780. Proved Dec. 1, 1781. Wife Hannah. Son Bernard and son-in-law Benjamin Paxson, exrs. Sons John (all Lands), Bernard, and Timothy. Daus. Hannah White and Deborah Paxson. Grandchildren, Mary Kinsey, James Gillingham, Sarah Conrad and Hannah Williams. Benj. White and other children of dau. Hannah. Children of dau. Esther Jones, dec'd. Relation Martha Beal. Falls Mo. Mtg. of Friends.
Wit: John Burroughs, John Buckman, Moses Smith.

Page 153. Solomon Lipecap of Nockamixon Twp., Yeoman. Aug. 3, 1780. Proved Dec. 21, 1781. Wife Caterine and son Jacob, exrs. Son Michael and Solomon. Daus. Mary Wolfinger, Margaret Pile, Caterine Groover, Elizabeth Shup, Hester Trauger, Magdalena Oldhouse and Mary Elizabeth Lipecap.
Wit: James Loughrey, John Loughrey, Amos Loughrey.

Page 154. Joseph White of Lower Makefield. 5th mo., 1775. Proved Dec. 22, 1781. "In 63d. year of my age" Wife Hannah and Bros.-in-law Bernard and Timonthy Taylor, exrs. 8 younger children, Hannah, Aby, Joseph, Esther, Deborah, Benjamin, William, and Rachel. "Hannah and Abi already married." Son Samuel and Hannah, his wife and his 3 sons Joseph, Benj. and William. Dau. Sarah Gillingham and Martha Kinsey. Codicil 2-14-1777.
Wit: to will John Merrick, Joshua Linton and Phebe. Wits to codicil William Field and Mary Yeardley.

Page 158. Elias Beidleman of Springfield Twp., Yeoman. Aug. 10,

1770. Proved Dec. 28, 1781. Wife Anna Maria. Sons Jacob and Adam, exrs. 7 sons Valentine, Jacob, Leonard, Adam, John, Samuel, and Abraham. Dau. Rosina, wife of George Hawke.
Wit: Peter Shuke, Henry Meier and Valentine ---.

Page 160. Jacob Hackman, of Bedminster Twp. Nov. 18, 1781. Proved Dec. 31, 1781. Wife Barbara. Bro. Ulry Hackman and Bro-in-law Jacob Latherman, exrs. Sons Jacob, Christian and Abraham. Daus. Elizabeth, Mary, Ann, Barbary.
Wit: Daniel Fretts and Rudolf Landis.

Page 162. John Palmer of Lower Makefield Twp. 7th mo., 27th day, 1774. Proved Jan. 5, 1782. Wife Ann. Son Benjamin, exr. James Thackeray, Junr and Joseph Gillingham, Trustees for son Joseph. Grandchildren, John Walker and Ann Lawrence, wife of Thos. Lawrence of Phila., late Ann Palmer, Junr and Jesse Palmer.
Wit: Jos. Gillingham, Stephen Sands, Timothy Brelsford.

Page 164. Michael Bishop of Lower Milford, Yeoman. Dec. 3, 1781. Proved Jan. 9, 1782. Codicil Dec. 13, 1781. Son Jacob and Saml. Foulke of Richland, exrs. Sons Jacob and Michael. Daus. Barbara, Ann Elizabeth wife of Andrew Stahlnecker, Margaret wife of John Rothrock and Susanna wife of John Shaw. Grandchildren, John and Mary Eve Dietz. Tan Yard and Grist Mill in Milford Twp., Land in Upper Saucon adj. Casper Yoder, Jacob Myer, Christopher Johnson and Ulrick Lutz. In Bucks Co. adj. John Lloyd and Jacob Witmer.
Wit: Jost. Erdman and John Landis.

Page 168. John Biehn of Rockhill Twp., Weaver. Sept. 7, 1779. Proved Jan. 13, 1782. Sons John and Jacob, exrs. Son Paul. Daus. Anne and Mary. Land in Hilltown Twp. adj. Abraham Cope and Levi Thomas. in Rockhill adj. Isaac Dirstine, Ernest Hair, Saml. Bechtel, and Jacob Sabelkool.
Wit: Isaac Dirstine and Abrm. Stout. Signed "Johannes Biehn.."

Page 169. Jacob Savelcool, of Rockhill Twp., Yeoman. Aug. 3, 1780. Proved Jan. 23, 1782. Wife Elizabeth. Son William and son-in-law Julius Kolb, exrs. Sons William and Isaac. Daus. Catharine, Eleanor, Susanna and Elizabeth. Gd.son Jacob Kolb. Land in Hilltown adj. Henry Hertzell, Leonard Seller, John Shellenberger, Philip Wagner and Jacob Appenzeller.
Wit: Isaac Dirstine, Jacob Clemmer, Abrm. Stout.

Page 171. Samuel Dyre of Northampton Twp. Mch. 2, 1771. Proved Feby. 6, 1782. Wife Hannah. Dau. Hannah Dyre and James Wildman exrs.
Wit: Joseph Wildman, William Richardson, Thomas Atkinson.

Page 172. Jacob Clements of Plumstead, Yeoman. Jan. 8, 1782. Proved Feby. 7, 1782. Wife Susanna. Children, Adam and Christina. Eldest son Valentine. Peter Loux and John Mayers, exrs.
Wit: Mathias Tenchman, John McCalla.

Page 176. Benjamin Hamelton of Warwick, Yeoman. Jan. 9, 1782.
Proved Feby. 16, 1782. Wife ---. Son John, John Jameson, and
Elijah Stinson, exrs. Sons Thomas, James and Benjamin. Dau.
Sarah Hamelton.
Wit: Wm. Scott, Alex Bunsted, Hugh Edams.

PAge 173. Michael Dirstine of Rockhill, Miller. Feby. 8, 1777.
Proved Jany. 23, 1782. Son Isaac and son-in-law Jacob Meyer,
exrs. Son Abraham. Grandson Michael Dirstine, son of son Jacob,
dec'd. Daus. Barbara wife of Jacob Meyer, Elizabeth wife of
Samuel Delp, Sarah wife of Peter Seller, and Hannah Dirstine.
Wit: Lewis Stannert, John Stannert.

Page 177. John Clemens, of Buckingham, Miller. Aug. 6, 1781.
Proved Feby. 21, 1782. "Far advanced in years." Wife Catharine.
Son Garet and his two eldest children, John and Elizabeth. Son
Jacob. Children of dau. Margaret Bugwalter, dec'd. 2 youngest
children of dau. Ann Springer, dec'd. Philip Krotz, of Plumstead
and Jacob Yodder of New Britain, exrs.
Wit: Gabriel Swartslander, Jacob Lapp and Abrm Stout.

Page 179. Martin Hoffman of Nockamixon, Yeoman. Feby. 6, 1782.
Proved Feby. 25, 1782. Wife Gertrout. 8 children, Ann, Mary,
Conrad, Magdlen, Elisabeth, William, Martin, Gertrout and
Catharine. Jacob Shupe and Nicholas McCarty, exrs.
Wit: Joseph Kohle, George Kohle.

Page 180. Mathias Harvye, of Upper Makefield, Yeoman. Jan. 5,
1775. Proved Mch. 12, 1782. Wife Ellen. Sons Mathias and John,
exrs. Daus. Jane, Ellen, and Sarah. 3 children of dau. Mary,
viz, Ellen, Thamer and Sarah.
Wit: John Burroughs, Abraham Harvye, John Chapman.

Page 182. John Erwin of Tinnecum Twp., Yeoman. Feby. 8, 1782.
Proved Mch. 13, 1782. Father Arthur Erwin of Tinnecum, exr. Bro.
Joseph of Phila., Merchant. Bros. William and Hugh. Land bought
of Robert Stewart, James Kennedy and Abraham Van Middleswart.
Wit: Ezekiel Everett, John Dakin, Neal McDuffee.

Page 184. Thomas Rickey of Lower Makefield, Cordwainer. Jan.
13, 1779. Proved Mch. 23, 1782. Wife Hannah and sons William,
Thomas, and Alexander, exrs. Daus. Mary White and Rachel Rickey.
Mary White dau. of dau. Hannah. Rebecca Rickey, dau. of son
Thomas.
Wit: John Larzeler, Benj. Vanhorn, and Martha Cottman.

Page 185. Robert Miller of Buckingham Twp. Apr. 4, 1777.
Proved Mch. 23, 1782. Wife Elizabeth. Son George. Other
children, Mary, Sarah, Samuel, Robert, Elizabeth, Isaac, Joseph,
and Rachel. Joseph Smith and John Terry, Junr., exrs.
Wit: John Tucker, David Worstall, Charles Carter.

Page 186. Timothy Smith of Upper Makefield Twp. 5th mo., 17th
day, 1768. Proved May (?) 11, 1776. Codicil 4th mo., 24th day,
1776. Wife Rachel. 6 children, Timothy, Isaac, Joseph,

Pleasant, Ruth, and Rachel. Wife and Nephew Timothy Smith and Joseph Smith, exrs. Dau. Rachel's legacy to be held during life time of her present husband.
Wit: Bernard Taylor, David Barton, and Jos. Tomlinson. To Codicil, Saml. Henderson and Abigail Curtis.

Page 190. William Smith of Wrightstown. 3rd mo., 13th day, 1770. Proved Apr. 15, 1782. Sons Stephen and Isaac, exrs. Oldest son Thomas. Daus. Sarah Betts, Mary, Rebecca, and Rachel.
Wit: Joseph Twining, Sarah Linton, Wm. Linton.

Page 188. Joseph Smith, of Wrightstown Twp. 8th mo., 3rd day, 1777. Proved Apr. 15, 1782. Wife Mary. Nephews Thomas and Joseph Smith, exrs. Niece Rachel Smith. Nephew Robert Smith, land in Md. Bros. Thomas, Timothy, Robert and Samuel. £50 to Wrightstown Mo. Mtg. for use of a Free School.
Wit: Stephen Hambleton, Joseph Worthington, William Linton.

Page 192. Robert Magill, of Warwick Twp., Yeoman. Sept. 6, 1781. Codicil Apr. 5, 1782. Proved Apr. 20, 1782. Wife Martha. Son William. Bros. Henry, James, and William. Sis. Letitia and Margaret Magill. Niece Jane Magill, dau. of Bro. William. exrs. Benj. Snodgrass and William Dungan and Guard.s of Son William.
Wit: John Crawford, David Evans. To Codicil Jesse Fell and David Evans.

Page 195. Edmund Lovett, of the Falls, Yeoman. Dec. 25, 1773. Proved Apr. 30, 1782. Wife Phebe and Friend Daniel Burgess, exrs. Sons Owen, Daniel and Evan. Sister Martha Priestly. Land bought of Saml. Burgess, Joseph Ashton and Joseph Ashton, Junr.
Wit: John Sotcher, Joseph Brown, Junr., Henry Fagan.

Page 198. Jacob Herwick of Lower Milford Twp., "Taylor." Nov. 9, 1779. Proved May 20, 1782. Wife Elizabeth and Friend Jacob Yodder of New Britain, exrs. Daus. Barbara, Elizabeth, Mary, Esther. Eldest dau. Anne (married). Sons John, Samuel, Jacob. Land adj. Casper Johnson, Samuel Foulke, and Theophilus Foulke in Richland Twp.
Wit: Peter Fluke, George Ackerman, and Abm. Stout.

Page 200. George Adam Hellapord, of Tinicum Twp. Feb. 16, 1777. Proved May 20, 1782. Wife Mary Philip Pene and Jacob Beidleman, exrs. Children, John, George, Adam, Barned, Henry, Frederick, Margaret, Elizabeth and one unborn.
Wit: John Nease, Jacob Nease.

Page 201. Edward Thomas of Richland, Yeoman. July 23, 1775. Codicil May 6, 1781. Proved May 31, 1782. Wife Alice. Bro. Thomas and Thomas Foulke exrs. Codicil ~Bro. Thomas being dec'd." makes son Samuel exr. in his stead. Daus. Margaret, Miriam Heacock, Martha and "infirm dau. Mary.."
Wit: Saml. Foulke, John Thomas, John Foulke.

Page 203. John Pursell of Bristol Twp., Yeoman. 5th mo., 31, 1777. Proved Apr. 8, 1783. Wife Mary. Bro-in-law James Moon and

Friend Joseph Merrick, exrs. Sons Jonathan and Mahlon to be
bound to trades "among Friends." Daus. Ann Pursell.
Wit: Jacob Lancaster, John Mitchell, Junr., Pierson Mitchell. 1st
two witnesses dec'd. handwriting proved by Samuel Waber.

Page 205. Evan Mathias of Hilltown, Yeoman. Dec. 7, 1775.
Proved June 10, 1782. Dau. Sarah Mathias, exr. Son Benjamin.
Ephrai Thomas and Mannaseth Thomas of Hilltown, Trustees.
Wit: Enoch Davis, Ebenezer Owen, Thomas Jones.

Page 206. John Wilkinson Esq. of Wrightstown. Feby. 11, 1782.
Proved June 10, 1782. Wife Hannah. Son Stephen and Kinsman John
Chapman exrs. Son Elisha. Daus. Tamar Wilkinson, Mary Twining,
Martha, Rachel, Ann and Hannah Wilkinson. Dau. Rachel's son
Aaron. Grandson John Wilkinson land adj. Tract confirmed to son
John in his life time. Grandsons Abraham Wilkinson, Amos
Wilkinson, and Elias Twining. Granddau. Rachel Twining.
Wit: Jos. Sacket, John Scott, John VanPelt.

Page 210. Philip Wood of Plumstead Twp., Yeoman. Jan. 3, 1782.
Proved June 11, 1782. Son Peter. Daus. Elizabeth Miller and
Deborah ---. Gd.son William Miller eldest son of dau. Elizabeth.
Benj. Fell and Wm. Mains, exrs. Caveat filed May 28, 1782. by
Peter Wood.
Wit: Joseph Britton, James Davis, Jesse Britton. "Great age and
infirmities." Will confirmed June 11.

Page 212. Henry Darroch of New Britain, Yeoman. Mch. 17, 1782.
Proved June 12, 1782. Wife Ann. Son William of age in 1788.
Children, James, William, John, George, Ann and Margaret and one
unborn. Sister, the widow Ann Davis. Wm. Dean, Wm. Scott, and
Wm. Roberts, exrs.
Wit: John Tayler, John Garvin, John Davis.

Page 214. William Michener of Plumstead Twp. 8th mo., 17th day,
1778. Proved June 19, 1782. Wife Ann. Sons William and
Meschach, exrs. Sons John, Mordecai, Joseph, Meschach, George
and William. Dau. Margaret.
Wit: Francis Goode, Sarah Goode, Jonathan Combs.

Page 215. Jacob Shouch of Haycock, Yeoman. Aug. 27, 1777.
Proved June 19, 1782. Wife Madlen and Son John, exrs. Sons Jacob
and Rudolf. Daus. Cateren and Eve.
Wit: Susan Winner, Stophel Shmidt, William Deile.

Page 216 (?). Jacob Myers of Hilltown Twp., Yeoman. Dec. 18,
1777. Proved Aug. 5, 1782. Bro. Samuel Meyer and Friend Jacob
Kolb exrs. Sons Christian and Jacob and Dau. Mary "their dec'd.
mother's portion." Wife Barbara. Sons Michael, Samuel, Joseph,
and David. Daus. Agnes and Barbara.
Wit: Jacob Agne, Jacob Beidler, Abrm. Stout.

Page 218. Jacob Meyer the younger of Hilltown. May 3, 1780.
Proved Aug. 5, 1782. Wife Susanna. Bro. Christian and Sister
Mary. Dau. Margaret. Wife and bro-in-law Jacob Kolb, exrs.

"Land devised by will of Father Jacob Meyer."
Wit: Isaac Kolb, Jacob Wismer, Abrm. Stout.

Page 222. Michael Meyer of Hilltown, Farmer. Sept. 1, 1780.
Proved Aug. 5, 1782. Uncle Isaac Dirstine, exr. Bros. Joseph,
Christian, Samuel and David. Sisters Mary, Agnes, and Barbara.
Sister-in-law Susanna Meyer. "Land devised by Father Jacob
Meyer."
Wit: Jacob Agne, Abrm. Stout.

Page 220. Michael Leatherman of Bedminster Dated Dec. 26, 1780.
Proved July 21, 1782. Wife Anna and Neighbor Rudolf Landis, exrs.
Children, Henry, Jacob, Elizabeth, and Ann Leatherman.
Wit: Dilman Culp and Jacob Leatherman. Letters granted to Rudolf
Landis, Anna Loux (late Leatherman), the widow renouncing.
Translated from German.

Page 221. Henry Leatherman of Plumstead. Dec. 7, 1778. Proved
July 21, 1782. Wife Elizabeth. Uncle Philip Johns and Rudolf
Landis of Bedminster exrs. Children, Jacob and Magdalene.
Sisters Catharine and Ann Leatherman.
Wit: Abraham Overholt and Samuel Mayer. Translated from German.
Joyner and Turner's Tools.

Page 223. Peter Buck, of Lower Milford, Blacksmith. July 19,
1782. Proved Aug. 13, 1782. Wife Mary. Children, Katharine,
Margaret, Henry, Mary, Peter, and Jacob. Jacob Singer of
Worchester Twp., Phila. Co., and Andrew Reed of Cosehopen sd. co.
exrs.
Wit: Geo. Weicher, George Swigmaster (?), Jos. Phillips.

Page 225. Jared Irwin of Hilltown, Blacksmith. Aug. 14, 1776.
Proved Oct. 8, 1782. Wife Rachel. Daus. Sarah, Mary, Elizabeth,
and Rachel. Son Charles, Lot in Phila. devised to wife Rachel by
will of John Morgan. Wm. Bryan of Haycock and John Garvin of New
Britain, exrs.
Wit: David Thomas, Nathaniel Jones. Letters to Jesse Bryan, exrs.
and Thos. Hughes and Rachel his wife, (late Irwin) the widow of
decedent having renounced.

Page 226. John Wharton of Lower Makefield, Yeoman. 2nd mo., 9th
day, 1777. Proved Oct. 10, 1782. Sons Joseph, William, and
Daniel exrs. Grandson Mahlon Wharton. Land adj. James Moon,
David Brelsford and Michel Hutchinson.
Wit: Joseph Gillingham, Jonathan Bradfield, Joseph Nutt.

Page 228. Peter Bright of Springfield, Joiner. Oct. 24, 1780.
Proved Oct. 11, 1782. Wife Mary Elizabeth. Children, John, Peter,
Elias, and David. Land surveyed out to mother Margaret Bright.
Neighbors John Trichler and Abraham Tayler, exrs.
Wit: David Zublin, Jacob Rothrock.

Page 230. Martin Young of Springfield, Weaver. 6-28-1775.
Proved Oct. 19, 1782. Wife Catren and John Man, exrs. Sons John
and Peter.

Wit: Michael and Wm. Deile.

Page 231. Thomas Paxson of Solebury, Yeoman. 6-28-1775. Proved Oct. 19, 1782. Wife. --- Son Joseph, exr. Sons Benjamin, Oliver, Jacob and Isaiah. Gdson Thomas Paxson.
Wit: Aaron Phillips, Mary Phillips, Miriam Betts.

Page 233. Agnes Gill of Buckingham. 10-9-1782. Proved Oct. 29, 1782. Sisters Grace Beal and Urel Bradfield. Sarah Thomson. Rachel, Mercy and Grace Beal, Jr. Jane Thompson. Susanna Williams, Gill, Isaac and Thomas Pennington, Marill Wood. Agnes Vankerk. Joseph, Thomas and William Beal. Wm. Beal and Jona. Fell, exrs.
Wit: Thomas Fell, Amos Fell.

Page 234. Lawrence Johnson, Senior, Bensalem, Yeoman. Mch. 8, 1776. Proved Jan. 31, 1782. Wife Mary and son Lawrence, exrs. Sons Jacob, Evan, Isaac and Jesse.
Wit: John Brown, Joseph Worrell, John Evans.

Page 236. John Boyd of the Falls Twp., Weaver. Jan. 28, 1782. Proved Nov. 9, 1782. Wife Catharine. Sons James and John, exrs. 6 sons Andrew, James, John, Jarrett, William and Mathew.
Wit: Samuel Hutchinson, John Milnor.

Page 238. Henry Keller of Haycock, Yeoman. Jan. 23, 1782. Proved Nov. 15, 1782. Wife Juliana. Son John, exr. Sons John, Peter, Christophel and Henry. Daus. Anamere, Dorothea, and Barbara. Son-in-law Philip Stiver and Solomon Grover.
Wit: Casper Berger, Henry Trach.

Page 244. Abraham Fretz of Bedminster, Yeoman. July 21, 1779. Proved Dec. 10, 1782. Wife Mary and brother John Fretz and Henry Overholt, exrs. Son Abraham, daus. Agnes, Barbara, Elizabeth, Mary and Sarah.
Wit: Henry Fretz, John Fretz, Junr.

Page 239. Alexander Brown of New Britain, Yeoman. 4-1-1782. Proved Dec. 3, 1782. Wife Esther. Son Josiah and son-in-law Andrew Ellicott and Wm. Shoemaker, exrs. Son Alexander, dec'd. Sons Josiah, John, Jonathan,. Son-in-law Ezekiel Haizley. Daus. Elizabeth Rich, Esther Ellicott, Martha Shoemaker and Mary Haizley. 3 of the children of dau. Elizabeth, viz. Mary Wells, Alexander and Joseph Rich. Tace Ellicott, dau. of dau. Esther. Susanna Brown, dau. of son John. Thomas Brown son of son Jonathan. Martha Haizley, dau. of dau. Mary. Levina Brown, dau. of son Alexander.
Wit: Robert Kirkbride, Jonathan Worthington, and Thomas Goode, Junr.

Page 242. Thomas Dawson of Solebury, Yeoman. 8-1-1776. Proved Dec. 7, 1782. Wife Agnes and Dau. Esther Blackfan, exrs. Sister Ann Brown, dau. Esther Blackfan's children, Elizabeth, Rachel, Hannah, Sarah, Agnes, John and Thomas Blackfan. Grandson Jonathan Smith, son of dau. Sarah, dec'd.

Wit: Thos. Ross, Thos. Whitson, Daniel Martin.

Page 245. Daniel Pennington of New Britain, Yeoman. 12-5-1775. Proved Dec. 14, 1782. Wife Elizabeth. Son-in-law, John Carlile and Robert Kirkbride, exr. Sons-in-law William Lukens and Joseph Conrad. Sons William, Daniel, John and Paul (dec'd.). Daus. Hannah Bradfield, Elizabeth Lukens, Sarah Carlile, Margaret David, Martha Conrad and Mary Pennington. Grandchildren, Daniel Lukens, Daniel Carlile, Paul, John and Priscilla Conrad and Rebecca, dau. of son Paul.
Wit: Edward Goode, Everad Conard, Margaret Conard.

Page 248. Rachel Rue of Middletown, Widow. Mch. 6, 1777. Proved June 16, 1783. Son Lewis Rue and Dau. Elizabeth Severns, exrs. Son Stoffell. Daus. Ann Inglesdue, Elizabeth Severns, Catharine Parker, Rachel Stackhouse, and Jesinah Richardson.
Wit: Anthony Rue, Rachel Rue, Robt. Brodnax.

Page 250. Enion Williams of Bristol Boro., Yeoman. 1-19-1780. Proved 1-17-1783. Kinsman Phineas Buckley, exr. Real estate adj. Wm. Tisom.
Wit: Joseph Church, Edward Church.

Page 251. Stephen Guyon of Bristol Twp., Yeoman. 9-11-1782. Proved 2-3-1783. Bro-in-law Jonathan Hibbs, exrs. Sisters Sarah and Elizabeth Hibbs. Mother Mary Rue. Bro. John Guyon. Nephews Stephen, John, Samuel Hibbs. Nieces Kezia and Jemima Hibbs. Sister Mary Vansant's children in Virginia, names unknown.
Wit: Thomas Cabe, John Sotcher.

Page 252. Thomas Gilbert of Buckingham, Yeoman. 1-9-1781. Proved 2-8-1783. Son David, exr. Sons Thomas, William, Jonathan, Caleb and David. Dec'd. son Joshua. Dec'd. dau. Sarah Hughes. Grandchildren, Samuel Gilbert, Sarah Hughes, and David Gilbert. Sister Sarah Roberts. Farm bought of Amos White, dower of Mary White, widow of Daniel White.
Wit: David Bradshaw, Amos Bradshaw.

Page 255. John Sellers of Hilltown, Blacksmith. 12-26-1782. Proved 2-13-1783. Wife Anne and Son Abraham, exrs. Sons Abraham, Samuel and John. Daus. Elizabeth. Land adj. Abrm. Wambold and Ernest Hair in Rockhill. Farm in Hilltown adj. Henry Hartzell, Adam Cobe, Abrm. Cobe and Abrm. Miller.
Wit: Job Thomas, Abraham Stout.

Page 257. John Mathews of New Britain, Yeoman. 11-9-1781. Proved 3-10-1783. Son Joseph, exr. Wife Diana. Sons Joseph and Benjamin. Daus. Margaret Young, Mary Barton, Rachel Meredith, Ann Doyle, and Susanna Mathews.
Wit: Thomas Mathews and Benjamin Thomas.

Page 259. Josiah Fenton of Buckingham. 1-19-1783. Proved 3-12-1783. Son John and James Shaw, Sr., exrs. Wife Sarah. Sons John, Eleazer, Ephraim. Daus. Jane, Judea, and Sarah.
Wit: William Bradshaw, Ambrose Poulton, Randel Fenton.

Page 261. George Shuman, of Springfield, Yeoman. 3-28-1782.
Proved 3-12-1783. Son Michael and Philip Stall,exrs. Wife Anna
Cathrina, dau. Christiana. Granddaus. Elizabeth, dau. of
Christiana and Barbara Keller.
Wit: Peter Gruber, Saml. Foulke.

Page 262. Margaret Gray, of Warrington, Widow. 4-5-1782.
Proved 3-13-1783. Bros. Son, Thomas Craig, exr. All Est. to
Margaret wife of James Barclay.
Wit: Wm. Walker, Daniel Craig, Alexander Nelans.

Page 263. Joseph Wharton of Falls, Yeoman. 2-28-1783. Proved
3-21-1783. Wife Mary and sons Joseph and Edward, exrs. Sons
John, Joseph, Edward, Israel and Benjamin. Dau. Sarah.
Wit: Daniel Wharton, William Young.

Page 264. Sarah Yardley widow of Wm. Yardley of Lower Makefield
Twp. 11-28-1782. Proved 3-28-1783. Bro. Robert Kirkbride and
son-in-law John Stabler, exrs. Sons Thomas, Mahlon, William, and
Joseph. Dau. Mary Woolston, Hannah Stabler, Achsah Yardley and
Letitia Willis.
Wit: Joseph Field, Joseph Taylor, William Field.

Page 266. Mahlon Kirkbride of Falls, Yeoman. 12-10-1777.
Proved 3-28-1783. Wife Ann. Bro. Robert and Friend Joseph
Gillingham, exrs. Bros. Stacy, Robert and Jonathan. Cousins
Mahlon Taylor, Ann Rickey, dau. of James Rickey, dec'd. and John
Sotcher.
Wit: Nathan Field, John Nutt, and Alexander Rickey.

Page 268. James Neeld of Lower Makefield Twp. 12-10-1773.
Proved 3-29-1783. Sons Richard and Eli, exrs. Wife Rachel.
Daus. Ann Paist and her son James Paist. Dau. Elizabeth Keys and
her dau. Ann Jessop.
Wit: James Moon, Moses Moon, James West.

Page 270. Christopher Carter of Penna. Dated 2-21-1782. Proved
3-31-1783. Wife Ann and Son Charles MacMicking, exrs. Son Jacob,
Benjamin, Charles and Ebenezer. dec'd. son Christopher. Daus.
Rachel and Mary MacMicking.
Wit: David Stockdale, Ralph Williams, William Curry.

Page 272. Asher Mott of Bucks Co. Dated 12-13-1781. Proved 4-1-
1783. Bro. John Mott and Bro-in-law William Biles exrs. Sons
William and John. Daus. Mary and Margaret.
Wit: Daniel Bunting, Joseph Bunting.

Page 273. Michael Hutchinson Lower Makefield, Merchant. Dated
10-23-1782. Proved 4-14-1783. Wife Margery, and nephew Mathias
Hutchinson, exrs. Daus. Mary Hutchinson and Owen Lovett. Dec'd.
Bros. Thomas, John, Joseph, and Randle. Bro. Samuel. Nephews
John and Thomas Hutchinson, sons of Bro. John dec'd. Niece
Rebecca Hutchinson, dau. of John. Mary Brown, Hannah Linton and
Joseph Hutchinson, children of brother Joseph, dec'd. Niece
Phebe Ashton's son Samuel. Joseph Hutchinson son, dec'd. Bro.

Thomas. Mahlon and James Hutchinson sons of dec'd. Bro. Randle.
Jonathan Kirkbride and Joseph Gillingham £50 in Trust for Free
School near Falls. Letitia Carter.
Wit: William Wharton, Jos. Hutchinson, Thos. Hutchinson. Widow
married John Chapman before settlement was filed.

Page 277. William Searbrough of Solebury. 2-27-1783. Proved 4-
23-1783. Daniel Stradling, Yeomans Gillingham, and Isaac
Scarbrough, exrs. Sarah, Daniel, and Joseph Stradling, Bro.
Euclides Scarbrough, Sarah Scott, Jonathan Thomas.
Wit: John Smith, Nathan Fell, Sarah Michener.

Page 278. John Cooper of Northampton Twp., Yeoman. 4-4-1783.
Proved 5-3-1783. Sons John and Henry, exrs. Son William. Daus.
Margaret Tomlinson, Sarah Campbell, and Mary Atkinson.
Wit: Joseph Buckman, Asenath Buckman, Wm. Linton.

Page 280. Joseph Fell of Buckingham, Yeoman. 12-15-1775.
Proved 5-5-1783. Son Joseph and Dau. Sarah Fell, exrs. Sons
Joseph and David. Daus. Sarah, Rachel, and Martha.
Wit: Paul Preston, Thomas Smith, Benjamin Harmer.

Page 281. Joseph Fentove of Northampton Twp., Yeoman. 2-8-1782.
Proved 5-19-1783. Sons Joseph and John, exrs. Wife Mary. Son
Benjamin. dec'd. Sons Thias and Cornelius. Dau. Helena Kroesen.
Grandchildren, Joseph Thomas, Mary and Martha Fenton and Joseph
and Mary Fenton.
Wit: Richard Leedom, Arthur Lefferts.

Page 283. Henry Kelso of New Britain, Gentlemen. 7-29-1782.
Proved 6-10-1783. Wife Agnes and Bro. Thomas, exrs. Bro. John.
Sisters Margaret and Jane. Nieces Jane, Mary, Ann, and Margaret
Kelso, nephew Thomas Kelso.
Wit: Geroge Congle, Philip Miller, John Davis.

Page 284. Philip Shull of Milford Twp., Miller. 3-18-1783.
Codicil 5-6-1783. Proved 6-10-1783. Father-in-law George
Weikard, Esq. and Bro. Peter, exrs. Wife Elizabeth. Sons Peter
and Elias. Father Peter Shull. Bros. Peter and Elias.
Wit: Jacob Wagoner, Stoffel Sacks, Christian Weikel.

Page 287. Benjamin Jones of Northampton Twp., Yeoman. 5-22-
1783. Proved 6-18-1783. Wife Kuertie, son Benjamin, and Dau.
Catharine Jones, exrs. Sons Benjamin, Lawrence and Joshua. Daus.
Catharine, Mary and Mercy.
Wit: Gilliam Cornell, David Dungan, John Kroesen.

Page 288. Thomas Betts, of Buckingham Twp. 4-12-1783. Codic
5-11-1783. Proved 6-19-1783. Wife Sarah and son John exrs.
William, John, Isaac, Stephen and Zachariah. Daus. Sarah Har
Ann Sample, Rebecca Rose, Susanna Mitchell and Mary Bettes.
Grandson Thomas Betts, son of dec'd. son Thomas.
Wit: William Newburn, Susanna Newburn, John Terry, Jr.

PaAge 291. Thomas Betts Jr. of Buckingham Twp. 3-18-177

Proved 6-19-1783. Bro. John, exr. Wife Elizabeth.
Wit: James Bonner, William Newburn, John Beaumont.

Page 292. Jacob Hammerstein of ---. 5-17-1783. Proved 6-21-
1783. Son Andrew and Frederick Funk, exrs. Dau. Margaret wife
of Michael Hartman of Berks Co.
Wit: George Fuhr, Anthony Shoemaker.

Page 293. Joshua Ely of Solebury Twp., Yeoman. 9-4-1776.
Proved 8-5-1783. Sons Joshua and George, exrs. Wife Elizabeth.
Sons Joshua, Geroge, Hugh, and John. Daus. Sarah Kitchin and
Jane Balderston, Grandchild Absalom Duberry and sister Hannah,
John Kitchin and Joshua Balderston.
Wit: Aaron Phillips, Thomas Phillips.

Page 296. Thomas Smith of Plumstead Twp. 9-13-1777. Proved 8-
23-1783. Son John, exr. Wife Sarah. Children not named.
Wit: Paul Preston, Ralph Cowgill, John Lewis.

Page 299. Robert Wilson of Tinicum Twp., Farmer. 9-7-1778.
Proved 10-3-1783. Son James, exr. Wife Jane. Sons James, Andrew
and Charles. Daus. Mary Patterson, Anne Snodgrass, Sarah
Patterson, Hester Abernathy and Elizabeth Horner and Judith
Wilson. Grandson Robert Wilson. Servant Jacob Robinson.
Wit: George Reigel, David Wilson, Rev. Alex Mitchell.

Page 297. Mary Kirkbride of Lower Makefield, widow of Mahlon
Kirkbride. Dated 9-14-1778. Proved 9-15-1783. Sons Robert and
Jonathan, exrs. Son Stacy. Daus. Mary Taylor, Sarah Yeardley.
Grandchildren, Mary, Sarah, and Prudence, children of Stacy.
Mary, Esther, Hannah, Sarah and Letitia children of Robert.
Mahlon and Mary, children of Jonathan. Mary, Hannah, Achsah, and
Letitia, children of Sarah Yeardly. Joseph, Letitia and Mary
Taylor and Hannah Field. Son Jonathan's wife Elizabeth.
Wit: Saml. Johnson, Joseph Johnson, Jr., Joseph Gillingham.

Page 301. Charles Polton of Buckingham, Yeoman. 10-26-1772.
Proved 10-14-1783. Wife Ruth and son Thomas, exrs. Sons Charles,
Thomas, John and Ambrose. Daus. Abigail, Barbara, Ruth and
Rachel.
Wit: Samuel Hanin, Joseph Willson.

Page 302. John Black of Bedminster Twp., Weaver. 11-4-1782.
Proved 10-24-1783. Son Andrew and Wife Catarina exrs. Daus.
Anna, Elizabeth, Barbara and Margaret.
Wit: Dilman Kolb, Jacob Overholt.

Page 304. Wilhemus Cornell of Southampton, Yeoman. 9-15-1782.
Proved 10-28-1783. Sons John and Gilliam, exrs. Wife Else.
Daus. Breehe (also spelled Brachget, Braeghe), Cornelia, wife of
William Craven, Margaret wife of Henry Courson and Elizabeth
Cornell. Farms bought of Jo. Addis and John VanDike adj. Daniel
Hoageland.
Wit: Abraham Cornell, Gilliam Cornell.

Page 306. Patrick Gregg of Middletown Twp. 10-11-1783. Proved
11-4-1783. Sons James and John, exrs. Son John, Michael,
Francis, William and James.
Wit: Jonathan Carlile, Thos. Jenks, Jr. James McMickin.

Page 307. Erasmus Kelly of Hilltown Twp., Yeoman. 7-7-1783.
Proved 12-10-1783. Wife Hannah, extx. Sons Erasmus and Benjamin.
Son-in-law Mathew Grier. Land in Posession of Wm. Godshalk
bought of Amos Vastine.
Wit: William Godshalk, Jane Jones, Thomas Jones.

Page 309. Rev. Mathew Light of Southampton N.D. Minister. Dated
9-20. Proved 12-10-1783. Gilliam Cornell, Jr. exr. Wife
Katharine. Dau. Elizabeth. Bro-in-law Peter Uredenburg, Jr. of
New Brunswick, Guardian.
Wit: Henry Wynkoop, Gilliam Cornell, John Kroesen.

Page 310. Grace Kirkbride of Middletown, Widow. 11-1-1783.
Proved 12-16-1783. Son Jonathan and son-in-law William Blakey,
exrs. Son Jonathan. Daus. Sarah Blakey and Hannah Biles. Niece
Sarah Woolston.
Wit: John Woolston, James Moon, Hannah Woolston.

Page 311. Isaac Bolton of Southampton Twp. 2-3-1783. Proved
12-18-1783. Wife Sarah and Bros-in-law Thos. Walmsby, exrs.
Children not named.
Wit: Thos. Austin, Joshua Comly, Henry Tomlinson.

Page 312. Richard Iliff of Nockamixon, Yeoman. 12-18-1783.
Proved 1-16-1784. Benjamin Williams, Sr. and son John, exrs.
Sons Joseph, James and John.
Wit: Anthony Shoemaker, Rebekah Baily.

Page 313. John Brelsford of Middletown, Yeoman. 11-23-1783.
Proved 2-7-1784. Wife Rebecca and son William, exrs. Daus.
Rachel Stackhouse, Mary Nields, Martha Nields and Hannah Sisom.
money due from Thomas Wilson.
Wit: John Brown, Samuel Brown, Christian Lundy.

Page 315. William Ashburne of Newtown Dated 1-14-1782. Proved
2-16-1784. Son John and Son in law John Thornton, exrs. Son
Jacob. Grandchildren, William Blaker, Mary Dyer. Elizabeth and
Patience daus. of son William, Dec'd. Ages Cary. Sarah Terry
and Hannah Beakes dau. of son John and Mary Griffith. Bro. Jacob
Ashburn.
Wit: Samuel Cary, Sarah Thornton, and Joseph Thornton.

Page 316. George Shittinger of Plumstead Twp. 1-19-1784.
Proved 2-9-1784. Wife Christina and Jacob Tensman Admrs. with
will annexed. Sons Abraham, John and Andrew. Daus. Elizabeth,
Catreen, Mary and Susanna. John Wilson, J.P., Abrm. Swartz,
Translator.
Wit: Nathan Huddleston, John Myers.

Page 317. Henry Seibel of Hilltown, Miller. Dated 3-10-1779.

Proved 2-18-1784. Son George and Friend Andrew Keichline, exrs. Son Conrad, Daus. Ursula, Eva, Hannah, and Elizabeth. Wit: Saml. Foulke, Saml. Mayer.

Page 318. Killian Zimmerman of Richland Twp. 7-31-1782. Proved 3-1-1784. Leonard Hinckel of Richland and Manuel Salletey of Tinicum, exrs. Housekeeper Margaret Hinckel. Catharine wife of Philip Hinckel. Margaret Gayrey. Magdalena wife of Leonard Hinckel, dec'd. Hannes Hud's wife. Wit: John Heany, Jr. and Peter Standt. Abrm. Swartz Translator.

Page 319. Nicholas Hill of Plumstead, Worsted Comber. Dated 4-8-1782. Proved 2-28-1784. George Geddes and John McMullen of Plumstead, Yeoman, exrs. Daus. Alice Smith and Elizabeth Craft. G.daus. Elizabeth Hill and Martha Simmonds. Wit: John Lewis, Mathew Adams, Silas Watts.

Page 320. Thomas Dungan of Warwick, Yeoman. 10-19-1781. Proved 3-6-1784. Sons Joseph and John, exrs. Son Jonathan. Daus. Deborah Stevens and Lucretia Rundle. Granddau. Mary Johnston. Grandson Thomas Stevens. Wit: Thos. Dungan, Isaac Stevens.

Page 322. John Plumly of Northampton, Yeoman. 2-11-1784. Proved 3-13-1784. Sons John and Edward, exrs. Wife Ayels. Sons William, Charles, Robert, George, Edward, and John. Daus. Mary, Susanna, Alice and Sarah Mitchener. Grandson John Gregg. Granddau. Anna Gregg. Wit: Jacob Vandegrift, Simon Vanarsdalen, John Rankin.

Page 326. Jane Slack of Lower Makefield Twp. 3-8-1784. Proved 3-25-1784. Sons Philip and John Slack, exrs. Father Thomas Winder. Wit: Cornelius Slack, Thomas Slack.

Page 323. Magdalena Morgan of Newtown Twp., Widow. 10-10-1783. Proved 3-16-1784. John Thornton, exr. Daus. Magdalena Bulger and Frances Clark, son Charles Morgan's children, John and Elinor. Son Peter Morgan's children, Thomas and Josiah. Dau. Elizabeth's children, Moses and John Neal. Granddaus. Magdalena Kreusen and Magdalena Gilbert. Grandson Joseph Dyer. Wit: John Roney, Agnes Gregg, Margaret Davids.

Page 325. Ulriah Hughes, Senr., of Buckingham, Yeoman. 4-5-1782. Proved 3-22-1784. Nephew Uriah Hughes, Jr. and David Forst exrs. Wife Jennet. Bros. Elias Hughes. Charity Hughes who has long live with me, Elizabeth, wife of Robert Smith dau. of Bro. Elias. Mathew Thomas, Isaac and Constantine, children of brother Mathew Hughes, dec'd. Cousin John Hughes (shoemaker). Wit: Samuel Harrold, William Bennet, John Large.

Page 327. George Brown, of Falls Twp., Yeoman. 3-17-1784. Proved 4-10-1784. Sons George and Thomas, exrs. Daus. Martha Barnes, Ann Dean, Mercy, Sarah and Susanna Brown. Land bought of Amos Shaw.

Wit: John MacKinney, John Moon, William Young.

Page 329. Alexnader Rickey of Phila. 11-20-1783. Proved 4-10-1784. Aunt Ann Kirkbride, extx. Sisters Elizabeth Vennal and Ann Rickey.
Wit: William Smith, John Carter, Jr.

Page 330. Joseph Penrose of Bristol Twp. 10-7-1783. Proved 4-10-1784. Cousin Jonathan Penrose of Phila. and Friend Saml. Benezet of Bucks Co. exrs. Natural children begat on body of Abigale Wyley, viz. Margaret, Elizabeth and Abraham Penrose.
Wit: Wm. Kinnersley, John Bennett.

Page 332. Christian Frats, Senr. of Tinicum Twp., Yeoman. 1-22-1777. Proved 4-26-1784. Son Daniel and son in law Jacob Yoder, exrs. Wife Elizabeth. Sons Daniel, Abraham, Christian and Mark. Daus. Barbara and Esther.
Wit: Edward Murphy, John Frats, Jacob Frats.

Page 334. John McIntyre of Warwick Twp. 7-5-1775. Proved 4-27-1784. Son John and Dau. Elizabeth exrs. Other children not named. Farm adj. John Walders.
Wit: John Ramsey, Alexander Ramsey.

Page 335. Rachel Pownal of Solebury Twp. 12-3-1773. Proved 4-28-1784. Friends Aaron Phillips and Oliver Paxson exrs. Rachel Pownal, dau. of Bro. Reuben. George and Elisha Pownal sons of Bro. Reuben Pownal. Cousin Rachel Pownal. Bro. Simeon Pownal.
Wit: Mary Phillips, Jonathan Johnson.

Page 336. Sarah Growden of Falls Twp., Gentlewoman, Widow of Lawrence Growdon. 1-15-1781. Codicil 6-16-1783. Proved 4-30-1784. Nephews William Biles and Richard Gibbs. Nephew Edward Pennington of Phila. exrs. Sister Hannah Janney. Nieces Mary Smith, Susanna Thorn and Nancy Mott. Polly Mott dau. of Asher Mott. Mary Borden wife of Joseph. Nancy dau. of Edward Pennington niece Nancy Mott's children, viz., William, John, Mary and Peggy. Samuel, Mary, Sarah, Betzey, Hannah, and Margery Gibbs. Hannah Barnes, Polly Sykes. Phebe and Peggy Mott. John Bates.
Wit: Elizabeth Moon, Catharine Clayton.

Page 340. Casper Yoder, of Milford Twp., Yeoman. 1-5-1781. Proved 5-1-1784. Son Jacob and son-in-law Jacob Kulp, exrs. Wife Barbara. Sons Casper, Jacob, Abraham, and John. Dau. Anne Kulp. Land in Richland adj. John Clemer, Thos. Blackledge.
Wit: John Clymer, Henry Baum, William Foulke.

Page 343. John Shidelwood, of Durham Twp., Yeoman. 4-19-1784. Proved 5-8-1784. Lutwick Afflerbach, exr. and sole legatee.
Wit: George Gresler, Andrew Barnet.

Page 343. James Thackray of Middletown, Weaver. 9-14-1767. Proved 5-13-1784. Son Isaac, exr. Sons James, Joseph, Isaac, and Ezer. Dau. Ruth.

Wit: Gilbert Hicks, George Merrick, Saml. Kirkbride.

Page 345. Joseph Thackray of Middletown Twp. 3-18-1784. Proved 5-13-1784. Son Isaac, exr. Bro. James and his three sons Amos, Joshua and Phineas. Bros. Isaac and Ezer. Sister Ruth Thackray. Wit: Isaac Watson, Joseph Hayhurst, Henry Huddleston.

Page 346. Joseph Church of Bristol Boro. Dated 11-1-1784. Proved 1-7-1785. Son Edward and son in law John Hutchinson, exrs. Son Joseph. Dau. Ann Hutchinson. Sister Solice Johnston. Sarah wife of Edward Church.
Wit: Phineas Buckley, Richard Hartshorne.

Page 348. Elizabeth Thomas of Hilltown, Widow. 10-4-1784. Proved 1-10-1785. Son Levi Thomas, exr. "Relict of Richard Thomas." Dau. Martha and her son Jonathan.
Wit: Benjamin Griffith, Jonathan Walton, Cadwd. Morris.

Page 349. Geoge Shaffer of Springfield Twp., Tinsmith. 5-3-1775. Proved 1-10-1785. Wife Barbara, exr. and sole legatee.
Wit: Peter Seen, Michael Ernst.

Page 350. John Warner of Wrightstown Twp. 4-21-1783. Proved 1-18-1785. Wife Elizabeth and sons David and Isaiah, exrs. Sons John, David, Isaiah, Jonathan, Simeon, and Amos. Daus. Rachel Weaber and Elizabeth Warner. Father in law David Daws. Joseph Chapman and Thomas Warner, Guardians.
Wit: Ruth Warner, Thomas Warner, Wm. Linton.

Page 353. William Bidgood, Bristol Twp., Yeoman. 9-20-1784. Codicil 11-1-1784. Proved 1-19-1785. Son William and sons-in-law Robert Kirkbride and Benjamin Palmer, exrs. Wife Hannah. Son William. Daus. Sarah Bunting, Mary Allen, Hannah Kirkbride, Ann Lovett and Esther Palmer. Grandchildren, Mark, William, Amos, and Hannah Watson. Hannah Kirkbride's children, viz., Mary, Esther, Hanna, Sarah, Letitia, Robert, David, Ann. Thos. Watson living on Lot in Bristol.
Wit: James Moon, John Brown, Abraham Swain.

Page 357. Samuel Eastburn of Solebury, Blacksmith. 11-20-1780. Proved 1-26-1785. Son Robert and grandsons Samuel and John Eastburn, exrs. Wife Elizabeth. Daus. Sarah Smith and Mary wife of Wm. Edwards. Dau-in-law Mary wife of son Joseph, dec'd. Grandchildren, Rachel Fell and Rebecca and Mary Eastburn, Elizabeth, Sarah, Phebe, Benjamin and Samuel Edwards, children of dau. Mary Edwards. Samuel, John, Amos and David, children of son Joseph, dec'd. Friends Oliver Paxson and Aaron Phillips, trustees.
Wit: Aaron Phillips, Abraham Paxson, Thomas Brown.

Page 359. John Smith of Milford Twp. 9-13-1769. Proved 1-28-1785. Friends John Moore, John Jameson Esq. and Thomas Foulke, exrs. Children, James, Mary, and John Smith.
Wit: James Heston, Jr., Rebeckah Simpson and Jonathan Willis.

Page 361. William Gosline of Middletown Twp. 8-26-1784. Proved
1-31-1785. Bro. John and son John, exrs. Sons John, Peter,
Ricahrd, William, Jacob, Levi and Ely. Daus. Elizabeth,
Rebeckah, Charity, Abigail and Mary.
Wit: William Vansant, Steples Thompson.

Page 362. Mary Yerkes, Wife of Harman Yerkes of Warminster, late
Mary Clayton. 5-10-1784, Proved 2-1-1785. Bro. Joseph Houghton
and Isaac Hough, exrs. Richard Houghton son of Joseph.
Elizabeth and Mary daus. of Bro. Joseph. Elizabeth wife of Isaac
Hough Jr. Nieces Sarah Vanhorne and Jane Livezey, dau. of Sister
Dinah, dec'd. Nephew John Houghton, dec'd. Friend Isaac Hough,
Sr.
Wit: Harman Yerkes, Mary Yerkes, Wm. Vanhorn.

Page 364. Peter Sager of Richland Twp., Yeoman. 4-25-1770.
Proved 2-10-1785. Bro in law John Stouver and Friend Peter Meyer
exrs. Wife Barbara. Bros. Gabrael, William and Conrad. Sister
Elizabeth Young. Peter son of Gabrael and Peter son of William.
Deed to be made to Hermanus Yost for land sold.
Wit: Abraham Taylor and Saml. Foulke.

Page 365. Samuel Allen, of Bensalem, Yeoman. 11-15-1782.
Proved 2-10-1785. Son Samuel, exr. Daus. Jane and Sarah Allen and
Ann Paul.
Wit: Joseph Allen, Joseph Paxson, John Ewers.

Page 368. Philip Parry of Buckingham Twp. 6-13-1781. Codicil
10-12-1784. Proved 2-28-1785. Wife Rachel and sons John and
Philip exrs. Son Thomas. Daus. Hannah, Jane, Grace, Rachel,
Mary.
Wit: Daniel Longstreth, John Longstreth, Isaac Longstreth, Thomas
Hill, and Jacob Walton.

Page 370. Diana Bryan of Milford Twp., Widow. 3-16-1783.
Proved 3-15-1785. Friends William Clark and Joseph Phillips exrs.
Gd.son William son of John Bryan late of Chester Co. dec'd.
Gd.son John son of Henry Bryan, late of New York, dec'd. and Mary
dau. of said Henry. Nephew Joseph Phillips, Senr.
Wit: Samuel Walton, Waller Clark, Samuel Clark.

Page 371. Charles Lydey of Hilltown Twp., Yeoman. 2-24-1784.
Proved 3-15-1785. Son Henry and son-in-law Conrad Shelliberry
exrs. Wife Ursula. sons Charles, Henry, Jacob and George.
Daus. Margaret, wife of Adam Buzard. Eve, wife of Conrad
Shelliberry. Hannah, wife of Christian Fluke. Mary, wife of
Philip Mumbrour. Elizabeth and Catharine Lydey.
Wit: Benj. Griffith, Jacob Chrisman, and Cadwallader Morris.

Page 375. John Grier, Senr., of New Britain, Yeoman. 12-16-
1784. Proved 3-16-1785. Sons Mathew and James exrs. Wife Agnes.
Sons Mathew, Joseph, John, James and Nathan. Daus. Martha wife
of John Jamison, Jean wife of Joseph Thomas and Frances Grier.
Farm formerly of Philip Wood. Joseph Grier of Hilltown.
Wit: Thos. Jones, John Kempler.

Page 379.   David Lewis of Upper Makefield Twp.   1-2-1784.   Proved
3-16-1785. Friends Robert Thompson and John Chapman, exrs.   Wife
Elizabeth.   Daus. Elizabeth and Rebecca Lewis.   Thomas Lewis son
of brother Zachariah, farm adj. John Chapman, Thomas Smith, and
Jonas Ingham.
Wit: Jonathan Cooper, Thomas Lewis, Jr., Peter D. Cattell.

Page 381.   Elizabeth Spear of Northampton Twp., Widow.   7-10-
1775.   Codicil 6-18-1785.   Proved 6-25-1785.   Friend John
Thompson (Miller), exr.   Son John Spear and dec'd. son David
Spear.   Daus. Jane Burley, Elizabeth Slack and Mary Johnston.
Elizabeth Spear dau. of son David.

INDEX

BALEY, Ann, 62
BALL, John, 29
  Plain, 47
BANES, Elizabeth,
  40
  James, 40
  Jesse, 40, 89
  Joseph, 40
  Mathew, 40
  Phebe, 40
  Thomas, 28
BANKSON, Daniel,
  12, 32
  Elizabeth, 12
  Mary, 41
  Rachel, 100
BARBUR, Elizabeth,
  27
BARCKLEY, James,
  100
  Margaet, 100
BARCLAY, James, 122
  Margaret, 122
BARCROFT, Ambrose,
  11
BARD, Mary, 66
  Peter, 66
  William, 73
BARGE, Israel, 108
BARNES, Earles, 93
  Hannah, 127
  Jane, 105
  John, 93
  Martha, 126
  Mary, 93
BARNET, Andrew, 127
BARNHILL, Jane, 100
  John, 100
  Robert, 44, 52
  Samuel, 100
  Sarah, 100
BARNSON, Christian,
  9
BARR, Adam, 87
  George, 87
  Hugh, 61
  Mary, 87
  Thomas, 48, 87
BARROL, Moses, 56
BARTHOLOMEW,
  Daniel, 106
  Hannah, 106
  Jeremiah, 7
  John, 27, 51
  Thomas, 48, 50

BARTLEY, Elizabeth,
  90
BARTON, Amey, 102
  David, 76, 117
  Elizabeth, 102
  Hannah, 102
  Henry, 8
  John, 102
  Joseph, 20, 55,
  87, 102
  Loy, 111
  Mary, 63, 121
  Thomas, 20, 84,
  87
BARWIS, Esther, 43
  Jane, 43
  John, 43
  Margaret, 43
  Phebe, 43
  Thomas, 43
BATE, Sarah, 59
  Thomas, 59
BATES, Grace, 27
  Hannah, 27, 63
  Jeremiah, 27
  Job, 66
  John, 17, 27, 66,
  127
  Sarah, 27, 66
  William, 27
BATHOLOMEW, John,
  33
BATTON, Thomas, 58
BAUM, Henry, 127
BAVINGTON,
  Jonathan, 46
BAXTER, Elizabeth,
  57
  Hannah, 57
  Hugh, 57
  John, 57
  Margaret, 57, 90
  Mary, 57
  Thomas, 57
BAYLEY, Edward, 81
  John, 81
  Thomas, 25
BAYLY, Ann, 107
  Edith, 107
  Edward, 107
  John, 107
  Mercy, 107
  Susanna, 107
  Tace, 107
  Thomas, 107

  William, 107
BAYNES, Ellin, 41
  Joseph, 22
  Thomas, 7
BEAKES, Edmund, 56
  Elinor, 2, 3
  Hannah, 125
  John, 16
  Lydia, 76
  Mary, 76
  Samuel, 6, 18
  Stacy, 76
BEAKS, Stacy, 96
  William, 1
BEAL, Alex, 68, 87
  Alexander, 5
  Ann, 5
  Elizabeth, 5
  Grace, 49, 120
  John, 5, 40, 68,
  72, 79, 87
  Jonathan, 72
  Joseph, 49, 120
  Martha, 5, 72,
  114
  Mercy, 120
  Phebe, 72
  Rachel, 120
  Rebecka, 5
  Sarah, 49, 94
  Thomas, 49, 120
  William, 5, 49,
  120
BEANS, Elinor, 88
  Elizabeth, 88,
  100
  Hester, 89
  Jacob, 88
  James, 88, 89
  Jesse, 88
  John, 89, 100
  Joseph, 88, 89
  Margery, 55
  Mary, 89
  Mathew, 76, 88,
  89
  Rebecca, 55
  Seth, 89
  Thomas, 88
  Timothy, 88
  William, 88
BEARD, John, 55, 57
BEARSON, Lawrence,
  11
BEATES, Hannah, 24

Jane, 97, 98
John, 23
Jonipher, 83
Langhorne, 24,
  27, 51, 63, 83
Lunhorne, 24
Margaret, 24, 27
Mary, 63
Molly, 83
Nancy, 83
Samuel, 51, 63,
  93
Sarah, 3, 24, 27,
  51, 83
Thomas, 13, 24,
  27, 51, 97, 98
William, 2, 3, 6,
  13, 22, 24, 27,
  63, 98, 122, 127
BIRNEY, William, 48
BIRTCH SWAMP, 12
BISHOP, Ann
  Elizabeth, 115
Barbara, 115
Jacob, 115
John, 18
Margaret, 115
Michael, 115
Susanna, 115
BLACK, Adam, 86
Andrew, 124
Anna, 124
Barbara, 124
Catarina, 124
Elizabeth, 124
John, 124
Margaret, 124
BLACKFAN, Agnes,
  95, 120
Crispin, 66, 70,
  89
Elinor, 89
Elizabeth, 89,
  95, 120
Esther, 95, 120
Hannah, 70, 95,
  120
John, 70, 120
Martha, 97
Rachel, 95, 120
Rebekah, 89
Sarah, 89, 120
Thomas, 120
William, 31, 70,
  80, 88, 89, 95

BLACKLEDGE, John,
  102
Thomas, 127
BLACKSHAW, Joseph,
  30
Mary, 8, 11, 30
Nehemiah, 4, 8,
  13, 30, 47
Phebe, 30
BLAKELY, william,
  76
BLAKER, Achilles,
  105
Catharine, 112
John, 105
Lydia, 112
Mary, 113
Paul, 100, 105
Peter, 35, 69,
  105, 112
Ruth, 6
Samuel, 21, 112
Sarah, 28
William, 42, 125
BLAKEY, Esther, 96
Joshua, 79, 95,
  96, 112
Sarah, 77, 79,
  96, 125
William, 77, 91,
  96, 112, 113,
  125
BLEAKEY, William, 5
BOARD, William, 73
BOARE, Joshua, 1, 2
Margaret, 1
Mary, 3
BODEN, Hugh, 83
BODER, Peter, 108
BODINE, James, 33,
  60
Joseph, 42
Sarah, 105
BOGART, Gysbert, 66
BOIZE, John, 106
William, 106
BOL, William, 29
BOLLARD, William,
  51
BOLTON, Charles, 47
Everard, 98
Isaac, 98, 125
Joseph, 98
Luezar, 113
Margaret, 98

Rachel, 98
Sarah, 98, 125
BOND, Abraham, 34
Benjamin, 34
Edward, 34
Hannah, 34
John, 32, 34
Joseph, 6
Joshua, 34
Rebecca, 34
Sarah, 34
BONNER, James, 124
BOOM, Elizabeth, 29
Joseph, 29
Ralph, 29
Solomon, 29
BOOMAN, Andrew, 64
BOON, Mary, 25
Neels, 25, 87
BOOROM, Aaron, 106
BOOSKIRK, Charity,
  100
BOOTH, John, 67
BORDEN, Joseph, 127
Mary, 127
BORE, Joshua, 1
BORELAND, Jane, 104
John, 104
BOTHER, Peter, 108
BOTTING, John, 41
Thomas, 41
BOUCHER, Anne, 105
BOURNE, Jonathan,
  19
Susanna, 22
BOWMAN, ---, 9
Elizabeth, 112
Jer., 28
BOWN, John, 5, 54
BOWNE, John, 10
BOY, Thomas, 72
BOYD, Andrew, 120
Catharine, 120
James, 49, 120
Jarrett, 120
John, 81, 120
Joseph, 59
Mathew, 120
William, 120
BOYDEN, James, 2, 3
BRACKENBRIDGE,
  Samuel, 107
Susanna, 107
BRADFIELD, Hannah, 121
Jane, 16, 56

Lydia, 97
Margaret, 97
Martha, 18, 37,
97
Mary, 18, 37
Nathaniel, 18, 37
Rebecca, 97
Rebekah, 89
Sarah, 18, 29
Thomas, 18, 26,
37, 97
BYER, Benjamin, 51
BYLE, Rebecca, 90
BYLES, Daniel, 51

-C-
CABE, Thomas, 121
CADIWALLADER, John,
24
CADWALLADER,
Abraham, 24
Elizabeth, 24
Isaac, 24
Jacob, 25, 56,
110
John, 16, 25
Margaret, 24
Mary, 24
Sarah, 24
Thomas, 42
CADWALLADER SWAMP,
12
CAHILL, Edmond, 49
CALDWELL, Agnes, 32
David, 32, 84
Francisca, 32
James, 32
Jean, 32
Mary, 32
CAMPBELL, George,
82, 107
James, 32
John, 20, 64
Sarah, 123
CANBY, Ann, 46
Anne, 38
Benjamin, 12, 38,
46, 86
Elizabeth, 46
Esther, 46
Jane, 46
Lydia, 46
Mary, 46
Oliver, 46
Phebe, 46

Rachel, 46
Samuel, 38
Sarah, 38
Thomas, 12, 13,
22, 38, 46, 68,
98
William, 38
CANLY, Thomas, 22
CARAH, Sarah, 29
CARLILE, Daniel,
121
Elizabeth, 25, 26
John, 26, 73, 95,
108, 121
Jonathan, 25, 26,
74, 78, 91, 125
Marcy, 78, 81
Sarah, 121
CARMAN, Elizabeth,
73
CARR, Adam, 96
Andrew, 56
Isabel, 56
John, 52, 56, 93,
96, 103
Joseph, 56
Margret, 56
Mary, 56
Norris, 88
William, 56, 103
CARRELL, Jacob, 63
James, 17
Sarah, 104
CARRIL, James, 65
CARRUTHERS, Mary,
28
Rachel, 28
CARTAR, William, 28
CARTER, Alice, 30
Ann, 6, 42, 87,
96, 122
Asher, 74
Benjamin, 6, 114,
122
Charles, 116, 122
Christopher, 74,
122
Ebenezer, 122
Edmund, 114
Grace, 7
Henry, 30
Isabella, 6
Jacob, 122
James, 6, 30, 43,
67, 114

John, 6, 30, 114,
127
Joseph, 6, 82,
87, 114
Katharine, 114
Letitia, 123
Martha, 7
Mary, 7, 43
Rachel, 87, 114
Rebecca, 78
Richard, 6, 87,
114
Robert, 6, 7
Sarah, 17, 43,
114
Susanna, 5, 6
Susannah, 4
William, 6, 7,
43, 78, 82, 87,
109, 114
CARVER, Benjamin,
98
Elizabeth, 62,
90, 98
Ely, 87
Henry, 40, 62,
90, 98
John, 24, 67, 98,
114
Joseph, 62, 90,
98, 99
Mahlon, 96
Mary, 62
Rachel, 98
Rebecca, 62
Sarah, 84
Thomas, 98
William, 40, 62,
84, 90, 98
CARY, Abigail, 24
Ages, 125
Ann, 79
Asa, 78
Bethula, 79
Bula, 79
Hannah, 24
Hannahmeal, 79
Hepsibah, 79
Jane, 24
John, 24
Joshua, 78
Margaret, 24, 83
Mary, 24
Phineas, 79
Samson, 24, 42,

DOWNEY, Hannah, 5,
68
James, 9, 12, 19,
68, 77
Sarah, 68
DOXAL, Edward, 23
DOYLE, Ann, 121
Clement, 49, 50,
90, 38
John, 90
Jonathan, 90
Margaret, 90
Martha, 31
Richard, 90
William, 108
DRACH, Adam, 88
Henry, 88
Marelas, 88
Rudolf, 88
DRACORDS, Philip,
90
DRACOTT, Philip, 10
DRAK, Peter, 88
DRAKE, Ann, 78
Aphie, 52
Benjamin, 78
Catharine, 52
Daniel, 78
David, 17
Deborah, 52
Elizabeth, 78
George, 52
Hannah, 78
Jacob, 78
Jaon, 78
Jonathan, 50, 52
Mary, 52, 78
Robert, 78
Zachariah, 78
DRIEDRICK, John, 60
DUBERRY, Absalom,
124
Hannah, 124
DUBOIAS, Yanica,
100
DUER, John, 44, 62,
106
Joseph, 42, 47,
63
Sarah, 55
DUFF, Thomas, 32
DUFFIELD, Thomas,
102
DUGIN, Michel, 31
DUNBAR, Andrew, 16

Mary, 16
Thomas, 77
DUNCAN, Edmund, 34
Jane, 67
John, 24, 28, 48,
70, 71
Mary, 34
Sarah, 5
William, 34
DUNGAN, Abel, 62
Ann, 112
Benjamin, 62
Catharine, 87
Clement, 2, 17,
112
David, 62, 79,
113, 123
Deborah, 3
Eleanor, 112
Elias, 112
Elizabeth, 2, 3,
62, 112
Enoch, 62
Esther, 62
Garret, 86
George, 17
Jacob, 63
James, 63, 85,
86, 112
Jaremy, 112
Jeremiah, 2, 3,
17, 87
John, 2, 63, 66,
87, 126, 103
Jonathan, 63, 126
Joseph, 63, 87,
126
Joshua, 87
Martha, 79, 102
Mary, 2, 17, 30,
83
Nathan, 87
Rachel, 33
Rebecka, 2
Samuel, 63
Sarah, 2, 62
Thomas, 2, 3, 17,
19, 62, 63, 126
William, 2, 3,
17, 79, 87, 103,
108, 117
DUNGWORTH, Charles,
105
Susanna, 105
DUNKAN, Ann, 67

Catharine, 67
Edmund, 36, 67,
68
Hellen, 67
Isaac, 36, 67
Jane, 67
John, 14, 68
Margaret, 14, 68
Mary, 67
Patrick, 68
Sarah, 14, 67
William, 14, 36,
60, 75, 67
DUNLAP, Allen, 44
James, 95
DUNN, Anna, 51
George, 12, 20,
71, 78, 97
Hannah, 12
Joseph, 97
Margaret, 12, 97
Mary, 12
Ralph, 12, 20, 97
Rebecca, 12
Rephane, 12
Sarah, 12
William, 12
DURHAM, Mathew, 10
DURSTEN, Abraham,
95
DYE, Ann, 64
Jonathan, 64
Josias, 64
Lydia, 64
William, 60, 64,
79
DYER, Abraham, 23
Benjamin, 85
Charles, 66
Deborah, 66
Edward, 66
Elizabeth, 23,
53, 66, 108
Esther, 108
Henry, 66
James, 62, 66
John, 23, 53, 108
Joseph, 23, 66,
98, 108, 126
Josiah, 23, 53,
108
Mary, 108, 125
Phebe, 108
Rachel, 108
Samuel, 23, 85

65
FETHER, Anna mary,
112
Philip, 112
FETTER, John, 72
FETTERS, Ann, 105
FIELD, Benjamin, 7,
25, 42, 48
Edward, 42
Elizabeth, 42
Hannah, 124
Jennings, 42
Joseph, 122
Mary, 42
Nathan, 122
Sarah, 42
Stephen, 62
Susanna, 33, 42
Thomas, 42
William, 114, 122
FINLEY, Alexander,
106
Archibald, 44
Henry, 44
James, 44, 106
Jane, 106
John, 44
Margaret, 44
Martha, 106
Mary, 106
Sarah, 106
William, 27
FISHER, Barak, 76
Deborah, 76
Elizabeth, 13
Henry, 77
John, 11, 13, 30,
38, 76
Joseph, 76
Katharine, 76
Mary, 13, 19
Robert, 76
Samuel, 76, 84
FISSLER, Anna Mary,
112
Barbara, 112
Christina, 112
Dordea, 112
Elizabeth, 112
Eva, 112
Jacob, 112
Mary, 112
Michael, 112
Susanna, 112
FITCHET, Constant,

25
James, 25
FITREY, Nicholas,
65
Sarah, 65
FITZRANDEL,
Benjamin, 16
FLACK, Ann, 102
FLEMING, Thomas, 92
FLUCK, Barbara, 108
Casper, 108
Christian, 108
Elizabeth, 108
Fredrick, 108
John, 108
Ludwick, 108
Philip, 108
FLUKE, Christian,
129
Hannah, 129
Peter, 117
FOGELMAN, Conrad,
107
FOLWELL, John, 94
Thomas, 89
FORMAN, Hester, 55
FORREST, John, 20
FORT, David, 126
FOSTBINDER, John,
100
FOSTER, Abraham,
111
Anne, 87
Hannah, 112
Joseph, 111
Sarah, 93
FOULKE, Amelia, 109
Edward, 33
John, 110, 117
Margaret, 109
Samuel, 61, 105,
109, 110, 117,
122, 126, 129,
115
Theophilus, 117
Thomas, 105, 109,
117, 128
William, 127
FOWLER, Adam, 92
John, 75
FOX, Jacob, 54
Joseph, 7
Martha, 108
FRANCIS, Elizabeth,
6

FRANK, Jacob, 56
FRANKLIN, Benjamin,
82
FRATS, Abraham, 127
Barbara, 127
Christian, 127
Daniel, 127
Elizabeth, 127
Esther, 127
Jacob, 127
John, 127
Mark, 127
FRAZER, John, 34
FRAZIER, Andrew, 41
FREAME, Anne, 52
Archibald, 52
Elizabeth, 52
James, 52
John, 52
Thomas, 52
William, 52
FREDERICKSON,
Michael, 10
FREISE, Christian,
93
FRELICH, Jacob, 78
FRETTS, Daniel, 115
FRETZ, Abraham, 120
Agnes, 120
Barbara, 120
Elizabeth, 120
Henry, 120
John, 120
Mary, 120
Sarah, 120
FRICKER, Anthony,
71
Catharine, 71
John, 71
Joseph, 71
Salome, 71
Theresia, 71
FRITZINGER,
Catharine, 113
John, 113
FROHOCK, Elizabeth,
28
Hugh, 40
John, 17, 18, 28,
36, 40
Joseph, 19
Thomas, 40
William, 40
FROST, Edmund, 6
Isaac, 6

Richard, 4, 5, 8,
26
Samuel, 38
Sarah, 32, 38,
46, 80, 96
Thomas, 38, 129
William, 5, 38,
39, 46, 79
HILLBORN, Abigail,
91
David, 91
Elizabeth, 9, 91
John, 9, 91
Joseph, 9, 91
Katharine, 7, 9
Margaret, 6, 9
Mary, 7, 91
Rachel, 9
Robert, 7, 9, 87
Samuel, 9, 87, 91
Thomas, 7, 9, 33,
80, 91
William, 91
HILLBORNE,
Elizabeth, 7
John, 21
Katharine, 7
Mary, 21
Miles, 21
Rachel, 21
Ruth, 21
Samuel, 6
Sarah, 21
Thomas, 6, 7, 30,
45
HILLBOURNE, John,
57
Widow, 58
HILLBURN, Thomas,
18
HILLBURNE, Ann, 13
HILLEBRANDT,
Christophel, 71
Elizabeth, 71, 72
HILLEGAS, Barbara,
102
Michael, 109
Peter, 102
HILLIARD,
Cornelius, 36
HILLTOWN, 8
HINCKEL, Catharine,
126
Leonard, 126
Magdalena, 126

Margaret, 126
Philip, 126
HINDS, Mathew, 55
HIRST, Martha, 87
Mary, 101
HISCOCK, William, 1
HITTIN, Robert, 12
HOAGELAND, Daniel,
124
HOCKLEY, Richard,
31
HOCUS, Margaret, 78
HODGSON, David, 81
Isaac, 107
John, 81
HOFF, John, 75
HOFFMAN, Ann, 116
Catharine, 116
Conrad, 116
Elisabeth, 116
Gertrout, 116
Magdlen, 116
Martin, 116
Mary, 116
William, 116
HOGELAND, Benjamin,
102
Daniel, 87, 102
Dirck, 102
Direk, 102
Elizabeth, 102
George, 102
John, 102
Mary, 102
Phebe, 102
Sarah, 102
HOLCOMBE,
Elizabeth, 36
Hannah, 36
Jacob, 13, 30,
35, 36
John, 11
Joseph, 95
Mary, 36, 62
Rebecca, 36
Richard, 62
Sarah, 36
Sophia, 36
Susanna, 36
Thomas, 13, 36
HOLLINGSHEAD,
Elizabeth, 88
Francis, 88
Thomasin, 88
William, 88

HOLLOMAN, Jacob, 80
HOLME, Thomas, 54
HOMER, Ester, 3
William, 3, 68
HOMMER, Joanna, 90
Mary, 90
HOOKER, Jacob, 91
HOOPER, Anthony, 51
Daniel, 81
Jacob, 25
HOPE, William, 79
HORN, Catharine,
112
James, 87
Stephen, 112
HORNECKER,
Catharine, 102
Elizabeth, 102
Isaac, 102
John, 102
Joseph, 102
Margaret, 102
Ulrick, 102
HORNER, Andrew, 81
Elizabeth, 124
Heath, 33
James, 112
John, 112
HOSKINS, Esther, 95
HOTE, William, 12
HOTTENSTEIN,
Catharine, 102
David, 102
HOUEY, John, 46
HOUGH, Barnard, 36
Benjamin, 37
Daniel, 29, 63
Edith, 54
Elenor, 29
Elinor, 19
Elizabeth, 129
Isaac, 56, 73,
110, 129
Jane, 29, 80
John, 8, 29, 80
Jonathan, 63, 80
Joseph, 8, 29,
50, 97
Letitia, 63
Margaret, 37
Margery, 2, 8
Martha, 80
Mary, 29
Michael, 7
Richard, 2, 8,

Mary, 28
Richard, 62
MUSGRAVES, Thomas, 24
MYER, Jacob, 115
MYERS, Agnes, 118
Barbara, 118
Christian, 118
David, 118
Jacob, 85, 86, 118
John, 125
Joseph, 118
Mary, 118
Michael, 118
Samuel, 118

-N-
NAGLE, Alexander, 101
Gasper, 101
NASE, George, 101
NASH, William, 64, 65
NAYLOR, John, 20, 22, 33
Joseph, 25
Richard, 33
Robert, 33
Susanna, 33
NEAL, Elizabeth, 126
John, 126
Moses, 126
NEASE, Jacob, 117
John, 117
NEELD, Eleanor, 84
Eli, 107, 122
Elizabeth, 98
James, 122
John, 84, 98
Judith, 84
Moses, 98
Rachel, 92, 122
Richard, 92, 107, 122
NEELE, James, 81
NEELEY, William, 111
NEESE, John, 82
NEFFUS, Cornelius, 53
John, 53
Peter, 53
Williamkee, 53

Yorus, 53
NELANS, Alexander, 122
NELSON, Alice, 24, 30
Hannah, 111
Henry, 7, 29, 30
Naomi, 51
Thomas, 30, 51, 55
Valentine, 51
NESBITT, David, 67
NESHAMINAH CREEK, 1
NEWBURN, David, 111
George, 78, 111
Jonathan, 111
Margaret, 111
Susanna, 123
William, 111, 123, 124
NEWTON, Ann, 46
Elizabeth, 46
George, 46
Henry, 46
Jean, 46
Robert, 46
NEWTOWN, Rebecca, 104
NICHLESON, Elizabeth, 85
NICKLESON, Elizabeth, 85
Thomas, 85
NIELD, James, 43
Jane, 43
John, 43
Judith, 43
Martha, 43
NIELDS, Martha, 125
Mary, 125
NIXON, Robert, 33
Samuel, 110
Thomas, 33, 48
William, 11, 29, 47
NOBLE, Elizabeth, 28, 83
Job, 37
William, 28
NODEN, Henry, 27, 28
NORRIS, Charles, 80
NORTON, John, 37, 44
NOX, Margaret, 32

Moses, 32
Samuel, 32
William, 32
NUTT, Ann, 42
Edmund, 42
Hannah, 42
John, 33, 42, 122
Jonathan, 42
Joseph, 119
Susanna, 50

-O-
OAT, George, 56
OBERBECK, Anna Maria, 98
Elizabeth, 98
Maria Magdalena, 98
OBERHOLTZER, Henry, 110
O'DANIEL, John, 63, 74
OELAH, Mary, 76
OGBURN, Samuel, 16
OGG, John, 30
O'HAIGHAN, Catharine, 91
Oliver, 91
OLDHOUSE, Magdalena, 114
OLIPANT, Anne, 108
OLIPHANT, William, 65
OLPHIN, Giles, 51
O'NEAL, Roger, 54
OPDYCKE, Wynchel, 41
ORR, Jane, 72
John, 72
Rebekah, 72
Thomas, 72
OSTERDAY, Adam, 86
OTT, Adelhite, 106
Henry, 113
Jacob, 113
John, 113
Michael, 113
Stephen, 106
OTTER, John, 2
OVERBACK, George, 64
OVERFELT, Abner, 57
Benjamin, 57
Rebecca, 57
OVERHOLD, ---, 54

RANKIN, John, 100,
113, 126
RANKINS, John, 97
Katharine, 84
RAPP, Catharine,
107
Christian, 107
Frederick, 107
Mary, 107
Philip Henry, 107
RAWLE, Francis, 9
RAY, David, 10
James, 10
Robert, 10
REA, John, 58
Joseph, 58
Mathew, 58
Moses, 58
Samuel, 58
Sidney, 58
READING, John, 23
REECE, William, 98
REED, Andrew, 119
Elizabeth, 16
James, 75
John, 16
Thomas, 4
REEDER, Charles, 17
Isaac, 17
John, 17
Joseph, 17
Margaret, 17
Sarah, 17
William, 17
REESE, Joseph, 66
REI, Jacob, 100
REIGEL, George, 124
RENBERRY, William,
40
RENNER, Adam, 113
Catharine, 113
Clara, 113
Ellisabeth, 113
Henry, 113
Jacob, 113
Magdalena, 113
Michael, 113
Peter, 113
Valentine, 113
RETTINHOUSR,
William, 24
REUP, Michel, 31
REYNOLD, ---, 62
RIALE, Hannah, 34
John, 34

Joshua, 34, 71
Mary, 34
Phebe, 34
Richard, 34, 92
RICE, Allen, 108
Catharine, 86
Lewis, 86
Mary, 86
Mathew, 86
Richard, 86
Sarah, 110
RICH, Alexander,
120
Elizabeth, 120
Isaac, 108
John, 35, 53
Joseph, 120
RICHARDS, Abraham,
20
Joshua, 21
Sarah, 17
RICHARDSON, Ann, 91
Elizabeth, 91
Francis, 15
Jane, 90
Jesinah, 121
John, 15
Joseph, 15, 24,
26, 28, 60, 71,
90, 20
Joshua, 90, 94
Marcy, 91
Mary, 26, 90, 94
Rachel, 91
Rebecca, 15, 90
Ruth, 90
Sarah, 90
William, 15, 90,
91, 115
RICHE, John, 41
Sarah, 41
RICHELIEU, 15
RICHMONT, Robert,
99
RICKERT, Henry, 110
RICKEY, Alexander,
61, 83, 116,
122, 127
Alexander A., 19
Ann, 61, 83, 122,
127
Hannah, 68, 116
James, 61, 83,
122
John, 61, 83, 100

Joseph, 62
Kairl, 61, 83
Keirll, 68, 109
Kevill, 83, 113
Mary, 61, 83
Rachel, 83, 116
Rebecca, 72, 116
Sarah, 61, 109
Thomas, 61, 68,
83, 95, 116
William, 116
RIDGE, Thomas, 114
William, 60
RIDGEWAY, Abigail,
105
David, 105
Rachel, 105
RIDGWAY, Elizabeth,
2
Richard, 2, 3
RIGBY, Sarah, 98
RIGG, William, 12
RIGGS, William, 26
RING, William, 13
ROAT, Ann, 113
ROBBINS, John, 98
ROBERTS, Edmond, 43
Edward, 11, 15,
38, 43, 112
Eldad, 57
Elizabeth, 15, 60
Ellis, 60
Grace, 55
Henry, 70
Jane, 43, 63, 70,
79, 84
John, 15, 25, 73,
86
Joseph, 53
Margery, 70
Mary, 43, 55, 64,
70, 84
Nathan, 110
Owen, 50
Priscilla, 108
Rebecca, 27
Richard, 70
Sarah, 121
Susanna, 73
Thomas, 21, 70,
105
Timothy, 15, 64
William, 15, 70,
84, 91, 104, 118
ROBINSON, Ebenezer,